IN THE NAME OF

ALLAH

THE ALL-COMPASSIONATE, ALL-MERCIFUL

Kitâb at-Tawheed
Explained
New & Revised Third Edition

- Title: Kitâb at-Tawheed Explained
- Author: Muhammad ibn 'Abdul-Wahhâb
- English Edition 1 (1999)
- New & Revised English Edition 3 (2010)
- Commentary compiled & translated by: Sameh Strauch
- Layout Design: IIPH, Riyadh, Saudi Arabia
- Filming and Cover Design: Samo Press Group

Kitâb at-Tawheed Explained

Explained

New & Revised Third Edition

شرح كتاب التوحيد

Muhammad ibn 'Abdul-Wahhâb

Commentary compiled & translated by

Sameh Strauch

الدار العالمية للكتاب الإسلامي

INTERNATIONAL ISLAMIC PUBLISHING HOUSE

Copyright © 2010 International Islamic Publishing House
King Fahd National Library Cataloging-in-Publication Data

Ibn 'Abdul-Wahhâb, Muhammad
  Kitâb at-Tawheed Explained. / Muhammad ibn 'Abdul-Wahhâb .-
Riyadh, 2010

  400 p ; 21 cm

  ISBN Hardcover: 978-603-501-078-8

  1- Oneness   I- Sameh Strauch (translator)
  II- Title

  240 dc   1431/4446

Legal Deposit no. **1431/4446**
ISBN Hardcover: **978-603-501-078-8**

International Islamic Publishing House (IIPH)
P.O. Box 55195 Riyadh 11534, Saudi Arabia
Tel: 966 1 4650818 / 4647213 — Fax: 966 1 4633489
E-mail: iiph@iiph.com.sa — iiphsa@gmail.com
www.iiph.com.sa

List of Contents

Arabic honorific symbols used in this book

(﷿): *Subḥânahu wa ta'âlâ* — 'The Exalted'

(ﷺ): *Ṣalla-Allâhu 'alayhi wa sallam* — 'Blessings and peace be upon him'

(ﷹ): *'Alayhis-salâm* — 'Peace be upon him'

(﷽): *Raḍiya Allâhu 'anhu* — 'May Allah be pleased with <u>him</u>'

(﷼): *Raḍiya Allâhu 'anhâ* — 'May Allah be pleased with <u>her</u>'

Pronunciation and Transliteration Chart

Arabic script	Pronunciation	Transliterated as:
أ	short 'a', as in *cat*	a
آ – ى	longer 'a', as in *cab* (not as in *cake*)	â
ب	/b/ as in *bell*, *rubber* and *tab*	b
ت	/t/ as in *tap, mustard* and *sit*	t
ة	takes the sound of the preceding diactrical mark sometimes ending in h (when in pausal form): ah, ih, or ooh; or atu(n), ati(n) or ata(n) when in uninterrupted speech	h or t (when followed by another Arabic word)
ث	/th/ as in *thing*, *maths* and *wealth*	th
ج	/j/ as in *jam*, *ajar* and *age*	j
ح	a 'harsher' sound than the English initial /h/, and may occur medially and in word-final position as well	ḥ
خ	as in *Bach* (in German); may occur initially and medially as well	kh
د	/d/ as in *do*, *muddy* and *red*	d
ذ	as in *this*, *father*, and *with*	dh
ر	/r/ as in *raw*, *art* and *war*; may also be a rolled r, as with Spanish words	r

Arabic script	Pronunciation	Transliterated as:
ز	/z/ as in *zoo*, *easy* and *gaze*	z
س	/s/ as in *so*, *messy* and *grass*	s
ش	as in *ship*, *ashes* and *rush*	sh
ص	no close equivalent in English, but may be approximated by pronouncing it as /sw/ or /s/ farther back in the mouth	ṣ
ض	no close equivalent in English, but may be approximated by pronouncing /d/ farther back in the mouth	ḍ
ط	no close equivalent in English, but may be approximated by pronouncing /t/ farther back in the mouth	ṭ
ظ	no close equivalent in English, but may be approximated by pronouncing 'the' farther back in the mouth	<u>dh</u>
ع	no close equivalent in English: a guttural sound in the back of the throat	'
غ	no close equivalent in English, but may be closely approximated by pronouncing it like the French /r/ in 'rouge'	gh
ف	/f/ as in *fill*, *effort* and *muff*	f

Arabic script	Pronunciation	Transliterated as:
ق	no close equivalent in English, but may be approximated by pronouncing /k/ farther back in the mouth	q
ك	/k/ as in *king, buckle* and *tack*	k
ل	/l/ as in *lap, halo*; in the word *Allah*, it becomes velarized as in *ball*	l
م	/m/ as in *men, simple* and *ram*	m
ن	/n/ as in *net, ant* and *can*	n
ـه – ه – هـ	/h/ as in *hat*; unlike /h/ in English, in Arabic /h/ is pronounced in medial and word-final positions as well	h
و	as in *wet* and *away*	w
و (as a vowel)	long u, as in *boot* and *too*	oo
ي	as in *yet* and *yard*	y
ي (as a vowel)	long e, as in *eat, beef* and *see*	ee
ء	glottal stop: may be closely approximated by pronouncing it like 't' in the Cockney English pronunciation of *butter*: *bu'er*, or the stop sound in *uh — oh!*	' (Omitted in initial position)

Diphthongs:

Arabic script	Pronunciation	Transliterated as:
و ، أَوَ	Long o, as in *owe*, *boat* and *go*	au, aw, ow
يَ ، أَي	Long 'a', as in *able*, *rain* and *say*	ay, ai, ei

Diacritical marks (*tashkeel*):

Name of mark	Pronunciation	Transliterated as:
́ faṭḥah	very short 'a' or schwa (unstressed vowel)	a
̖ kasrah	shorter version of ee or schwa (unstressed vowel)	i
̗ Dammah	shorter version of oo	u
́ shaddah	a doubled consonant is stressed in the word, and the length of the sound is also doubled	Double letter
̊ sukoon	no vowel sound between consonants or at the end of a word	Absence of vowel

About the word *Lord*

The word *lord* in English has several related meanings. The original meaning is 'master' or 'ruler', and in this sense it is often used to refer to human beings: 'the lord of the mansion' or 'Lord So-and-So' (in the United Kingdom, for example). The word *Lord* with a capital L is used in the lexicon of Islam to refer to the One and Only God — Allah. In Islam, there is no ambiguity about the meaning of this word. While it is true that one may occasionally use the word *lord* (whether capitalized or not) to refer to a human being, in Islamic discourse the reference of this term is always clear from the context. Whereas for Christians, Hindus and other polytheists, the word *Lord* with a capital 'L' may refer to Allah, to Jesus or to some imagined deity, for Muslims, there can be no plurality of meaning. Allah alone is the Lord, and the Lord is Allah — not Jesus, not Rama, not any other being.

The Editor

Publisher's Note

*A*ll praise and thanks belong to Allah alone, the One, the Almighty, and All-Merciful. Blessings and peace be upon Prophet Muhammad, the last of His Messengers and Prophets, and upon his family, his Companions and all those who follow in his footsteps until the end of time.

Without question, the most important subject for a Muslim to comprehend is *'Aqeedah*; without it, no act of worship or good deed is accepted by Allah, Most Glorified, Most High, nor rewarded in the Hereafter. And without any doubt, one of the finest — if not the finest — books on the subject is *Kitâb at-Tawheed* by the great Muslim scholar and reformer, the *mujaddid* (reformer and revivalist) of his age, Muhammad ibn 'Abdul-Wahhâb. However, this book was not intended for the average person in the street, but for the student of knowledge; therefore, it is not easily understood by those without the requisite learning. For this reason, although the text of this book has been available in translation for some years, the translator and compiler, Sameh Strauch felt it important to provide an explanation for this estimable book, gleaned from the authoritative Arabic works of Muslim scholars. It is with great pleasure therefore, that we present this, the second edition of *'Kitâb at-Tawḥeed — Explained'*. We ask Allah, the Almighty, the All-powerful, that He accept it and make it of benefit to English-speaking Muslims around the world.

May Allah accept the efforts of all those who contributed to the production of this book, and may it be acceptable to Him, *âmeen.*

Muhammad ibn 'Abdul Mohsin Al-Tuwaijri

Managing Director
International Islamic Publishing House
Riyadh, Saudi Arabia

Commentator's Foreword

$\mathcal{A}$ll praise be to Allah, and may the peace and blessings of Allah be upon our Prophet Muhammad and upon all his family and Companions.

When I embraced Islam in 1983, by the grace of Allah, one of the first books which I was given to read was a translation of *Kitâb at-Tawheed* by the renowned scholar, Muhammad ibn 'Abdul-Wahhâb. I understood very little of it and was driven to the conclusion that this was because I was new to Islam and therefore lacked knowledge. It was only later, when I studied the book *Tayseer al-'Azeez al-Hameed* in Arabic, that I realized that not even Arabic speakers try to understand *Kitâb at-Tawheed* without the benefit of explanatory notes or texts.

It has therefore been in my mind for some time to try to provide English-speakers with an explanation of this great work; however, other projects diverted me until now.

In compiling this explanation, I have relied mainly on *Al-Jadeed fee Sharh Kitâb at-Tawheed* by Shaykh Muhammad al-Qar'âwi, *Tafseer Ibn Katheer*, and a number of books of *Hadith* [the collected statements and actions of Prophet Muhammad (ﷺ)].

I ask Allah that He accept this humble effort from me and make it of benefit to my brothers and sisters in Islam.

Sameh Strauch

﴿ ... رَبَّنَا لَا تُؤَاخِذْنَا إِن نَّسِينَا أَوْ أَخْطَأْنَا رَبَّنَا وَلَا تَحْمِلْ عَلَيْنَا إِصْرًا كَمَا حَمَلْتَهُۥ عَلَى ٱلَّذِينَ مِن قَبْلِنَا رَبَّنَا وَلَا تُحَمِّلْنَا مَا لَا طَاقَةَ لَنَا بِهِۦ وَٱعْفُ عَنَّا وَٱغْفِرْ لَنَا وَٱرْحَمْنَآ أَنتَ مَوْلَىٰنَا فَٱنصُرْنَا عَلَى ٱلْقَوْمِ ٱلْكَٰفِرِينَ ﴿٢٨٦﴾

(سُورَة البَقَرَة: ٢٨٦)

﴾...Our Lord! Punish us not if we forget or fall into error, our Lord! Lay not on us a burden like that which You laid on those before us; our Lord! Put not on us a burden greater than we have strength to bear. Pardon us and grant us forgiveness. Have mercy on us. You are our Protector; and give us victory over the disbelieving people.﴿

(Qur'an 2: 286)

About the author of
Kitâb at-Tawḥeed

$\mathcal{S}$haykh Muhammad ibn 'Abdul-Wahhâb was a leading revivalist of the 12th H (18th CE) century who is famous for his call to return to the original teachings of Islam. His influence remains felt into modern times. Today, the appellation 'Wahhâbi' is sometimes used to refer to those who follow in his path; and regrettably, the term 'Wahhâbi' is also used erroneously to refer to groups that act in opposition to what Shaykh Muhammad taught. The Shaykh did not establish a new or separate school of jurisprudence or thought, rather his focus remained on reform within orthodox Sunni Islam.

Shaykh Muhammad was born to a religious family of the Tameemi tribe in Al-Uyaynah, a small town about 30km from the city of Riyadh in Saudi Arabia. His education began at home, as his first formal teacher was his father. The Shaykh memorized the entire Qur'an before he had reached the age of ten. Later, he travelled to further his studies in the religious centres of Makkah, Madinah, and Basra.

Returning to his Saudi hometown around the year 1152 H (1740 CE), Shaykh Muhammad had already begun his career as a reformer. He called upon Muslims to return to the basic tenets of Islam as taught in the original sources of Islam, which are the verses of the Noble Qur'an and the authentic Hadith of the Prophet's Sunnah. The Shaykh refuted all innovations and deviations from these teachings and spent the rest of his lifetime devoted to the call of enjoining all that is good and right and forbidding all that is evil and wrong. He focused on purification which started with the internal correction of basic beliefs and the purity of intention. He rejected the blind following practiced by many followers of the different schools of thought, and he rebuffed the division this caused among the Muslims.

Upholding tawḥeed, the fundamental Islamic teaching of monotheism, was his primary concern. Though the Shaykh mostly instigated change through religious instruction and debate rather than physical acts, he also caused great controversy at the time by supporting his belief in tawḥeed with appropriate actions. The people of his day were strongly attached to their polytheistic practices. The Shaykh encouraged Muslims to level graves and pull down the structures built over them for the purpose of venerating the pious people who were buried there. Thus, many shrines of the so-called Muslim saints and martyrs were destroyed to prevent ignorant Muslims from visiting them to pray to them and seek their intercession. The Shaykh also participated in cutting down supposedly 'magical' trees which people visited to get blessings and ask for cures.

The Shaykh's preaching earned him enemies, who mainly opposed him in the name tradition or politics. Some of his enemies tried to have him killed. Throughout these difficulties, the Shaykh continued to be a lecturer and teacher. He also served as a judge and gave rulings based on the texts of the Qur'an and the Sunnah. The weakness of his opponents, even to this day, is that they attacked him without being able to disprove his writings.

The Shaykh was not the leader of a jihad movement, as reformation, not jihad, was his major theme. He did, however, have influence on what would eventually become the formation of the modern Saudi state, which officially came into existence more than a hundred years after his death. Around 1157 H (1744 CE), the Shaykh made an alliance with Muḥammad ibn Saʻood, the patriarch and founder of current ruling family of Saudi Arabia. This partnership gave the Shaykh the support he needed to propagate the original Islamic teachings throughout the Arabian Peninsula.

Shaykh Muhammad ibn 'Abdul-Wahhâb died in 1206 H (1792 CE). His children, grandchildren, and students continued on with his message of revival, purification, and return to the Islamic fundamentals, and this continues among them even today. There have been many scholars among his descendents, who are known by the family name Âl ash-Shaykh, or 'House of the Shaykh'.

Kitâb at-Tawheed remains the Shaykh's most famous book. It has been translated into many languages, and this English translation by Sameh Strauch is particularly useful due to the concise notes that are added to clarify the importance of each Qur'anic verse and hadith which the Shaykh has quoted.

Introduction to the concept of tawheed

It is impossible to overstate the importance of *tawheed* for all of humankind. Tawheed is the fundamental teaching of all divinely-originated religion. It is the message of all the Prophets and Messengers who appeared since the beginning of time. It is the very basis of all Islamic belief and practices. Tawheed is the concept of perfect monotheism: There is one and only one god, Allah, who creates and sustains all of creation, and nothing must be worshipped except for Him.

The word tawheed is itself derived from the Arabic word which means 'one'. Tawheed is the absolute unity of the Deity which is expressed concisely in the Islamic statement of faith: There is no god but Allah. Traditionally, Islamic scholars broke down the teaching of tawheed into three categories to help clarify all aspects of tawheed and those acts and beliefs which contradict it:

1. Oneness of Lordship (*Tawḥeed ar-Ruboobiyah*) — It is Allah alone who created all that exists, and it is He alone who continues to maintain, provide for, and control His creation.

2. Oneness of Worship (*Tawḥeed al-'Ibâdah*) — All forms of worship, inward and outward, should be directed only to Allah.

3. Oneness of Allah's names and attributes (*Tawḥeed al-Asmâ' was-Ṣifât*) — This involves acceptance of all the attributes which were revealed to the Prophet Muhammad (ﷺ) to describe Allah, while maintaining that these names and attributes are free from any type of human deficiencies or limitations, and without distorting them or twisting their meanings.

The opposite of compete tawḥeed is defined in Islam as *shirk*. Shirk literally means to take partners with Allah in any aspect of His divinity. Shirk is the antithesis of Islam, which is based on the belief that full acceptance of tawḥeed leads to eternal salvation and corruption of tawḥeed leads to damnation. Thus, there is a vital need for books like this one to explain the details of tawḥeed and warn about actions which are considered shirk.

The teachings of Islam strictly guard the concept of monotheism without allowing for any deviation from its purity. This renowned book evaluates verses of the Noble Qur'an and additional statements made by the Prophet Muhammad (ﷺ) and some of the well-known scholars for the guidance they offer in understanding tawḥeed. Many actions which have implications of tawḥeed or shirk are clearly obvious; however, there are other acts and beliefs which cause many people to fall inadvertently into committing serious errors. This book will shed light on those errors. The concise style and thoroughness of *Kitâb at-Tawḥeed* has kept it a standard and widely published text for more than two hundred years since it was first written.

Chapter 1

Taw̲ḥeed

1.1

*A*llah (*Subḥânahu wa Ta'âlâ* — Glorified and Exalted is He) says:

﴿وَمَا خَلَقْتُ ٱلْجِنَّ وَٱلْإِنسَ إِلَّا لِيَعْبُدُونِ ۝ مَآ أُرِيدُ مِنْهُم مِّن رِّزْقٍ وَمَآ أُرِيدُ أَن يُطْعِمُونِ ۝ إِنَّ ٱللَّهَ هُوَ ٱلرَّزَّاقُ ذُو ٱلْقُوَّةِ ٱلْمَتِينُ ۝﴾

(سورة الذَّارِيَات: ٥٦-٥٨)

﴿I created the jinn and humankind only so that they should worship me. I seek no provision from them, nor do I ask that they should feed Me. Verily, Allah is the All-Provider, Owner of Power, the Most Strong.﴾ *(Qur'an 51: 56-58)*

Allah, the Exalted, informs us that it is He who created humans and the *jinn* (non-human, rational beings created by Allah from fire, often referred to as 'demons' or 'devils'). The wisdom behind that creation was that they worship Him alone and reject the worship of any other. He did not create them for any benefit for Himself, only that they should worship Him. He has undertaken to provide sustenance for them, and He is the Most Truthful in keeping His promises. He is Able to fulfil them, for He is All-Powerful, Most Strong.

Benefits derived from this verse:

1. The wisdom behind Allah's creation of the jinn and humankind is that they worship Him alone.
2. The verse confirms the presence of the jinn.
3. Allah is completely independent of His creation.
4. The source of all sustenance is Allah, but the jinn and humankind are still commanded to do all in their power to work to attain their needs.
5. The verse confirms two of Allah's names: *Ar-Razzâq* (the All-Provider) and *Al-Mateen* (Owner of Power).

Relevance to the subject of tawḥeed

These Qur'anic verses show that the wisdom behind the creation of humans and the jinn is the worship of Allah alone and the rejection of all objects of worship besides Allah.

1.2

Allah (ﷻ) says:

﴿وَلَقَدْ بَعَثْنَا فِى كُلِّ أُمَّةٍ رَّسُولًا أَنِ اعْبُدُوا اللَّهَ وَاجْتَنِبُوا الطَّاغُوتَ فَمِنْهُم مَّنْ هَدَى اللَّهُ وَمِنْهُم مَّنْ حَقَّتْ عَلَيْهِ الضَّلَالَةُ فَسِيرُوا فِى الْأَرْضِ فَانظُرُوا كَيْفَ كَانَ عَاقِبَةُ الْمُكَذِّبِينَ ۝﴾ (سورة النحل: ٣٦)

❰Verily, We have sent among every community a Messenger [proclaiming]: Worship [only] Allah and avoid ṭâghoot.[1] Then of

---

[1] *ṭâghoot*: all that is worshipped or obeyed in disobedience to Allah and His Messenger (ﷺ). There are many kinds of ṭâghoot. The leader of tâghoot is Satan — Allah's curse be upon him — and tâghoot includes all those who=

them were some whom Allah guided, and of them were some upon whom the straying was justified. So travel through the land and see what was the end of those who denied [the truth].❯ *(Qur'an 16: 36)*

Allah, Most Glorified, informs us in these verses that He has sent to every human community a Messenger, who conveyed to them the Message and ordered them to believe in only One God, Allah, and to reject all false gods and objects of worship other than Him. The people who heard from these Messengers are divided into two groups. The first are those whom Allah guided to goodness and who responded positively to the guidance of the Messengers and abstained from all that was forbidden to them. The second group were forbidden from success and rejected the truth, and therefore they were losers, both in this world and the hereafter. Whoever travels throughout the earth, seeking to learn from it, will see the evidence of Allah's retribution upon some of those who stubbornly rejected the guidance of Allah and His Messengers. Examples of rebellious communities which Allah destroyed are the people of 'Âd, Thamood,[2] and Pharaoh.

Benefits derived from this verse

1. The verse is evidence that humankind has not been neglected and left without guidance.

2. The verse shows the universality of the Message to all nations, and the details of the Message brought by each new Messenger abrogated that of the previous Messenger.

=change the judgement of Allah; all those who judge by other than that which Allah has revealed; all those who call to the worship of others besides Allah; and all those who are worshipped besides Allah when they are pleased with that worship.

[2] 'Âd and Thamood: ancient communities that Allah destroyed because of their disbelief and rejection of the Messengers

3. The mission of the Messengers was to call people to the worship of Allah and call them to reject all false deities.

4. Only Allah grants guidance and success.

5. The fact that Allah has ordained something for a person does not necessitate that Allah is pleased with it.

6. It is desirable to travel in the land with the intention of taking heed of the example of the communities of old, whom Allah has destroyed because of their disbelief.

Relevance to the subject of tawḥeed

This Qur'anic verse proves that worship of Allah is of no benefit if the worship of others besides Him is not rejected.

1.3

Allah (ﷻ) says:

﴿ ۞ وَقَضَىٰ رَبُّكَ أَلَّا تَعْبُدُوٓاْ إِلَّآ إِيَّاهُ وَبِٱلْوَٰلِدَيْنِ إِحْسَٰنًا إِمَّا يَبْلُغَنَّ عِندَكَ ٱلْكِبَرَ أَحَدُهُمَآ أَوْ كِلَاهُمَا فَلَا تَقُل لَّهُمَآ أُفٍّ وَلَا تَنْهَرْهُمَا وَقُل لَّهُمَا قَوْلًا كَرِيمًا ۝ وَٱخْفِضْ لَهُمَا جَنَاحَ ٱلذُّلِّ مِنَ ٱلرَّحْمَةِ وَقُل رَّبِّ ٱرْحَمْهُمَا كَمَا رَبَّيَانِي صَغِيرًا ۝ ﴾

(سورة الإسراء: ٢٣-٢٤)

❲Your Lord has decreed that you worship none but Him, and that you be dutiful to your parents. If one of them or both of them attain old age in your life, say not to them a word of disrespect [such as 'uff!'], nor shout at them, but address them in terms of honour. And lower unto them the wing of submission and humility through mercy, and say: My Lord! Bestow on them Your Mercy as they did bring me up when I was a child.❳   *(Qur'an 17: 23-24)*

Allah, Most Glorified, commands all those who are obligated to obey Him to worship Him alone and to observe filial piety and devotion. Allah affirms the right of parents upon their offspring immediately after mentioning His own right upon His slaves. Then He describes some ways to show respect to parents, especially when they become frail and elderly, such as not displaying annoyance with them and not raising one's voice or scolding them, instead speaking to them in tones of gentleness and kindness, and supplicating to Allah on their behalf — both while they are alive and after their death.

Benefits derived from these verses

1. It is an obligation to worship Allah alone.
2. It is an obligation upon every Muslim to show filial piety and devotion to both parents.
3. It is a communal responsibility of the Muslim society to ensure the rights of parents upon their offspring.

Relevance to the subject of tawheed

These Qur'anic verses prove the obligation of worshipping Allah, alone and without partners.

1.4

Allah (ﷻ) says:

﴿ ۞ وَٱعْبُدُواْ ٱللَّهَ وَلَا تُشْرِكُواْ بِهِۦ شَيْـًٔا ۖ وَبِٱلْوَٰلِدَيْنِ إِحْسَٰنًا وَبِذِى ٱلْقُرْبَىٰ وَٱلْيَتَٰمَىٰ وَٱلْمَسَٰكِينِ وَٱلْجَارِ ذِى ٱلْقُرْبَىٰ وَٱلْجَارِ ٱلْجُنُبِ وَٱلصَّاحِبِ بِٱلْجَنۢبِ وَٱبْنِ ٱلسَّبِيلِ وَمَا مَلَكَتْ أَيْمَٰنُكُمْ ۗ إِنَّ ٱللَّهَ لَا يُحِبُّ مَن كَانَ مُخْتَالًا فَخُورًا ۝ ﴾

(سورة النِّساء: ٣٦)

❨Worship Allah and join none with Him in worship, and do good to parents, kinfolk, orphans, the poor, the neighbour who is near of kin, the neighbour who is a stranger, the companion by your side, the wayfarer, and those [slaves] whom your right hands possess. Verily, Allah does not love those who are proud and boastful.❩ *(Qur'an 4: 36)*

Sincerity is the foundation upon which true religion is built, and Allah commenced this verse by commanding sincerity in worship and the rejection of all false deities. He followed this up by mentioning the obligation to show goodness to parents because parents are the means by which we are brought into the world and cared for when we are young. Allah, the Exalted, did not neglect the rights of the kinfolk, for they are also most deserving of a Muslim's benevolence and kindness.

Then, in order that the rest of a Muslim's brothers and sisters in Islam be not downhearted, Allah made clear the rights of others who are close to the Muslim. He enjoined kindness to the orphans and the poor, whether close relatives or not. Allah mentioned first the neighbour who has familial rights and Islamic rights over the Muslim, then the nearby resident who is not related, such as a non-Muslim neighbour. Then Allah mentions the rights of close companions, which also include a Muslim's spouse and a Muslim's travelling companion. Islam has encouraged the Muslim to travel in the land with the intention of doing business and taking heed of the punishment meted out to former peoples. Because of this, Allah has obliged the Muslim to help the traveller who is in need — whether it be with material assistance or otherwise.

Allah, Most Glorified, affirmed the obligation of fairness and justice in dealing with other Muslims, and He has not forgotten the slaves. In fact, Allah requires us to give them their Islamic rights, to treat them with gentleness and mercy, and to recognize their human rights. Because all these deeds cited in the verse are righteous deeds, they bring about a fear of Allah and prevent a Muslim from becoming proud and self-absorbed, two attributes that would cause the reward of one's deeds to be lost.

Benefits derived from this verse

1. It is an obligation to worship Allah alone.
2. Filial piety and obedience are required as long as it does not entail disobedience to Allah and His Prophet (*ṣalla Allâhu 'alayhi wa sallam* — blessings and peace be upon him) nor cause harm, for Allah's Messenger (ﷺ) said: «Do not harm others nor reciprocate (when harm is done to you).» (a reliable hadith recorded by Aḥmad and Ibn Mâjah)
3. It is a legal obligation to maintain close family ties, according to the closeness of the relationship.
4. It is a duty to treat the orphans in one's care well by guiding them, directing their affairs, and properly managing their wealth.
5. Kindness to the poor and needy is a virtue, and the varieties of such kindness are numerous.
6. It is an obligation to give neighbours their rights.
7. The verse is an exhortation to Muslims to help all of their companions who request assistance, whether travelling companions or resident friends.
8. It is a duty to help the lost wayfarer.
9. Kindness to slaves is an obligation.
10. The traits of pride and vanity are forbidden.
11. The verse is an affirmation of Allah's attribute of love.

Relevance to the subject of tawḥeed

This Qur'anic verse proves the obligation of sincerity and purity of worship for Allah alone and the rejection of all other objects of worship.

Important note

In an Islamic society, neighbours fall into three categories:

1. The first has three rights: (i) the right of kinship, (ii) the right of a Muslim, and (iii) the right of a resident neighbour.

2. The second has two rights: (i) the right of a Muslim, and (ii) the right of a resident neighbour.

3. The third has only one right: (i) the right of a neighbour. This category is comprised of the non-Muslim neighbours who live in the Islamic state.

1.5

Allah (ﷻ) says:

﴿ قُلْ تَعَالَوْا أَتْلُ مَا حَرَّمَ رَبُّكُمْ عَلَيْكُمْ أَلَّا تُشْرِكُوا بِهِ شَيْئًا وَبِالْوَالِدَيْنِ إِحْسَانًا وَلَا تَقْتُلُوا أَوْلَادَكُم مِّنْ إِمْلَاقٍ نَّحْنُ نَرْزُقُكُمْ وَإِيَّاهُمْ وَلَا تَقْرَبُوا الْفَوَاحِشَ مَا ظَهَرَ مِنْهَا وَمَا بَطَنَ وَلَا تَقْتُلُوا النَّفْسَ الَّتِي حَرَّمَ اللَّهُ إِلَّا بِالْحَقِّ ذَٰلِكُمْ وَصَّاكُم بِهِ لَعَلَّكُمْ تَعْقِلُونَ ﴾

(سورة الأنعام: ١٥١)

﴿Say [O Muhammad!]: Come, I will recite what your Lord has prohibited for you: join not anything in worship with Him; be good and dutiful to your parents; kill not your children because of poverty — We provide sustenance for you and for them; come not near to shameful sin [such as adultery and fornication], whether committed openly or in secret; and kill not anyone whom Allah has forbidden except for a just cause [in accordance with Islamic law]. This He has commanded you that you may understand.﴾   *(Qur'an 6: 151)*

Allah, Most Glorified, ordered His Prophet, Muhammad (ﷺ), to call the people to come forth and listen to the commands of Allah concerning what has been prohibited for them. Because it is the people who commit *shirk*[3] who most often oppose good deeds, Allah began by warning them to abstain from associating partners with Him. Then He mentioned many of the evil deeds which they used to commit and forbade such actions.

Allah, the Exalted, ordered them to be kind and dutiful to their parents and forbade them from killing their offspring, for such acts are evil and result in the serious sin of cutting family relations. He mentioned poverty here because the fear of poverty was the most common reason for the killing of children in the days of ignorance.[4] To assuage their fear of poverty, Allah stated that He has undertaken the responsibility of sustaining them and their children.

Then He prohibited all acts of disobedience — both open and secret. The extra-judicial killing of any person is a great sin, whatever the reason. Unlawful killing causes many problems in society, such as social unrest, the breakdown of law and order, revenge killing, and vigilantism. Thus, Allah laid great stress upon the prohibition of unlawful killing, by ending the verse saying: ❨This He has commanded❩ — so that His slaves may understand and act in accordance with it.

Benefits derived from this verse

1. Shirk is the greatest of sins and no other deed will accepted by Allah if a person does not reject shirk.[5] Because of its importance,

---

[3] *shirk*: associating partners with Allah or directing worship to something other than Allah. Shirk is the opposite of tawḥeed.

[4] days of ignorance (*jâhiliyyah*): the time of ignorance and polytheism prior to Islam

[5] ❨Verily, Allah forgives not [the sin of] setting up partners [in worship] with=

Allah mentioned it first.

2. Being good and dutiful to parents is an obligation.

3. It is forbidden to kill one's children in Islam. This includes abortion if it is carried out after forty days from the start of the pregnancy.[6]

4. Allah has undertaken the responsibility of providing for all humankind.

5. Attempting to prevent pregnancy due to fear of poverty is an act from the days of ignorance.

6. Shameful sins, such as adultery and fornication and all that leads up to them (like flirting, dating, kissing, and caressing), are forbidden in Islam.

7. It is prohibited to kill any person whose life has been forbidden by Allah, except by judicial means in accordance with Islamic law.

8. Allah has not defined here what is meant by 'judicial means', but the Prophet (ﷺ) mentioned something about it in an authentic *hadith* [statement of the Prophet (ﷺ)] concerning adultery, disbelief after belief, and the taking of a life for a life.[7]

Relevance to the subject of tawḥeed

This Qur'anic verse warns against shirk in any shape or form.

=Him, but He forgives whom He wills sins other than that.⟩ (*Qur'an 4: 116*)

[6] This does not mean that abortion before forty days is legal, but that before forty days it is not considered murder; it is still forbidden, unless there is some life-threatening danger to the mother.

[7] Abu Dâwood. This hadith means that it is not permissible to take the life of a Muslim except for three reasons:

(i) adultery,

(ii) apostasy, and

(iii) murder.

1.6

It is reported that Mu'âdh ibn Jabal (*raḍiya Allâhu 'anhu* — may Allah be pleased with him) said: «I was riding behind the Prophet (ﷺ) on a donkey, when he said to me: Mu'âdh, do you know what the right of Allah is upon His slaves and what the right of the slaves is upon Allah? I said: Allah and His Messenger know best. He (ﷺ) said: The right of Allah upon His slaves is that they worship Him and do not associate anything with Him; and the right of the slaves upon Allah is that those who do not associate anything with Him will not be punished. I said: O Messenger of Allah, shall I not inform the people (of this)? He (ﷺ) said: Do not inform them, lest they rely upon it.» (recorded by Bukhari and Muslim)

Mu'âdh ibn Jabal (ﷺ) informs us that he was riding behind the Prophet (ﷺ) on a donkey one day, and the Prophet (ﷺ) wished to favour him with the answers to certain important questions. In order to achieve this, the Prophet (ﷺ) chose to ask Mu'âdh some rhetorical questions to arouse his curiosity. Mu'âdh did not wish to venture an opinion on a matter of which he had no knowledge, so he replied to the questions by saying that Allah and His Messenger know best. Then the Prophet (ﷺ) explained to him two important truths: the obligation which Allah has placed upon His slaves and the bounty and grace which He has made incumbent upon Himself. Because Mu'âdh cared so much about the welfare and happiness of the Muslims, he asked the Prophet's permission to tell them about this good news, but the Prophet (ﷺ) refused his request, for he feared that the Muslims might depend upon this promise and stop competing with each other in the performance of good deeds, which wipe out their bad deeds and elevate them in status. However, Mu'âdh eventually did inform the other Muslims of this, since he was fearful of concealing anything of the Guidance from them, although the reason for the Prophet's warning his people against depending upon these words is clear.

Benefits derived from this hadith

1. It is legitimate to ride behind another person if it does not overtax the riding beast.
2. The Prophet (ﷺ) showed humility by sharing his donkey with another person.
3. The sweat of the donkey is not impure.
4. Muʿādh ibn Jabal (ﷺ) was a virtuous Companion of the Prophet (ﷺ).
5. Asking rhetorical questions is an Islamic way of teaching.
6. It is forbidden for people to venture to discuss matters about which they have no knowledge.
7. The first obligation of the slave towards Allah is to worship Him alone.
8. Those who die while believing and practising tawḥeed are saved from the torment of hellfire as long as they do not commit any of the major sins which would cause them to be punished in the Fire.
9. Although it is mentioned in an authentic hadith that the Prophet (ﷺ) said: «If a person conceals knowledge, Allah will make him wear a bridle of fire on the Day of Resurrection» (Abu Dâwood and at-Tirmidhi, who said it was reliable), there is no contradiction here. The forbiddance of concealing knowledge in this hadith is general, while the hadith of Muʿādh contains an exception to that forbiddance in special circumstances: it permits one to conceal knowledge if there is a fear that revealing it will cause disorder or strife in the Muslim community.

Relevance to the subject of tawḥeed

This hadith proves that the right of Allah over His slaves is that they worship Him and do not associate any partners with Him.

Chapter 2

Tawḥeed's superiority and how it wipes away sins

2.1

Allah (ﷻ) says:

﴿ٱلَّذِينَ ءَامَنُوا۟ وَلَمْ يَلْبِسُوٓا۟ إِيمَٰنَهُم بِظُلْمٍ أُو۟لَٰٓئِكَ لَهُمُ ٱلْأَمْنُ وَهُم مُّهْتَدُونَ ﴾

(سورة الأنعام: ٨٢)

﴿It is those who believe and do not adulterate their faith [in Allah's Oneness] with wrongdoing [such as associating partners with Him], for them [only] is there safety, and they are rightly-guided.﴾

(Qur'an 6: 82)

Allah informs us that those who practise tawḥeed, without corrupting their faith with shirk, have His promise of safety from hellfire in the hereafter, and He will guide them to the Straight Path[8] in this life.

Benefits derived from this verse

1. When faith is adulterated by shirk, faith has no value.

---

[8] Straight Path: the path of tawḥeed, which is the only path to ultimate success

2. Allah refers to shirk as wrongdoing, injustice, and oppression.[9]
3. Those who do not confuse their belief with shirk are promised safety from punishment in the hereafter.

Relevance to the subject of tawḥeed

This Qur'anic verse proves that those who die practising tawḥeed and having turned to Allah in repentance from any major sins they committed will be saved from punishment in hellfire. Those who die practising tawḥeed but having committed major sins without having repented will be saved from eternal damnation in the Fire, although they may be first punished in it or forgiven, as Allah wills.

2.2

It is reported on the authority of 'Ubâdah ibn aṣ-Ṣâmit (رضي الله عنه) that Allah's Messenger (ﷺ) said: «Whoever testifies that none is worthy of worship except Allah alone, without partners, and that Muhammad is His slave and Messenger, and that 'Eesâ (Jesus) is His slave and Messenger and His Word which was bestowed upon Maryam (Mary) and a Spirit [created] from Him, and that paradise and hell are realities, then Allah will admit him to paradise, whatever his deeds might be.» (recorded by Bukhari)

This hadith tells us the characteristics of those who will enter paradise, in spite of their deeds. They are those who pronounce the Islamic testimony of faith,[10] understand its meaning, and act in accordance with it in their worship. They affirm their belief in the

---

[9] meanings of the Arabic word *dhulm*, found in the verse under discussion
[10] testimony of faith: the declaration of faith made by every Muslim that there is no god but Allah, none has the right to be worshipped but Him, and that Muhammad (ﷺ) is His Messenger

status of Muhammad as Allah's slave and Messenger. Likewise, they believe in 'Eesâ's status as a slave and Messenger of Allah. They believe that 'Eesâ was created within Maryam (may Allah's peace be upon both of them) by Allah's Word, the command ﴾Be!﴿, and that Allah absolved Maryam from the charges levelled against her by certain iniquitous Jews. They also affirm their belief that paradise will be the abode of the believers and that hell is for the disbelievers. Those who die upon this state of belief will have their sins forgiven.

Benefits derived from this hadith

1. The Muslim testimony of faith is the essence of the religion.

2. The testimony of faith is not valid except from one who understands its meaning and acts accordingly.

3. Mentioning together the Prophet Muhammad's status as both slave and Messenger is a refutation of those who make exaggerated claims about him (ﷺ).[11]

4. Affirming the status of 'Eesâ (*'alayhi as-salâm* — peace be upon him) as Allah's slave and Messenger is a rebuttal of the claims of divinity made for him by the Christians.

5. 'Eesâ was created from Maryam (may Allah's peace be upon them both) without a father by Allah's Word ﴾Be!﴿; and this is a refutation of the claims of certain Jews, who had accused Maryam of the sin of fornication.

6. The mention of Allah's Word is an affirmation of Allah's attribute of (the power of) speech.

7. Humankind will be resurrected on the Day of Judgement.

8. The hadith confirms the existence of paradise and hell.

9. Sinful Muslims will not dwell eternally in hellfire.

---

[11] Such as the deviant Braillawis of the Indian subcontinent who have elevated him (ﷺ) to the status of a deity — may Allah save us from such blasphemy!

Relevance to the subject of tawḥeed

This hadith proves that whoever dies while adhering to and practising tawḥeed will enter paradise, whatever the person's deeds may have been.

2.3

'Itbân (ﷺ) reported that the Prophet (ﷺ) said: «Indeed, Allah has forbidden hell for the person who testifies that none is worthy of worship except Allah, seeking nothing by it but Allah's Countenance.» (recorded by Bukhari and Muslim)

This hadith informs us that Allah, the Exalted, will save from the punishment of hellfire all those who confirm His Oneness and act in accordance with that, as long as their intentions are only to get close to Allah by obeying Him and pleasing Him and not to do good deeds to show off or gain a good reputation.

Benefits derived from this hadith

1. No one who sincerely believes in the Oneness of Allah will enter hellfire.
2. Words and deeds are of no value without the intention of getting closer to Allah.
3. The hadith is a confirmation of Allah's attribute of a Face.

Relevance to the subject of tawḥeed

This hadith proves that whoever dies while believing sincerely in the Oneness of Allah will be saved from hellfire.

2.4

Abu Saʿeed al-Khudri (ﷺ) reported that the Messenger of Allah (ﷺ) said: «Moosâ (Moses) said: Lord, teach me something by which I may remember You and supplicate to You. Allah answered: Say, '*Lâ ilâha illâ Allâh.*'[12] Moosâ said: Lord, all of Your slaves say that. Allah said: Moosâ, even were the seven heavens and all that they contain other than Me[13] and the seven earths as well all put on one side of a scale and 'Lâ ilâha illâ Allâh' put on the other, the latter would outweigh them.» (a sound hadith recorded by Ibn Ḥibbân and al-Ḥâkim)

Our Prophet (ﷺ) informs us that Allah's Messenger Moosâ (ﷺ) asked Allah to teach him a special act of worship by which he might praise Him and get closer to Him. So Allah taught him the words of sincerity, which are 'Lâ ilâha illâ Allâh'. Moosâ asked Allah to teach him something else because this testimony of faith was already well-known to the people. Allah responded that were this testimony to be weighed against the seven heavens and the seven earths and all that is in them, it would outweigh them, for it is the essence of every religion and the foundation of every community of believers.

Benefits derived from this hadith

1. It is permissible to ask Allah for something special for oneself.
2. The Messengers do not know anything about the Unseen except

---

[12] *Lâ ilâha illâ Allâh*: There is no god but Allah [and none has the right to be worshiped except Him]

[13] This must not be understood to mean that Allah is contained in His creation, as Allah has confirmed in numerous places in the Qur'an that He is above His creation.

what Allah reveals to them.

3. The hadith confirms Allah's attribute of speech.

4. The seven heavens, which are layered one above the other,[14] contain inhabitants.

5. The seven earths are, like the seven heavens, inhabited.

6. This hadith is evidence of the difference between some deeds and others.

7. This hadith clearly demonstrates the greatness and virtue of the Islamic testimony of faith.

Relevance to the subject of tawḥeed

This hadith proves that the words of tawḥeed, 'Lâ ilâha illâ Allâh', are the best way to remember, glorify, and worship Allah, and they are the weightiest deed in value.

2.5

Anas (رضي الله عنه) reported that he heard Allah's Messenger (ﷺ) say: «Allah, the Exalted, said: O son of Adam! Were you to come to Me with the world full of sins and meet Me without associating any partner with me, I would come to you with a similar amount of forgiveness.» (a reliable hadith recorded by at-Tirmidhi)

Allah, the Exalted, informs us in this *hadith qudsi* [communicated to Prophet Muhammad (ﷺ) by Allah, but not part of the Qur'an] that those who die while having sincerely believed in the Oneness of Allah and having rejected all manner of shirk will find that Allah replaces all their bad deeds with good, even if their sins were so numerous as to fill the earth or almost fill it.

---

[14] See *Qur'an 67: 3*

Benefits derived from this hadith

1. The hadith confirms Allah's attribute of speech.
2. It is proof of the vastness of Allah's generosity and mercy.
3. Dying in a state of belief in the Oneness of Allah is a condition for obtaining Allah's forgiveness; and this matter necessitates further explanation:

> (i) Whoever died while accepting major shirk[15] will dwell eternally in hellfire.
>
> (ii) Whoever died rejecting both major shirk and minor shirk[16] will dwell eternally in paradise.
>
> (iii) Whoever died without committing major shirk, but was guilty of a small amount of minor shirk, will enter paradise if the person's good deeds outweigh the person's sins.
>
> (iv) Whoever died without committing major shirk, but was guilty of a small amount of minor shirk, will enter the Fire if the person's sins outweigh the person's good deeds, but will not remain in hellfire forever.

Relevance to the subject of tawḥeed

This hadith proves that whoever dies without being guilty of any kind of shirk will enter paradise, even when the person's sins are many.

---

[15] major shirk: examples include giving the characteristics of divinity to anything other than Allah and directing any type of worship to other than Allah; it takes one out of the fold of Islam.

[16] minor shirk: examples include swearing an oath by other than Allah and doing a good deed to be praised by the people rather than doing it solely to please Allah; it is a major sin but does not take one out of the fold of Islam.

Chapter 3

Entering paradise without a reckoning

3.1

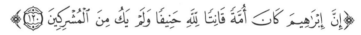

﴾إِنَّ إِبْرَٰهِيمَ كَانَ أُمَّةً قَانِتًا لِّلَّهِ حَنِيفًا وَلَمْ يَكُ مِنَ ٱلْمُشْرِكِينَ ۝﴿

(سورة النحل: ١٢٠)

﴾Verily, Ibrâheem [Abraham] was an *ummah* [a leader having all the good and righteous qualities], obedient to Allah, ḥaneefan [worshipping none but Allah], and he was not one of the polytheists.﴿

(Qur'an 16: 120)

Allah, Most Glorified, informs us in this verse that His Messenger Ibrâheem (﷽) was a leader in religion, a teacher of goodness, and a worshipper who was always humble and obedient to his Lord. Ibrâheem rejected shirk in all its manifestations and devoted himself exclusively to the worship of Allah without falling into shirk, either in word, deed, or belief.

Benefits derived from this verse

1. Tawḥeed is the basis of all true religion.
2. It is an obligation to follow Ibrâheem (﷽) by sincerely worshipping only Allah.
3. It is an obligation upon those who call others to Islam to set a good

example for the people in all that they do.

4. The nature of true worship, as exemplified by the prophets, is unchanging.

5. Tawheed is not acceptable without rejection of shirk.

6. The claim of Quraysh (the people of Makkah), in the days of ignorance, that in practising polytheism they were following the religion of Ibrâheem (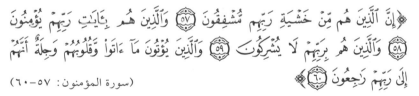) is rejected.

Relevance to the subject of tawheed

This Qur'anic verse proves that whoever exemplified these four attributes — worships Allah, obeys Allah, practices goodness, and rejects shirk — has earned the right to paradise, as did Ibrâheem (), without reckoning or punishment.

3.2

Allah () says:

$$\text{﴿إِنَّ ٱلَّذِينَ هُم مِّنْ خَشْيَةِ رَبِّهِم مُّشْفِقُونَ ۝ وَٱلَّذِينَ هُم بِـَٔايَـٰتِ رَبِّهِمْ يُؤْمِنُونَ ۝ وَٱلَّذِينَ هُم بِرَبِّهِمْ لَا يُشْرِكُونَ ۝ وَٱلَّذِينَ يُؤْتُونَ مَآ ءَاتَوا۟ وَّقُلُوبُهُمْ وَجِلَةٌ أَنَّهُمْ إِلَىٰ رَبِّهِمْ رَٰجِعُونَ ۝﴾}$$

(سورة المؤمنون: ٥٧-٦٠)

❲Those who live in awe for fear of their Lord, and those who believe in the Signs of their Lord, and those who join not anyone as partners with their Lord [in worship], and those who give that which they give [of their charity] with their hearts full of fear [whether their charity has been accepted or not] because to their Lord they must return.❳

(Qur'an 23: 57-60)

In these verses, Allah, Most Glorified, describes the believers by four of their attributes, for which they deserve praise and commendation. They fear the punishment of their Lord, the All-

Mighty, the All-Powerful. They believe in the revealed signs of Allah (such as the Scriptures) and His natural signs (such as the planets, the stars, the seasons, the animals, the birds, and the plants) which prove His existence, and they believe in the truth of the Message of Muhammad (ﷺ). They are guided by these signs and do not associate partners with Allah, either openly or secretly. Because of their strong faith, they fear that Allah will not accept their charity or their good deeds. Allah testifies to their mutual rivalry in performing virtuous deeds, and He informs us that they precede others in doing so.

Benefits derived from these verses

1. It is an obligation to fear Allah.
2. It is an obligation to believe in the signs of Allah.
3. Shirk, in all its manifestations, is forbidden.
4. The believers are concerned about whether or not their deeds will be accepted.
5. It is recommended to encourage each other by competing in the performance of good deeds.

Relevance to the subject of tawheed

These Qur'anic verses prove that those who personify these four attributes and purify themselves from shirk, which would nullify their good deeds, will have the right to enter paradise without a reckoning and without punishment. They have achieved the purest tawheed, and paradise is their reward.

3·3

It is reported that Ḥusayn ibn ʿAbdur-Raḥmân said: «I was with Saʿeed ibn Jubayr and he asked: Who among you saw the shooting star last night? I answered that I had seen it, and I explained to him that I had not been at prayer because I had been stung (by a scorpion). He asked: Then what did you do? I replied: I used *ruqyah*.[17] He asked: What made you do that? I answered: A hadith I heard from ash-Shaʻbi. He asked: What did he tell you? I said: He reported from Buraydah al-Ḥuṣayyib who said that ruqyah is not permitted except in the two cases of the evil eye and stings. He said: He who limits himself to what he has heard, has done well, but Ibn ʻAbbâs (رضي الله عنهما) reported to us that the Prophet (ﷺ) said: All the nations were made to pass before me, and I saw a prophet with a small group, and a prophet with only one or two people, and a prophet with no one. Then there was shown to me a large number of people which I thought to be my *Ummah* (community or nation), but it was said to me: This is Moosâ and his people. Then I looked and saw a huge crowd, at which it was said to me; These are your people. Among them are seventy thousand who will enter paradise without a reckoning or punishment. Then the Prophet (ﷺ) got up and went to his house, and the people began to discuss who they might be. Some of them said: Perhaps they are the Companions of the Messenger of Allah (ﷺ). Others said: Perhaps they are those who were born in Islam and have never associated any partners with Allah. While they were talking about it, the Messenger of Allah (ﷺ) came out, and they told him (about what they had been saying). He (ﷺ) said: They are those who do not treat themselves with ruqyah, nor practise treatment by cauterization, nor believe in good or bad omens, but depend upon and trust in their Lord (alone). Upon hearing this ʻUkkâshah ibn Miḥṣan (رضي الله عنه) stood up and said: Ask Allah for me that I be one of them. He (ﷺ) said: You are one of them. Then another man stood up and said: Ask Allah that I (also) be one of them. He (ﷺ) said:

---

[17] *ruqyah*: to recite a part of the Qurʼan (such as *Soorat al-Fâtiḥah*) or to supplicate to Allah using words prescribed by the Messenger of Allah (ﷺ) in authentic hadiths in order to obtain relief from illness

'Ukkâshah has preceded you.» (recorded by Bukhari and Muslim)

Ḥusayn ibn 'Abdur-Raḥmân (رضي الله عنه) informs us of a discussion which took place between him and the *tâbi'ee* [18] Sa'eed ibn Jubayr concerning the use of ruqyah. Ḥusayn had been stung by a scorpion, for which he resorted to using ruqyah, in accordance with the *Sunnah* [words and deeds of the Prophet (صلى الله عليه وسلم)].

When Sa'eed asked him for a proof for his action, Ḥusayn informed him of the hadith of ash-Sha'bi, which permits the use of ruqyah for the treatment of the evil eye and stings. Sa'eed praised him for his adherence to the hadith, but related to him a hadith which advocates the rejection of ruqyah. This hadith from Ibn 'Abbâs (رضي الله عنهما) also mentions the rejection of cauterization and belief in omens and requires us to have complete trust in Allah and depend upon Him alone. The hadith of Ibn 'Abbâs says that when 'Ukkâshah (رضي الله عنه) requested that the Prophet (صلى الله عليه وسلم) ask Allah to make him one of the seventy thousand who would enter paradise without reckoning and without punishment, the Prophet (صلى الله عليه وسلم) said that he was one of them; but when another man made the same request, the Messenger of Allah (صلى الله عليه وسلم) gently but firmly closed the door upon any further requests by saying: «Ukkâshah has preceded you.»

Benefits derived from this hadith

1. The *salaf* (pious, early generations of Muslims) used to keep away from *riyâ'* (showing off, especially in acts of worship) and anything that might lead to it.

2. It is an obligation to ask for proof before accepting anything in the religion.

---

[18] *Tâbi'ee*: a Muslim who met and reported from one or more of the Companions of the Prophet (صلى الله عليه وسلم)

3. It is permissible to use ruqyah to treat the evil eye and stings on the condition that the ruqyah is of a kind endorsed by the Islamic law — from the Qur'an or the authentic supplications of the Prophet (ﷺ) in the Arabic language.

4. The salaf had profound knowledge.

5. Acting in accordance with the Qur'an and the Sunnah takes precedence over all personal opinions.

6. The hadith shows the virtue of the salaf and their good manners and politeness in passing on Islamic knowledge.

7. There is a disparity in the number of followers of the different prophets, and some prophets had no followers.

8. The number of followers a person may have is not necessarily an indication of the truth or falseness of the message.

9. The hadith shows the virtue of Moosâ (ﷺ) and his people.

10. It also shows the excellence of the Ummah of Muhammad (ﷺ) in comparison with other communities.

11. The Companions loved all good deeds.

12. It is permissible to engage in debate in religious matters.

13. Whoever possesses the four attributes mentioned in the hadith has perfected tawheed and will enter paradise.

14. It is permissible for us to ask virtuous persons, who are still living, to supplicate to Allah on our behalf.

15. There is no contradiction between the hadith of Ash-Sha'bi, which permits ruqyah when the conditions for its acceptance are met, and the hadith of Ibn 'Abbâs (ﷺ), which forbids ruqyah when those conditions are not met.

Relevance to the subject of tawheed

This hadith proves that whoever possessed the four attributes mentioned — not practicing ruqyah or cauterization, not believing in omens, instead depending upon Allah alone — has perfected tawheed and will enter paradise without reckoning or punishment.

Chapter 4

Fear of shirk

4.1

Allah (ﷻ) says:

﴿إِنَّ اللَّهَ لَا يَغْفِرُ أَن يُشْرَكَ بِهِۦ وَيَغْفِرُ مَا دُونَ ذَٰلِكَ لِمَن يَشَآءُ وَمَن يُشْرِكْ بِاللَّهِ فَقَدِ افْتَرَىٰٓ إِثْمًا عَظِيمًا ۝﴾ (سورة النِّسَاء: ٤٨)

﴿Verily, Allah forgives not that partners be set up with Him [in worship] but He forgives other than that to whom He pleases; and whoever sets up partners with Allah [in worship], he has indeed invented an enormous wrong.﴾ *(Qur'an 4: 48)*

Shirk is the most dangerous of all sins, and the wickedest, and the most severely punished. Shirk dishonours and denigrates the Lord, All-Mighty, All-Powerful, and entails likening Allah to His creation. Allah informs us in this verse that He will not forgive the one who commits shirk and dies still committing shirk. As for those who die believing in the Oneness of Allah, although they may have committed some sins, Allah has promised them forgiveness, in accordance with His will. Then Allah explains why the ones who practice shirk will not be forgiven, saying that by their association of partners with Him, they have rejected Him and belied Him and committed a sin the like of which there is no other.

Benefits derived from this verse

1. Those who die being guilty of major shirk will assuredly go to hellfire.

2. Those who die believing in the Oneness of Allah, although they may have committed major sins, may be forgiven if Allah, the Exalted, so wills.

3. This verse is a reply to the Kharijites,[19] who charged those guilty of major sins with disbelief, and to the Mutazilites,[20] who believed that those guilty of major sins would spend eternity in the Fire.

4. This verse confirms the divine will, which is one of Allah's attributes.

Relevance to the subject of tawheed

This Qur'anic verse proves that Allah will not forgive those who are guilty of shirk, and this should be a warning to all.

4.2

Allah (ﷻ) says:

﴿وَإِذْ قَالَ إِبْرَٰهِيمُ رَبِّ ٱجْعَلْ هَٰذَا ٱلْبَلَدَ ءَامِنًا وَٱجْنُبْنِى وَبَنِىَّ أَن نَّعْبُدَ

ٱلْأَصْنَامَ ٣٥﴾   (سورة أبراهيم: ١٣)

﴿[Remember] when Ibrâheem said: My Lord! Make this city one of peace and security, and keep me and my sons away from worshipping idols.﴾   *(Qur'an 13: 35)*

---

[19] Kharijites: a deviant sect who claimed that committing major sins takes a person out of the fold of Islam

[20] Mutazilites: a deviant sect who denied the divine attributes of Allah and claimed that the believers who committed major sins would dwell eternally in hell

Allah informs us that Ibrâheem (عليه السلام) supplicated to Him to make Makkah a place of safety and stability because fear and chaos prevent people from worshipping and performing their religious duties. Then Ibrâheem followed this with another request to his Lord: that Allah preserve him and his family from idol worship, for he knew the danger of that, and he knew how easily people can be seduced by it.

Benefits derived from this verse

1. This verse shows the virtue of Makkah over other cities.
2. Ibrâheem prayed for the security and stability of Makkah.
3. This verse is evidence of the benefit of supplication.
4. The original religion of all the Messengers is one: belief in the Oneness of Allah.
5. It is desirable to supplicate on behalf of one's family.
6. It is forbidden to worship idols.

Relevance to the subject of tawḥeed

This Qur'anic verse proves that Ibrâheem (عليه السلام), even with his strong faith, feared for himself and his family that they might be affected by shirk. Thus, the obligation upon us to fear shirk is that much greater due to our weaknesses.

4·3

It is reported that the Prophet (صلى الله عليه وسلم) said: «Of the things which I fear for my Ummah, the thing which I fear most is minor shirk.» Then he was asked to explain what minor shirk is, and he said: «It is riyâ'.» (recorded by Aḥmad with a sound chain of narration)

The Prophet (ﷺ) informs us in this hadith that he fears for us and what he fears most is that we would fall into the sin of committing minor shirk. This shows how kind-hearted and compassionate the Prophet (ﷺ) was towards his Ummah and how concerned he was for their good. He knew the dangers of minor shirk and how it can strongly manifest itself in the community and pollute the pure monotheism of the Muslims, especially since it can afflict them without them even knowing it. This is why the Prophet (ﷺ) warned us to beware of it.

Benefits derived from this hadith

1. The Messenger of Allah (ﷺ) showed care and concern for his Ummah.
2. Shirk is divided into two categories: major shirk and minor shirk.
3. Riyâ', or showing off, is considered shirk.
4. It is an obligation to ask the people of knowledge about matters which confuse us.

Relevance to the subject of tawheed

This hadith proves that Allah's Messenger (ﷺ) feared for his Companions (may Allah be pleased with them) that they might unwittingly fall into minor shirk, in spite of their strong faith and understanding of Islam and tawheed. Therefore, we, with our comparatively weak faith and little knowledge, are even more obligated to fear both major and minor shirk.

4.4

It is reported on the authority of Ibn Mas'ood (ﷺ) that the Messenger of Allah (ﷺ) said: «Whoever dies while supplicating to a deity other than Allah will enter the Fire.» (recorded by Bukhari)

The Prophet (ﷺ) informs us that those who adulterate that which should be purely for Allah, by worshipping others besides Him, and die in this state, will have an eternal abode in hellfire.

Benefits derived from this hadith

1. Those who die practicing shirk will enter hellfire. If it was major shirk, they will abide in the Fire forever. If it was minor shirk, then Allah will punish them as much as He wills, then they will be allowed to leave the Fire.
2. People will be judged based upon their last actions in this world.[21]

Relevance to the subject of tawheed

This hadith proves that people who die while upon the path of calling upon a deity other than Allah will enter hellfire; therefore, it is incumbent upon us to fear shirk.

4.5

It is reported on the authority of Jâbir (ﷺ) that Allah's Messenger (ﷺ) said: «Whoever meets Allah without associating partners with Him will enter paradise, and whoever meets Allah associating anything with Him will enter the Fire (of hell).» (recorded by Muslim)

---

[21] It is reported on the authority of 'Abdullâh ibn 'Amr (ﷺ) that Allah's Messenger (ﷺ) said: «Verily, he whose abode will be paradise, his final deed will be of the deeds of the people of paradise, whatever he did (previously). And verily, he who is destined for hell, his final deed will be of the deeds of the people of hell, whatever he did (previously).» [recorded by Aḥmad and at-Tirmidhi, who said it was *hasan-saheeh-ghareeb*, i.e., somewhere between the classifications of authentic and reliable, though narrated at some point(s) in its chain of narrators by only one narrator.]

The Prophet (ﷺ) informs us that those who die without associating any type of partner with Allah in His divinity, either in His Lordship, or worship, or in His divine names and attributes, is promised an abode in paradise, while those who die practising shirk will abide in hellfire.

Benefits derived from this hadith

1. This hadith confirms the existence of paradise and hell.
2. People will be judged based upon their last actions in this world.
3. Whoever dies believing in the Oneness of Allah will not dwell forever in hellfire. Such a person will find an eternal abode in paradise.
4. Whoever dies while still committing shirk must dwell eternally in hellfire.

Relevance to the subject of tawheed

This hadith proves that whoever dies upon the path of shirk will enter the Fire, and the knowledge of this obliges us to fear shirk, in all its manifestations.

Chapter 5

The call to tawḥeed

5.1

*A*llah (ﷻ) says:

﴿قُلْ هَـٰذِهِۦ سَبِيلِىٓ أَدْعُوٓاْ إِلَى ٱللَّهِ عَلَىٰ بَصِيرَةٍ أَنَا۠ وَمَنِ ٱتَّبَعَنِى وَسُبْحَـٰنَ ٱللَّهِ وَمَآ أَنَا۠ مِنَ ٱلْمُشْرِكِينَ ۝﴾ (سورة يُوسُف : ١٠٨)

﴿Say [O Muhammad]: This is my way. I invite unto Allah [to the Oneness of Allah] with sure knowledge, I and whoever follows me [must also invite to the Oneness of Allah]. Glorified and Exalted is Allah, and I am not of the polytheists.﴾ *(Qur'an 12: 108)*

In this verse, Allah commands His Prophet (ﷺ) to teach the people and make clear to them the religion and his Sunnah and his way of life and that of those who follow the call to Allah's religion. Through practicing tawḥeed, the Prophet (ﷺ) and those who believe in him and obey him are following divine guidance and acting upon knowledge and clear evidence. They exalt their Lord and glorify Him above all that those who commit shirk associate as partners with Allah, in His Lordship, in worship, and in His divine names and attributes. Thus, the Prophet (ﷺ) is innocent of the beliefs, words and deeds of the polytheists, including their shirk.

Benefits derived from this verse

1. Sincerity and purity of faith are an obligation when calling to the religion of Allah.

2. The call should be based upon a foundation of truth and evidence.

3. It is an obligation to stay free from shirk and its followers.

4. Deeds are not accepted unless they are in conformity with that which was brought by the Messenger of Allah (ﷺ).

5. It is an obligation to exalt Allah above all that is not becoming His Majesty.

Relevance to the subject of tawheed

This Qur'anic verse proves that the way of the Prophet (ﷺ) and those who follow him is to call the people to the religion of Allah, and this embodies the testimony that none is worthy of worship except Allah.

5.2

It is reported on the authority of Ibn 'Abbâs (رضي الله عنهما) that when Allah's Messenger (ﷺ) was sending Mu'âdh (رضي الله عنه) to Yemen, he (ﷺ) told him: «You are going to a people who are People of the Scripture (Jews and/or Christians). So the first thing to which you call them should be the testimony that none has the right to be worshipped except Allah. [Another narration uses the words 'that they testify to the Oneness of Allah'.] If they obey you in that, then inform them that Allah has made compulsory upon them five prayers every day and night. If they obey you in that, then inform them that Allah has made incumbent upon them *zakâh* (obligatory charity), which is to be taken from the rich among them and given to their poor. If they obey you in that, then be careful not to take the best of their wealth (as zakâh), and be careful of the supplication of those who have suffered injustice, for there is no obstacle between such supplication and Allah.» (recorded by Bukhari and Muslim).

The Prophet (ﷺ) sent Mu'âdh ibn Jabal (ﷺ) as his representative to Yemen, and he advised Mu'âdh about what was required of him there, beginning with the call to worship Allah alone, without partners. The Prophet (ﷺ) said that if the people accepted tawheed, then Mu'âdh must inform them of the greatest obligations upon them after tawheed, which are the prescribed prayers and zakâh. If the people followed this guidance, then it became incumbent upon Mu'âdh to maintain justice with them. This included not wronging them or causing them to suffer by taking the best of their property as zakâh, for that would constitute an injustice to them and might provoke them and cause them to invoke Allah against him — and the invocation of the oppressed and the wronged is never rejected by Allah.

Benefits derived from this hadith

1. The first thing to which the callers of Islam must call is tawheed — the Oneness of Allah.
2. It is an obligation to call to Allah with wisdom, step-by-step, beginning with the most important topic, then the next most important, and so on.
3. It is an obligation to observe the five daily prayers.
4. The *witr* prayer [22] is not obligatory.
5. Those who have more than they need to fulfil their basic everyday needs must pay zakâh.

---

[22] *witr* prayer: literally, odd prayer; so called because it consists of an odd number of units. It is performed any time after *'ishâ'* (evening) prayer until time for the *fajr* (dawn) prayer. Even though it is not obligatory, it is strongly recommended, for the Prophet (ﷺ) never abandoned it, even when travelling.

6. Zakâh is not paid to the unbeliever.[23]

7. The poor, even those who do not beg, are legitimate recipients of zakâh.

8. It is permissible to pay zakâh to one category of recipients from amongst the permitted categories.

9. It is not permissible to pay zakâh outside of one's country, unless there is no one in need of zakâh within it.

10. It is not permissible to pay zakâh to the wealthy.

11. It is forbidden to take zakâh from the best of the people's wealth.

12. Any kind of injustice is forbidden.

13. The invocations of the wronged and oppressed are answered.

Relevance to the subject of tawḥeed

This hadith proves that the first thing with which the Islamic callers must begin their message is the call to testify that there is no god but Allah and none has the right to be worshipped except Him.

Important notes

1. Although they are two of the five pillars of Islam, fasting and Hajj pilgrimage have not been mentioned in this hadith. This is because at the time Allah's Prophet (ﷺ) made this statement, those pillars which had been made obligatory upon the Muslims were tawḥeed and belief in the prophethood of Muhammad (ﷺ), prayer and zakâh — all of

---

[23] Unless the unbeliever is one of those whose heart is inclined to Islam, for Allah, the Exalted says: ﴾*Aṣ-Ṣadaqât* [charity — here referring to zakâh] are only for the *fuqarâ'* [the poor who do not beg], the *masâkeen* [the poor who beg], those who are employed to collect [the zakâh], those whose hearts have been inclined [towards Islam], to free the captives, for those in debt, for [those waging struggle in] Allah's cause, and for the wayfarer [the traveller who is cut off from everything] — a duty imposed by Allah, and Allah is All-Knowing, All-Wise.﴿ (*Qur'an 9: 60*)

which were made incumbent from the beginning of Islam, while the time of fasting and Hajj had not yet come.

2. This hadith mentions the obligation to be careful of the supplication of those who have been wronged, because there is no obstacle between the supplication and Allah. Allah has said about Himself in the Qur'an: ❲Is not He Who responds to the distressed one when he calls Him [better than your so-called gods]?❳ *(Qur'an 27: 62)*. It is mentioned in another hadith (a sound hadith recorded by at-Tirmidhi) that the answer to the one who calls upon Allah is of three types:

(i) The request is granted quickly.

(ii) Some of the person's sins will be blotted out in accordance with the measure of the supplication.

(iii) A reward for the supplication will be stored up for the person on the Day of Resurrection.

We may reconcile this hadith with the above narration by saying that the latter concerns the one who is not oppressed or distressed, while the former concerns the supplication of one who suffers oppression or distress, for it is answered, even if after some time, and Allah alleviates the person's distress and bestows His mercy upon the person.

5.3

It is reported that Sahl ibn Saʻd said: «On the day of the Battle of Khaybar, Allah's Messenger (ﷺ) said: Tomorrow I shall indeed give the flag (that will be carried into battle) to someone who loves Allah and His Messenger and is loved by Allah and His Messenger, and Allah will grant victory under his leadership. The people spent the night absorbed in discussion about who might be given the flag. In the morning, they came eagerly to Allah's Messenger (ﷺ), each of them hoping to be given the flag. Allah's Messenger (ﷺ) asked: Where is 'Ali ibn Abi Țâlib? They replied: He is suffering from an eye ailment. He was sent for and brought to the Prophet (ﷺ) who spat in his eyes and prayed for him, whereupon he was cured as if he had not been in pain before. Allah's Messenger (ﷺ) then gave him the flag and said: Advance with ease and gentleness until you arrive in their midst; then call them to Islam and inform them of their duties to Allah in Islam. By Allah! If He guides through you a single person to Islam, it would be better for you than red camels.» (recorded by Bukhari and Muslim)

Benefits derived from this hadith

1. This hadith is evidence of the virtue of 'Ali ibn Abi Țâlib (﵁).
2. The hadith is a confirmation of Allah's divine attribute of love.
3. The Prophet (ﷺ) performed a miracle which healed 'Ali.
4. The hadith shows the love of the Companions for all that is good.
5. A leader should ask about the individual members of his congregation and show concern for their welfare.
6. It is an obligation to believe in divine ordainment and predestination, as was shown by the Companions when the flag was given to the one who did not ask for it.
7. It is an obligation of the leader to behave in a good manner, with gentleness, but with firmness.
8. It is an obligation to begin with the call to Islam before engaging in battle, for the benefit of those who have not heard the message.
9. The testimony of belief in the Oneness of Allah and the divine mission of His Prophet, Muhammad (ﷺ), is not sufficient unless accompanied by deeds.
10. It is permissible to swear by Allah's name concerning one's pronouncements as a means of emphasis.

11. It is permissible to invoke Allah's name without calling upon Him for a definite purpose.

12. It is a virtue to call people to Allah and teach them.

Relevance to the subject of tawḥeed

This hadith proves that the first pillar of Islam and the first thing with which the caller to Islam should begin is the testimony that there is no god but Allah, none has the right to be worshipped except Him, and that Muhammad is the Messenger of Allah.

Important note

The legal positions of the Islamic leader in regards to disbelievers are two. If the unbelievers are People of the Book (Scripture), then the leader gives them three choices, in this order: to embrace Islam; if they refuse then they are ordered to pay the *jizyah*,[24]; if they refuse then they are considered enemies of Islam and must be fought. As for idol-worshipers, their choices are but two: to embrace Islam or to be fought.[25]

---

[24] *jizyah*: a tax levied on the people of the Scriptures when they are under the protection of a Muslim government; it is in lieu of the alms tax paid by Muslims

[25] It is authentically reported that the Prophet (ﷺ) said: «I was ordered to fight the people until they testify that there is no god but Allah and none has the right to be worshipped except Him.» (recorded by Bukhari) It is also reported that the Prophet (ﷺ) wrote to Mundhir ibn Sâwâ, who was the leader of the people of Ḥajar: «As for the (pagan) Arabs, do not accept anything from them except Islam or (to be killed by) the sword; and as for the People of the Book and the Magians, accept from them the jizyah.» (narrated by al-Kalbi)

Chapter 6

The meaning of tawḥeed and 'There is none worthy of worship other than Allah'

6.1

*A*llah (ﷻ) says:

﴿أُوْلَٰٓئِكَ ٱلَّذِينَ يَدْعُونَ يَبْتَغُونَ إِلَىٰ رَبِّهِمُ ٱلْوَسِيلَةَ أَيُّهُمْ أَقْرَبُ وَيَرْجُونَ رَحْمَتَهُۥ وَيَخَافُونَ عَذَابَهُۥٓ إِنَّ عَذَابَ رَبِّكَ كَانَ مَحْذُورًا ٥٧﴾ (سورة الإسراء : ٥٧)

❨Those whom they supplicate [created beings, such as prophets, pious men, or angels] desire [for themselves] means of access to their Lord, as to which of them should be the nearest, and they [the prophets, pious men, and angels] hope for His mercy and fear His punishment. Verily, the punishment of your Lord is [something] to be afraid of.❩ *(Qur'an 17: 57)*

Allah informs us in this verse that those whom the polytheists worship besides Allah, the All-Mighty, the All-Powerful, such as the angels and the pious people, are themselves trying to get nearer to Allah by obeying Him, worshipping Him, carrying out His commands, and hoping for His mercy. In fear of His punishment, they abstain from those things which He has prohibited because every true believer fears and dreads His punishment.

Benefits derived from this verse

1. The polytheists' worship of deities other than Allah is false since the objects of their worship are themselves seeking nearness to Allah, hoping for His mercy, and fearing His punishment.
2. The piety of those who are worshipped does not validate the act of worshipping them.
3. This verse confirms Allah's divine attribute of mercy.
4. The true believer approaches Allah in a state between fear and hope, except at the time when death approaches, then hope becomes stronger.

Relevance to the topic of the chapter

This Qur'anic verse proves that the meaning of tawheed and the testimony that there is no god but Allah and nothing worthy of worship except Him is the abandonment of the deeds of the polytheists, such as calling upon prophets and other righteous persons and requesting their intercession with Allah. The verbal recitation of the testimony is not sufficient if the worship of everything besides Allah is not rejected.

6.2

Allah (ﷻ) says:

﴿وَإِذْ قَالَ إِبْرَٰهِيمُ لِأَبِيهِ وَقَوْمِهِۦٓ إِنَّنِي بَرَآءٌ مِّمَّا تَعْبُدُونَ ۝ إِلَّا ٱلَّذِي فَطَرَنِي فَإِنَّهُۥ سَيَهْدِينِ ۝﴾ (سورة الزّخرُف : ٢٦-٢٧)

﴿[Remember] when Ibrâheem said to his father and his people: Verily, I am innocent of what you worship, except Him Who originated me, and He will certainly guide me.﴾ *(Qur'an 43: 26-27)*

Allah informs us in this verse, that His Messenger and *khaleel*,[26] Ibrâheem (﷽), told his father, Âzar, and his people that he was totally blameless and guiltless of any association with their worship of their deities, except the worship of Allah. Allah is their creator, the One alone Who can grant them success, and by Whose Hand they are allowed to receive all that they get, whether beneficial or harmful.

Benefits derived from these verses

1. The basis of the religion taught by all the prophets was one: tawḥeed.
2. Speaking out in the cause of Truth is an essential attribute of all Messengers.
3. It is an obligation to condemn that which is detestable, even though it may be found among one's closest relatives.
4. It is an obligation to declare oneself free, in word and deed, from the wickedness of shirk.
5. Ibrâheem's people used to worship Allah, but they also associated partners with Him.
6. The guidance of success comes only from Allah.

Relevance to the subject of tawḥeed

These Qur'anic verses prove that a people's tawḥeed is not correct if they do not declare, by word and deed, their innocence of the worship of anything besides Allah.

---

[26] *khaleel*: beloved friend; Ibrâheem (﷽) is referred to by Allah as *khaleelullâh*, meaning 'The Beloved of Allah'. The common translation of khaleelullâh as the 'Friend of Allah' is far from doing justice to this illustrious title, for according to scholars of Arabic language, the word *khalla*, from which the word khaleel is derived, indicates a greater degree of love than is conveyed by the word 'friend'.

6.3

Allah (ﷻ) says:

$$﴿ٱتَّخَذُوٓاْ أَحۡبَارَهُمۡ وَرُهۡبَٰنَهُمۡ أَرۡبَابٗا مِّن دُونِ ٱللَّهِ وَٱلۡمَسِيحَ ٱبۡنَ مَرۡيَمَ وَمَآ أُمِرُوٓاْ إِلَّا لِيَعۡبُدُوٓاْ إِلَٰهٗا وَٰحِدٗاۖ لَّآ إِلَٰهَ إِلَّا هُوَۚ سُبۡحَٰنَهُۥ عَمَّا يُشۡرِكُونَ ٣١ ﴾$$

(سورة التَّوبَة: ٣١)

❴They have taken their rabbis, priests, and monks to be lords besides Allah, and [they take as their lord] the Messiah, the son of Maryam, though they were not commanded but to worship One God. There is none worthy of worship but He. Glorified is He; [far is He] above that which they associate [with Him].❵   *(Qur'an 9: 31)*

Allah, the Most High, informs us in this verse that the Jews and Christians have gone astray from the Straight Path. They have done what they were never commanded to do: they raised their scholars and other people of religion to the status of gods, worshipping them besides Allah. By obeying their religious leaders when they declared that which Allah has forbidden to be permissible and obeying them when they declared what Allah has permitted to be forbidden, the People of the Book elevated them to the level of lords, since only the Lord, the Exalted, ordains what is permissible and what is forbidden. Indeed, the Christians, not content with this, began to worship 'Eesâ (ﷺ) and considered him a son of Allah, though they were not ordered in the Torah and the Gospel[27] except to worship Allah alone. Far above that which they attribute to Him is He, Allah, the Lord of the worlds.

---

[27] The original divine Gospel as revealed to 'Eesâ (Jesus), not the versions now in circulation that have been added to and changed by human beings.

Benefits derived from this verse

1. Obedience to other than Allah, in contradiction to Allah's commands, constitutes shirk.

2. It is forbidden to obey one of Allah's created beings, if in doing so, one is disobedient to the Creator.

3. Deeds will not be considered righteous unless two conditions are met: (i) the deeds are done purely for Allah, and (ii) they conform to the teachings of the Messengers.

4. The scholars of religion are not infallible.

5. The Jews and the Christians have gone astray from the correct precepts of their religion. They have strayed from tawheed.

6. Misguided scholars are a danger to the Ummah.

Relevance to the subject of tawheed

This Qur'anic verse proves that the meaning of tawheed and the testimony that there is no god but Allah entails confirming the Oneness of Allah by obedience to Him and to His Messenger (ﷺ) because whoever obeys the Messenger has obeyed Allah.

6.4

Allah (ﷻ) says:

﴿وَمِنَ ٱلنَّاسِ مَن يَتَّخِذُ مِن دُونِ ٱللَّهِ أَندَادًا يُحِبُّونَهُمْ كَحُبِّ ٱللَّهِ وَٱلَّذِينَ ءَامَنُوٓا أَشَدُّ حُبًّا لِّلَّهِ وَلَوْ يَرَى ٱلَّذِينَ ظَلَمُوٓا إِذْ يَرَوْنَ ٱلْعَذَابَ أَنَّ ٱلْقُوَّةَ لِلَّهِ جَمِيعًا وَأَنَّ ٱللَّهَ شَدِيدُ ٱلْعَذَابِ ۝﴾ (سورة البقرة: ١٦٥)

❴Among people are those who take [for worship] others besides Allah as equals [with Allah]. They love them as they should love Allah. Those who believe love Allah more [than anything else]. If only the wrongdoers could see, when they will see the punishment, that to Allah belongs all power, and Allah is stern in punishment.

(Qur'an 2: 165)

Allah, Most Glorified, informs us in this verse that some of humankind set up for themselves objects of worship which they love more than they love Allah. Allah explains that the believers are stronger in their love for Him than the polytheists because the believers are pure and sincere in their love of Allah alone, while the polytheists divide their love between Allah and their false gods.

Then Allah promises those who associate partners with Him that when they see the punishment which He has prepared especially for them on the Day of Resurrection, they will wish that they had not associated others with Allah, either in love, or in anything else. Then they shall know with certain knowledge that all power belongs to Allah and that Allah is severe in enforcing His punishment.

Benefits derived from this verse

1. Love is a kind of worship.
2. The polytheists love Allah, but this will not benefit them as long as they are guilty of shirk.
3. Those who commit shirk by loving other deities beside Allah negate their faith.
4. The verse confirms Allah's divine attribute of all-embracing power.

Relevance to the topic of the chapter

This Qur'anic verse proves that the meaning of tawḥeed and the testimony that there is no god but Allah is to confirm the Oneness of Allah in a foundation of love, which entails purity and sincerity in all acts of worship for Allah alone.

6.5

It is authentically reported that the Prophet (ﷺ) said: «As for those who say 'There is no god but Allah' and reject all that is worshipped besides Allah, (know that) Allah has forbidden the taking of their property and the spilling of their blood and their account will be for Allah, the Almighty, the All-Powerful.» (recorded by Muslim)

Whoever pronounces the testimony that there is no god but Allah, understands its meaning, acts upon all that it entails, and rejects all that is worshipped besides Allah is a true believer. Such people have accepted the testimony by heart, tongue, and action. Thus, it is forbidden for the Muslims to take their property (except what is required by law, such as the payment of zakâh) or to take their lives (except as the law requires, such as the punishment for adultery, apostasy, or murder), and their accounts will be for Allah to decide. That is, on the Day of Resurrection, Allah will reward them if they were truthful in their testimony, and if they were insincere in their testimony, He will punish him.

Benefits derived from this hadith

1. A virtue of Islam is that it protects the life and property of whoever embraces it.
2. It is obligatory to desist from having enmity towards the disbeliever upon the disbeliever's embracing of Islam, even if it is done during a battle, unless it should be proved that the person's testimony was false.
3. Some people say that there is no god but Allah, but they fail to reject that which is worshipped besides Him.
4. The conditions of acceptance of faith include pronouncing the testimony of faith and rejecting all that is worshipped besides Allah.

5. Judgement in this world is based on appearances; only Allah knows all that is in a person's heart.

6. It is forbidden to appropriate the property of the Muslim unless it is ordained by Islamic law, such as zakâh or a legally imposed fine in compensation for that which a person has destroyed (be it property or a life).

Relevance to the topic of the chapter

This hadith proves that the meaning of tawheed and the explanation of the testimony of faith 'There is no god but Allah' are not complete without a categorical rejection of all that is worshipped besides Allah.

Important note

The disbelieving polytheist has only two choices:
  (i) to embrace Islam or
  (ii) to be fought.

The People of the Book have three choices, in this order:
  (i) to embrace Islam,
  (ii) to pay the jizyah, or
  (iii) to be fought.

Chapter 7

Wearing talismans

7.1

Allah (ﷻ) says:

﴿ ... قُلْ أَفَرَءَيْتُم مَّا تَدْعُونَ مِن دُونِ ٱللَّهِ إِنْ أَرَادَنِيَ ٱللَّهُ بِضُرٍّ هَلْ هُنَّ كَٰشِفَٰتُ ضُرِّهِۦ أَوْ أَرَادَنِي بِرَحْمَةٍ هَلْ هُنَّ مُمْسِكَٰتُ رَحْمَتِهِۦ قُلْ حَسْبِيَ ٱللَّهُ عَلَيْهِ يَتَوَكَّلُ ٱلْمُتَوَكِّلُونَ ﴿٣٨﴾ ﴾

(سورة الزُّمَر : ٣٨)

﴿...Say [O Muhammad]: Tell me then, the things that you invoke besides Allah — if Allah intended some harm to me, could they remove His harm? Or if He intended some mercy for me, could they withhold His mercy? Say: Sufficient for me is Allah; in Him those who trust [such as the true believers] must put their trust.﴾

(Qur'an 39: 38)

In this verse, Allah commands His Prophet, Muhammad (ﷺ), to reject those powerless, graven images worshipped by the polytheists. The polytheists put their trust in things which can neither remove any harm which might befall a person by Allah's decree nor prevent any sustenance or blessings which might come to a person from Him. Allah commands that we place our trust in Him, for He is Sufficient to bring benefit or prevent harm for all who sincerely depend upon Him.

Benefits derived from this verse

1. It is an obligation to reject the abominable.
2. Idol-worship is utter falseness.
3. The removal of harm and the giving of what is beneficial comes only from Allah.
4. It is an obligation to trust in Allah, depend upon Him, and be free from dependence upon any other, and this does not conflict with the requirement to take whatever legal measures one can in order to achieve one's objectives.

Relevance to the topic of the chapter

This Qur'anic verse proves that protection from harm is only from Allah. So entrusting oneself to any other protector or talisman, such as a ring, twisted threads, or other objects, is an act of shirk.

7.2

It is reported on the authority of 'Imrân ibn Husayn (رضي الله عنه): «Allah's Messenger (ﷺ) saw a man with a brass ring on his hand, and he asked him: What is this? The man replied: It is for protection from rheumatism. The Prophet (ﷺ) answered: Remove it at once, for verily, it will only weaken you, and were you to die while wearing it, you would never be successful (in attaining paradise).» (recorded by Ahmad with an acceptable chain of narrators)

'Imrân ibn Husayn (رضي الله عنه) informs us that the Prophet (ﷺ) saw a man who was wearing a brass ring, and he asked him why he was wearing it. The man answered that he was wearing it to protect him from illness, at which the Prophet (ﷺ) ordered him to remove it. He (ﷺ) informed him that it would not protect him from illness at all and that should he die while wearing it and believing in its power to protect him, he would not succeed in the hereafter and would not know eternal bliss.

Benefits derived from this hadith

1. It is permissible to request detailed information from the mufti.[28]
2. This hadith shows the importance of intentions.
3. The method of reproof and rejection may differ according to the individual concerned. So if there is a likelihood that words of wisdom will suffice, one should not resort to force.
4. This hadith is evidence of the ignorance of the polytheists before Islam.
5. Seeking a cure by the use of that which is prohibited is not allowed.
6. Prohibited things are of no benefit at all. Even though they may help to some degree, the harm which they cause is greater.
7. The ignorant person is not excused from the obligation to seek knowledge.
8. It is by a person's last actions that the person will be judged on the Day of Resurrection.

Important notes

1. This hadith does not contradict the alleged hadith of 'Ali ibn al-Ḥusayn in which the Prophet (ﷺ) supposedly states: «Plough (the earth) well; for verily, ploughing is a blessed task. And sow many seeds.» This is one of the *mursal*[29] narrations from Abu Dâwood, and Abu Dâwood has not vouched for the authenticity of his mursal narrations. Even if it were authentic, the reference is to seeds, and according to a large number of scholars, it means taking the required precautions to ensure the success of one's endeavours, such as

---

[28] mufti: an Islamic scholar who is qualified to deliver formal legal verdicts which are based on the Qur'an and the Sunnah

[29] *mursal*: an incomplete chain of narrators, not reaching to the Prophet (ﷺ)

planting many seeds to ensure a good crop or using permitted medicines to alleviate illness. It does not endorse things like some supposed treatments for fever which involve the laying of hands on the skull[30] of the patient. Taking reasonable precautions is not to be compared to resorting to the forbidden in order to achieve one's goals.

2. The enquiry made by the Prophet (ﷺ) might be construed as a rhetorical one, indicating disapproval, and it could also be understood as a genuine request for more information.

3. Some of the scholars have said that wearing a ring or other amulet in order to protect oneself against harm is an act of minor shirk, but what is understood from the hadith of 'Imrân is that it constitutes major shirk because it is mentioned in the hadith that to die while doing so would result in failure to achieve everlasting bliss in the hereafter. It could be that the definition depends upon the beliefs and intentions of the perpetrator. If the person believed that it could cure of itself, without Allah's help, then it would be major shirk, while if the person believed it be a cause of the cure, while Allah is the One Who grants health, then it would be considered to be minor shirk — and Allah knows best.

Relevance to the topic of the chapter

This hadith proves that it is obligatory to reject the wearing of rings, bangles, chains, and other talismans as a means of protection against harm. Causing good and avoiding harm are the prerogative of Allah alone, and seeking such help from other than Allah means associating partners with Him.

---

[30] The Arabic word for skulls and the Arabic word for seeds can both be *jamâjim* (جَمَاجِم).

7.3

It is reported on the authority of 'Uqbah ibn 'Âmir (ﷺ) that Allah's Messenger (ﷺ) said: «Whoever wears a talisman or amulet,[31] Allah will never see his wishes fulfilled; and whoever wears a *wada'ah*[32] Allah will never grant him peace and tranquillity.» In another narration, it says: «Whoever wears a talisman or amulet has committed an act of shirk.» (Both are narrated by Aḥmad.)[33]

'Uqbah ibn 'Âmir (ﷺ) informs us that the Messenger of Allah (ﷺ) supplicated against the people who wear talismans or seashells believing that they will benefit them in place of Allah. Allah will not allow them to achieve any of their goals nor fulfil their wishes or dreams. Rather, He, the Almighty, will prevent them from ever finding security and tranquillity. Such actions are nothing but falsehood. Indeed, in another narration, Allah's Messenger (ﷺ) informed us that amulets and talismans are a form of shirk because the people who use them believe that they will benefit them without the help of Allah.

Benefits derived from this hadith

1. This hadith is a denial of any benefit from believing in or wearing sea-shells or other amulets.

2. In general, it is permissible to make supplication against disobedient people.

---

[31] talisman or amulet: *tameemah* in Arabic

[32] *wada'ah*: a sea-shell resembling an oyster shell that is worn as an amulet

[33] They are reported in a *marfoo'* form, in other words, with a chain of narrators reaching to the Prophet (ﷺ).

3. If some of the Companions (may Allah be pleased with them) were ignorant about talismans, what can be said of those who came after them? It is imperative to pass along the correct teachings of Islam. 4. Using or believing in talismans or amulets is a kind of shirk.

Relevance to the topic of the chapter

This hadith proves that wearing an amulet or talisman and believing that it can cause some benefit is an act of shirk. Help and protection come only from Allah, the All-Mighty, the All-Powerful.

7.4

It is reported by Ibn Abi Ḥâtim that the Prophet's Companion Ḥudhayfah (ﷺ) said that he saw a man with a thread on his hand to protect him from fever. Ḥudhayfah took it and broke it, and he recited the Words of Allah, Most High: ﴾And most of them do not believe in Allah, except that they associate partners with Him.﴿ *(Qur'an 12: 106)*

Ibn Abi Ḥâtim narrated that Ḥudhayfah (ﷺ) visited a sick man and found him wearing a thread on his wrist. When he asked the man to explain the purpose of it, he told him that it was a protection from fever. Upon hearing this, Ḥudhayfah (ﷺ) broke the thread and declared it to be a form of shirk. As proof, he recited the Words of Allah, Most High: ﴾And most of them do not believe in Allah, except that they associate partners with Him﴿ — and the meaning of this verse is that many people believe in Allah, but they adulterate their belief with shirk.

Benefits derived from this narration

1. A person can forbid the detestable with one's own hand, even though the perpetrator may object.

2. The use of threads and other objects of superstition to protect from harm is an act of shirk.

3. It is an obligation to reject the detestable.

4. The Prophet's Companions (may Allah be pleased with them) had deep understanding and broad knowledge.

5. Shirk is present even amongst the people of this Ummah.

6. The heart of a person may contain faith and shirk at the same time.

Relevance to the topic of the chapter

This narration proves that the use of threads or twisted chains as protection from harm is an act of shirk because protection from harm comes only from Allah, the All-Mighty, the All-Powerful.

Chapter 8

Incantations, spells, and amulets

8.1

$\mathcal{J}$t is authentically reported on the authority of Abu Basheer al-Anṣâri (﷽) that he was with the Messenger of Allah (﷽) on one of his journeys when he sent a messenger to tell the people: «If any necklace of bowstring, or any other kind of necklace, remains on the necks of your camels, cut it off.» (recorded by Bukhari and Muslim)

Abu Basheer al-Anṣâri (﷽) informs us that he was travelling with the Messenger of Allah (﷽) who sent an announcer, Zayd ibn Ḥârithah[34] (﷽), to order the people to cut the bowstring necklaces that were tied on their camels. This was because the people in the days of ignorance used to believe that tying certain things around the necks of their camels was a protection against the evil eye.

Benefits derived from this hadith

1. It is an obligation to reject the detestable.
2. It is acceptable to take and follow the information from one reliable person.
3. It is falseness to believe in the benefit supposedly derived from wearing certain necklaces, whatever their kind.

---

[34] According to Imam Muslim the messenger was 'Abdullâh ibn Abu Bakr. (Editor)

4. The representative of the leader may act on the leader's behalf in matters entrusted to him or her.

Relevance to tawheed and the subject of the chapter

This hadith proves that it is forbidden to wear a necklace in order to protect against harm. This hadith shows that wearing good-luck charms are a form of shirk because protection from harm comes only from Allah.

8.2

It is reported that Ibn Mas'ood (ﷺ) said: «I heard the Messenger of Allah (ﷺ) say that incantations, spells, amulets, and *tiwalah*[35] are all forms of shirk.» (a sound hadith recorded by Ahmad and Abu Dâwood).

Ibn Mas'ood (ﷺ) informs us that the Prophet (ﷺ) said that spells and incantations; amulets, which are made from beads and such and are hung around the necks of children; and tiwalah, which is a spell made to cause a person to love another, are all forms of denying the Oneness of Allah.

Benefits derived from this hadith

1. Incantations are forbidden and are a form of shirk, except what has been permitted by Islamic law, such as the recitation of Qur'an and authentic supplications of the Allah's Messenger (ﷺ).
2. Amulets are forbidden and are a form of shirk.
3. Tiwalah is also forbidden and is a form of shirk.

---

[35] *tiwalah*: bewitchment, in order to make one person fall in love with another

Relevance to tawḥeed and the subject of the chapter

This hadith proves that incantations, spells, amulets, and tiwalah are all forms of shirk.

Important notes

1. Incantation is permissible if three conditions are met:

   (i) It contains the Words of Allah, or mention of His names and attributes, or a supplication to Allah, or a request for His aid.

   (ii) It is in Arabic, and its meaning is clearly understood.

   (iii) It is not believed that the incantation can, of itself, bring about any positive result, but that the benefit comes by the command of Allah and His divine decree.

When these conditions are met, the incantation is considered ruqyah. 2. Scholars have disagreed concerning amulets that contain writing from the Qur'an. Some have forbidden it since they infer a general prohibition from this hadith. Others have permitted it and compared it to ruqyah, which may be from the Qur'an and is permissible, but the first saying is more correct, and Allah knows best.

8.3

The following was reported on the authority of 'Abdullâh ibn 'Ukaym (ﷺ): «Whoever wears a talisman or amulet will be put in its charge.» (a sound hadith recorded by Aḥmad and at-Tirmidhi)

'Abdullâh ibn 'Ukaym (ﷺ) tells us that the Prophet (ﷺ) taught him that people who need something should entrust their affairs to Allah. Those who depend upon Allah alone to fulfil their needs will find that Allah relieves their distress and make their affairs easy, but those who depend upon something other than Allah, and entrust their affairs to it, will be left in the charge of what they trust. They will have no help from Allah because it is only by the Hand of Allah that goodness is achieved, and no one but He can provide the benefit that is sought.

Benefits derived from this hadith

1. It is an obligation to depend upon Allah alone, and this does not contradict the obligation to undertake all possible, permissible measures to ensure success.
2. Whoever seeks benefit from other than Allah will be abandoned.

Relevance to tawheed and the subject of the chapter

This hadith proves that it is forbidden to seek benefit from other than Allah. This hadith proves that whoever depends upon other than Allah to bring benefit or protection from harm will be abandoned. Granting benefit and protecting from harm are the prerogative of Allah, and seeking such things from others is an act of shirk.

8.4

It is reported by Ruwayfâ' (رضي الله عنه) that Allah's Messenger (صلى الله عليه وسلم) said to him: «Ruwayfâ', it is likely that your life will be a long one, so inform the people that whoever ties his beard, or wears a bowstring, or cleans his privates using animal dung or a bone (should know that) Muhammad (the Messenger of Allah) is innocent of him.» (recorded by Ahmad)

Ruwayfâ' (رضي الله عنه) tells us that the Prophet (صلى الله عليه وسلم) informed him that he would live a long life. Therefore it was incumbent upon him to tell the people in the future that he, Muhammad (صلى الله عليه وسلم), was free from blame in the case of anyone who tied his beard, or hung a bowstring around his neck or around the neck of his riding beast in order to be protected from the evil eye, or cleaned his private parts with animal dung or a bone after relieving himself. The Prophet (ﷺ) had conveyed the message that such actions were shirk and forbidden in Islam.

Benefits derived from this hadith

1. It is a miracle of the Prophet (ﷺ) that he knew Ruwayfa' (رضي الله عنه) would live a long life.
2. It is acceptable to take information from a single, reliable source.
3. Tying the beard is forbidden — though, according to some scholars, this means during prayer, and Allah knows best.
4. Tying a bowstring around one's neck, or the neck of a riding beast, to try to ward off the evil eye is a forbidden act.
5. Cleaning one's private parts using animal dung or a bone is a forbidden act. According to a hadith recorded by Bukhari, dung and bones are food for the jinn and other creatures.

Relevance to tawheed and the subject of the chapter

This hadith proves that it is forbidden to wear a bowstring, or other object, in order to protect oneself. The Prophet (ﷺ) declared himself free from those wore amulets as a means of protection. Bestowing benefit and granting protection from harm come from Allah alone, and whoever asks them from other than Allah has committed an act of shirk.

8.5

Wakee' reported that Sa'eed ibn Jubayr (رضي الله عنه) said, "If someone cut (and removed) an amulet from a person, it will be for him as if he had freed a slave." (recorded by Ahmad)

Wakee' also narrated that Ibrâheem an-Nakhâ'i said, "The Companions (may Allah be pleased with them) used to hate amulets, and they used to remove them (wherever they found them), whether the amulets were from the Qur'an or from other sources." (recorded by Ibn Abi Shaybah in his *Musannaf*)

In the first narration, Sa'eed ibn Jubayr (رضي الله عنه) informs us that whoever removed an amulet or talisman from a person would have a reward equivalent to the one who freed a slave, because by doing so, a person became freed from the Fire and freed from following vain desires and shirk.

In the second narration, the reporter informs us that the Companions of the Prophet (ﷺ) used to hate and forbid the wearing of talismans and amulets and ordered their removal, whether they included writing from the Qur'an or not.

Benefits derived from the two narrations

1. The narrations show the virtue of rejecting the forbidden.
2. Talismans and amulets, in all their forms, are forbidden.
3. The freeing of a slave is a very high and noble action.
4. The Companions prohibited the use of amulets, whether they contained verses from the Qur'an or something else.

Relevance to tawḥeed and the subject of the chapter

Both of these narrations prove the prohibition of wearing amulets or talismans, whether they contain Qur'anic verses or not. These narrations prove that it is forbidden to wear amulets and talismans as a protection against harm because protection from harm comes from Allah alone, and seeking it from other than Him is an act of shirk.

Chapter 9

Seeking blessing from trees, stones, or other things

9.1

*A*llah (ﷻ) says:

﴿أَفَرَءَيْتُمُ ٱللَّـٰتَ وَٱلْعُزَّىٰ ۝ وَمَنَوٰةَ ٱلثَّالِثَةَ ٱلْأُخْرَىٰ ۝ أَلَكُمُ ٱلذَّكَرُ وَلَهُ ٱلْأُنثَىٰ ۝ تِلْكَ إِذًا قِسْمَةٌ ضِيزَىٰ ۝﴾

(سورة النَّجْـم : ١٩ – ٢٢)

﴿Have you seen al-Lât and al-'Uzzâ? And another, the third, Manât? What! Is the male sex for you and the female for Him? That would indeed be a most unfair division!﴾   *(Qur'an 53: 19-22)*

Allah, Most Glorified, reviles all idol-worshipping polytheists in general and in particular, those who worship the three idols: al-Lât,[36] the idol of the people of Ṭâ'if;[37] al-'Uzzâ,[38] worshipped by the people of Wâdi Nakhlah; and Manât,[39] the idol of the people of

---

[36] *Al-Lât*: derived from the word *Al-Ilâh*, which means 'The Deity'

[37] Ṭa'if: a city in the mountains east of Makkah, in present-day Saudi Arabia

[38] *Al-'Uzzâ*: derived from the name *Al-'Azeez*, which means 'The Almighty', and said to be the name given to a tree in Wâdi Nakhlah, which is on the road between Makkah and Ṭa'if. The pagans had erected a building over the tree and covered it with curtains and a gate, and it was worshipped by Quraysh and the tribe of Banu Kinânah.

[39] *Manât*: derived from *Al-Manân*, which means 'The Benefactor', it was a=

Mushallal. Allah challenges them concerning these idols, Can their idols benefit them in any way by bringing them good or protecting them from harm? Or are they simply names which they have given themselves, not sanctioned by Allah?

Allah also reviles their unfair division. They appoint those whom they themselves despise, especially the weaker females, as children for Allah, the All-Mighty, the All-Powerful, while they prefer for themselves sons, embodying the characteristics of manliness, strength, and power. That being the case, if this is injustice to women, then how about Allah? Allah is far above that which they attribute to Him of sons and daughters.

Benefits derived from these verses

1. It is an obligation to reject the forbidden.
2. Idol-worship is utter falseness.
3. It is an obligation to reject the attribution of sons and daughters to Allah.
4. The polytheists have corrupted their *fitrah*.[40] They attributed daughters to Allah, even though they despised them for themselves, and they claimed that their idol-worship was only to bring them closer to Allah.

Relevance to the topic of the chapter

These Qur'anic verses show that the polytheists worshipped their idols as a means of seeking protection from harm. Anyone who

---

=structure in Mushallal, near the town of Qadeed, between Makkah and Madinah; it was worshipped by the tribes of Khuzâ'ah, Aws and Khazraj, and they used it as a starting point when making pilgrimage to Makkah.

[40] *fitrah*: the natural state in which we are born, which includes the innate belief in the Oneness of Allah

seeks blessing from a tree or a grave or worships any other created thing by seeking from it some benefit or protection from harm is imitating the polytheists and commits an act of shirk like them.

It has been said concerning al-Lât that he was a pious man, who used to prepare food for the pilgrims to Makkah, and that when he died, they began to worship at the site of his grave. It was also said that al-Lât was a name given to a carved stone. In reconciling these two statements, we may say that the carved stone was near to the grave (and graves are often marked with stones) and the edifice the polytheists erected covered both of them, thus making them into one object of worship.

9.2

It is reported that Abu Wâqid al-Laythi (رضي الله عنه) said: «We were travelling with the Prophet (ﷺ) to Ḥunayn when we had only recently abandoned disbelief. The polytheists had a lote tree (zizyphus spina-christi; in Arabic: *sidr*) at which they used to worship and upon which they used to hang their weapons (for blessings). They called it *Dhâtu Anwât*. So we said to Allah's Messenger (ﷺ): Make for us a Dhâtu Anwât like theirs. The Messenger of Allah (ﷺ) responded: *Allâhu Akbar*! ('Allah is the Greatest', here used as an expression of astonishment) Verily, that which you have said — by Him in Whose Hand is my soul — is the same as was said by the Children of Isrâ'eel (Israel) to Moosâ: 'Make for us a god such as the gods which they [the polytheist] have.' Then he (ﷺ) said: Verily, you are an ignorant people, who will follow the way of those who were before you.» (a sound hadith recorded by at-Tirmidhi)

Abu Wâqid al-Laythi (رضي الله عنه) informs us in this hadith that he accompanied the Prophet (ﷺ) on a journey to the Battle of Ḥunayn.

At that time, the Companions knew that the polytheists had a lotus-tree from which they used to seek blessings and near which they would remain to worship. Because they were new to Islam and because they did not fully realize its goals to call people to the worship of Allah alone, they asked the Prophet (ﷺ) to designate a tree like it for them, so they might also seek blessings from it and worship in its vicinity, like the pagans. At this, the Prophet (ﷺ) exclaimed in vexation: 'Allâhu Akbar!' Then he explained to them that such ignorance was the same as that displayed by the people of Moosâ (ﷺ) who asked him to make for them an idol to worship, like the pagan Egyptians — and this was after Allah had saved them from Fir'awn and his people. Then the Prophet (ﷺ) informed them that this Ummah will do as the Jews and Christians did in everything, including following them in shirk.

Benefits derived from this hadith

1. It is a virtue to make clear the facts which would refute the charge of backbiting, for example, by saying, 'When we had recently abandoned disbelief...'
2. People often experience difficulty in ridding themselves of ingrained habits.
3. Devotion to a particular place is an act of worship.
4. Those who are ignorant are excused by virtue of their ignorance, so long as they cease their mistake once knowledge comes to them.
5. It is prohibited to imitate ignorant people, such as the polytheists and others.
6. It is permissible to say 'Allâhu Akbar!' when one is surprised.
7. It is an obligation to close off all possible routes leading to shirk.
8. Shirk will occur in this Ummah.

9. It is permissible to invoke Allah's name when delivering a legal verdict.

10. When there is a good reason, it is permissible to swear without the intention of making an oath.

11. There will be segments of this Ummah who will follow the Jews and Christians in their mistakes.

12. The evil deeds done by the Jews and Christians should serve as a warning to us.

Relevance to the topic of the chapter

This hadith proves that taking trees as a source of blessing and carrying out devotions in their vicinity is shirk. This also includes every stone or other object of worship from which blessings are invoked.

Important note

It has become very common nowadays for people to invoke blessings by the sweat of righteous people, or by touching them or their clothes, or by having a righteous person do the *tahneek*[41] of their children. They base this upon the action of the Prophet; however, this is unacceptable because this was something purely and solely for the Prophet (ﷺ), not a Sunnah for all Muslims. His Companions — who were the best of people in following him and implementing his Sunnah — did not seek such blessings from other people, either during the Prophet's lifetime or after his death.

---

[41] *tahneek*: putting chewed date juice and saliva into the mouth of an infant. It is reported on the authority of 'Â'ishah (ؓ): «The first child born in the Islamic State (of Madinah) amongst the Emigrants was 'Abdullâh ibn az-Zubayr. They brought him to the Prophet (ﷺ). The Prophet (ﷺ) took a date, and after chewing it, put its juice in the baby's mouth. So the first thing that went into the child's stomach was the saliva of the Prophet (ﷺ).» (recorded by Bukhari)

Chapter 10

Slaughtering an animal in
the name of other than Allah

10.1

*A*llah ( ) says:

﴿قُلْ إِنَّ صَلَاتِي وَنُسُكِي وَمَحْيَايَ وَمَمَاتِي لِلَّهِ رَبِّ الْعَالَمِينَ ۝ لَا شَرِيكَ لَهُ
وَبِذَٰلِكَ أُمِرْتُ وَأَنَا أَوَّلُ الْمُسْلِمِينَ ۝﴾ (سورة الأنعام: ١٦٢-١٦٣)

﴿Say: Verily, my prayer, my slaughter, my life and my death are [all]
for Allah, the Lord of the worlds; He has no partner. This am I
commanded, and I am the first of those who submit.﴾

(Qur'an 6: 162-163)

Allah commands His Prophet, Muhammad ( ), to inform the
polytheists that his prayers — both obligatory and supererogatory,
his slaughter of animals, everything which he does in his life, and the
correct Islamic Monotheistic beliefs and righteous deeds upon which
he will die are all directed purely to Allah alone, without partners.
The Prophet Muhammad ( ) was the first of this Ummah to submit
himself to the will of Allah, the All-Mighty, the All-Powerful.

Benefits derived from these verses

1. Prayer and slaughter are acts of worship.
2. All of the slave's righteous deeds in this life will become acts of worship if they are done seeking nearness to Allah.
3. What counts in deeds are one's final actions.
4. Sincerity in dedicating one's deeds to Allah alone is a condition of their acceptance.

Relevance to the topic of the chapter

These Qur'anic verses prove that the slaughtering of animals is not acceptable unless it is done in Allah's name, so that it becomes an act of worship. Dedicating acts of worship to other than Allah is shirk.

10.2

Allah, (ﷻ) says:

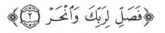

(٢ :سورة الكَوثَر)

❨Therefore pray to your Lord and slaughter [animals in His name only].❩   *(Qur'an 108: 2)*

Allah orders His Prophet, Muhammad (ﷺ), to approach these two acts of worship with humility and urgency, towards Allah alone, trusting in Him, and desiring to draw near to Him. Both the prayer and slaughter of animals in accordance with Islamic rites are physical actions, and the slaughtering is financial act as well.

Benefits derived from this verse

1. It is an obligation to draw near to Allah.
2. It is an obligation to draw near to Allah by slaughtering animals for

meat according to the rules and methods outlined in Islam — dedicating the act purely and solely for Him.

Relevance to the topic of the chapter

This Qur'anic verse proves that drawing near to Allah by slaughtering animals will not be achieved unless it is done purely and solely for Allah. Invoking the name of anyone or anything other that Allah while slaughtering an animal is an act of shirk.

Important note

Some people quote a narration in which 'Ali (رضي الله عنه) was said to have explained the word of Allah in this verse ❰slaughter❱ as meaning raising the hands in prayer. This narration is rejected by the scholars of hadith, and no one should put trust in it or follow it.

10.3

It is reported that 'Ali (رضي الله عنه) said: «Allah's Messenger (ﷺ) told me four things: Allah has cursed the one who slaughters in the name of other than Him; Allah has cursed the one who curses his parents; Allah has cursed the one who protects and shelters a criminal or wrongdoer; and Allah has cursed the one who alters landmarks.» (recorded by Muslim)

'Ali (رضي الله عنه) informs us that the Prophet (ﷺ) told him that Allah's curse is upon every person who attempts to get nearer to Allah by slaughtering an animal in the name of other than Him, Most High. Allah's curse is also upon people who curse their parents, either directly or by inciting others to do so, upon people who give shelter to a known criminal or malefactor, and upon people who alter the landmarks or borders in order to unlawfully seize the land which does not belong to them.

Benefits derived from this hadith

1. Slaughtering an animal in other than Allah's name is prohibited.
2. It is forbidden to curse one's parents, either directly or by inciting others to do so.
3. It is prohibited to aid or abet criminals.
4. It is forbidden to change borders in order to unlawfully acquire property or territory.
5. In general, it is permissible to curse those who are wilful and unrepentant wrongdoers.

Relevance to the topic of the chapter

This hadith proves that it is prohibited to slaughter an animal in other than Allah's name because directing an act of worship to others besides Allah is an act of shirk.

10.4

It is reported that Ṭâriq ibn Shihâb (راك) said: «The Prophet (صلى) said: A man entered paradise because of a fly, while another entered the Fire because of a fly. Those (who heard) asked: How was that possible, Messenger of Allah? He replied: Two men passed by a people who had an idol, and these people did not allow anyone to pass without making a sacrifice to it. The people said to the first man: Sacrifice (something). He said: I have nothing with which to do so. They said: Sacrifice something, even if it is only a fly. So he did, and they allowed him to continue on his way, and so he entered hellfire. Then they said to the second man: Sacrifice (something). But he said: I will not sacrifice anything unless it be to Allah, the All-Mighty, the All-Powerful. So they struck his neck (beheaded him) and he entered paradise.» (a sound hadith recorded by Aḥmad, but its chain stops at Salmân al-Fârisi)

The Messenger of Allah (ﷺ) informs us in this hadith that two men — possibly Children of Israel — were travelling through the land of a people who had an idol. They requested that the two men sacrifice something to their idol, even if the sacrifices were only something small. The first of them sacrificed a fly, and because of this, he was thrown in hellfire. The second, due to his strong faith and complete tawḥeed, refused to sacrifice to the idol. So the people killed him, and he entered paradise.

Benefits derived from this hadith

1. Shirk is an enormous sin, even though the act of shirk may be only slight.
2. The hadith confirms the existence of paradise and hell.
3. Even among the idol-worshipers, the action of the heart — the intention — is directed to a certain goal.
4. Humans are ever so close to ending up in paradise or hell.
5. This is a warning against sin, even though it may be considered a small sin.
6. This hadith is evidence of the breadth of Allah's forgiveness and the severity of His punishment.
7. The most important deeds are the last ones we do in life.

Relevance to the topic of the chapter

This hadith proves that it is forbidden to slaughter something as a sacrifice to other than Allah, for such is an act of worship and shirk.

Important note

This hadith does not contradict the words of Allah, Most High: ﴿...except he who is forced to do so, while his heart remains steadfast in faith. *(Qur'an 16: 106)* In the hadith about the fly, the Messenger of Allah (ﷺ) used the Arabic word *faqarrab* which implies that the man attempted to draw closer to Allah by sacrificing the fly to the idol. This indicates his acceptance of the deed. It is this which caused him to enter hellfire because his heart was inclined towards the act and did not remain steadfast in faith.

Chapter 11

Slaughtering at a place where animals are slaughtered in the name of other than Allah

11.1

ᏗAllah (ﷻ) says:

﴿لَا تَقُمْ فِيهِ أَبَدًا لَّمَسْجِدٌ أُسِّسَ عَلَى التَّقْوَىٰ مِنْ أَوَّلِ يَوْمٍ أَحَقُّ أَن تَقُومَ فِيهِ فِيهِ رِجَالٌ يُحِبُّونَ أَن يَتَطَهَّرُوا وَاللَّهُ يُحِبُّ الْمُطَّهِّرِينَ ۝﴾

(سورة التوبة: ١٠٨)

❴Do not ever stand [in prayer] therein. There is a mosque whose foundation was laid on piety from the first day. It is more worthy of your standing [for prayer] therein. In it are men who love to be purified; and Allah loves those who purify [themselves].❵

(Qur'an 9: 108)

Allah, Most Glorified, forbids His Prophet (ﷺ) in this verse from praying in the 'Mosque of Harm and Disbelief',[42] which was the first mosque to be built on a foundation of wicked intentions.

---

[42] This mosque known as *Masjid Ḍirâr*, or 'the Mosque of Harm and Disbelief', was built by the hypocrites of Madinah in an attempt to prove their allegiance to Allah and His Messenger (ﷺ).

Allah commands the Muslims to pray in the mosque which was built from the beginning upon a foundation of obedience to Him and His Messenger (ﷺ).[43] Then Allah praises the people of that mosque, and He tells us that they are meticulous in their cleanliness and ablutions. He informs us that He loves those who purify themselves from all unclean things, especially when coming from the toilet or after sexual intercourse, and those who purify themselves from the spiritual filth of shirk.

Benefits derived from this verse

1. It is prohibited to encourage that which is false.

2. It is an obligation to turn away from those deeds which are rejected and whose perpetrators are abandoned.

3. This hadith is evidence of the danger of the hypocrites to this Ummah and the obligation to warn against them.

---

[43] It is commonly believed that the mosque referred to in this verse is Qubâ' Mosque, on the outskirts of Madinah, as this is the first mosque built by the Muslims after the migration of the Muslims from Makkah to Madinah. Ibn Katheer states that some of the salaf held this view, while he says that a larger number held that it was the Prophet's Mosque in Madinah that was referred to in the verse. While there are some proofs for both views, those who held the latter view drew support from the hadith reported by Muslim, Aḥmad, Ibn Abi Shaybah and others, on the authority of Ḥumayd al-Kharrât, who said: «I heard Abu Salamah ibn 'Abdur-Raḥmân say: 'Abdur-Raḥmân ibn Abi Sa'eed al-Khudri (ﷺ) visited me, and I asked him: What did you hear from your father, concerning the mosque which was built upon a foundation of piety? He replied: My father said: I visited the Messenger of Allah (ﷺ) in the house of one of his wives, and I asked him: Messenger of Allah, which of the two mosques is it that was built upon a foundation of piety? The Prophet took a handful of stones and beat the earth with them; then he said: It is this, your mosque, the Mosque of Madinah. Abu Salamah then said: I testify that I heard your father say likewise.» Ibn Jareer aṭ-Ṭabari agreed with this, while Ibn Katheer said that there was no contradiction in saying that both mosques were intended — and Allah knows best.

4. This hadith shows the superiority of the Prophet's Mosque or Qubâ' Mosque or both.

5. This hadith is a confirmation of Allah's divine attribute of love.

6. Islam encourages cleanliness and purity, both physical and spiritual.

7. It is forbidden to pray in the Mosque of Harm and Disbelief, or in the place where it stood, forever, till the Day of Resurrection.

Relevance to tawheed and the subject of the chapter

This Qur'anic verse proves that it is forbidden to carry out an act of obedience to Allah and His Prophet (ﷺ) in a place that is known for carrying out acts of disobedience to Allah and His Messenger (ﷺ). That includes slaughtering animals in a place where animals are slaughtered for others besides Allah. This verse proves the prohibition of all things which might lead in the end to shirk.

11.2

It is reported that Thâbit ibn ad-Dahhâk (ﷺ) said: «A man vowed to sacrifice a camel at a place called Buwânah, and he asked the Prophet (ﷺ) about it. The Prophet (ﷺ) asked him: Does the place contain any of the idols from the days of ignorance? They said: No. He (ﷺ) then asked: Did the disbelievers hold any of their (religious) festivals there? They replied: No. So the Messenger of Allah (ﷺ) said: Then fulfil your vow, for verily, vows which entail disobedience to Allah or that which is beyond the capacity of the son of Âdam should not be fulfilled.» (recorded by Abu Dawood with a sound chain)[44]

---

[44] The hadith has a chain of narrators that meets the conditions of acceptance laid down by Bukhari and Muslim.

Thâbit ibn aḍ-Ḍahhâk (⁕) informs us that a man made a vow to slaughter a female camel in a place called Buwânah. So the Prophet (⁕) enquired about whether it had been used as a place of worship for the idols of the days of ignorance, or whether any of their pagan festivals had been celebrated there. When it was made clear to him that this was not the case, he ordered the man to fulfil his vow. In addition to this, he then gave a general ruling, binding upon his Ummah until the Day of Resurrection, prohibiting the fulfilment of vows made in disobedience to Allah or which require of a person what is beyond his or her capacity.

Benefits derived from this hadith

1. It is obligatory to fulfil one's vows, so long as it does not entail disobedience to Allah or some impossible act.
2. It is lawful for the mufti to make enquiries before delivering judgement.
3. It is prohibited to carry out an act of obedience in a place where acts of disobedience are performed.
4. It is forbidden to fulfil vows which entail disobedience — instead, an act of recompense is required.[45]
5. A vow should not be taken to do something which is beyond a person's ability.

---

[45] It is reported on the authority of Ibn 'Abbâs (⁕) that the Prophet (⁕) said: «If anyone takes a vow to do an act of disobedience, its atonement is the same as that for an oath.» (recorded by Abu Dâwood with a reliable chain of narration) Concerning the atonement for an oath, Allah, Most High, says: ⦃Allah will not call you to account for your unintentional oaths, but He will hold you to account for your deliberate oaths. For expiation, feed ten poor persons, on a scale of what is average for the food of your families, or clothe them, or give a slave his freedom. If that is beyond your means, fast for three days. That is the expiation for the oaths you have sworn.⦄ (*Qur'an 3: 89*)

6. It is permissible to specify a place or a time for the fulfilment of a vow.

Relevance to tawḥeed and the subject of the chapter

This hadith proves the prohibition of carrying out an act of obedience to Allah in a place where acts of disobedience to Him are performed. This includes slaughtering animals in a place where animals are dedicated to other than Allah. This hadith shows that it is forbidden to perform an act which may lead in the end to shirk.

Chapter 12

Making a vow in the name of other than Allah

12.1

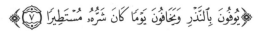

$c\mathcal{A}$llah (ﷻ) says:

﴿يُوفُونَ بِٱلنَّذْرِ وَيَخَافُونَ يَوْمًا كَانَ شَرُّهُۥ مُسْتَطِيرًا ۝﴾   (سورة الإنسان: ٧)

❰They fulfil their vows, and they fear a Day whose evil is spread far and wide.❱   *(Qur'an 76: 7)*

Allah, Most Glorified, praises His righteous slaves in this verse because they fulfil the vows which they have made incumbent upon themselves desiring nearness to Allah. Their belief in the Day of Resurrection is certain, as is their fear of Allah's severe chastisement, which will be delivered far and wide on that Day.

Benefits derived from this verse

1. It is an obligation to fulfil one's vows, so long as they do not involve disobedience to Allah.
2. Fear of the Day of Resurrection is one of the attributes of the believers.
3. This verse confirms the resurrection of humankind on that Day.

Relevance to tawḥeed and the subject of the chapter

This Qur'anic verse praises the fulfilment of vows. Allah does not praise something unless it is obligatory, or it is strongly preferred, or it refrains from a thing which is prohibited. This is why fulfilment of a vow is considered to be an act of worship, and dedicating an act of worship to other than Allah is an act of shirk.

12.2

Allah (﷽) says:

﴿وَمَآ أَنفَقْتُم مِّن نَّفَقَةٍ أَوْ نَذَرْتُم مِّن نَّذْرٍ فَإِنَّ ٱللَّهَ يَعْلَمُهُ وَمَا لِلظَّٰلِمِينَ مِنْ أَنصَارٍ ﴾ ۞

(سورة البَقَرَة: ٢٧٠)

❴Whatever you spend in charity or whatever vow you make, be sure Allah knows it all. But the wrongdoers have no helpers.❵

(Qur'an 2: 270)

Allah, Most Glorified, informs us in this verse that He knows whatever a person gives in the way of charity and whatever vows a person makes, seeking nearness to Him, even if the person were to keep the act a secret. Allah will reward the person for it. Then, Allah warns the people against injustice in charity, in their vows, and in all their deeds. He informs them that they will find none to help them or protect them should He punish them for their sins.

Benefits derived from this verse

1. This verse is evidence of the breadth of Allah's knowledge and the fact that it encompasses every single thing.
2. Taking a vow is an act of worship.
3. All types of injustice are prohibited.

Relevance to tawḥeed and the subject of the chapter

This Qur'anic verse proves that Allah (ﷻ), has knowledge of each and every vow, and that He rewards those who fulfil the vows they make. Therefore, fulfilling a vow is an act of worship, and dedicating an act of worship to another besides Allah is shirk.

12.3

It is authentically reported on the authority of 'Â'ishah (ﭬ) that the Prophet (ﷺ) said: «Whoever vowed to obey Allah, should do so; and whoever vowed to disobey Him, should not do so.» (recorded by Imam Mâlik)

Benefits derived from this hadith

1. It is an obligation to fulfil vows, as long as they are in obedience to Allah.
2. It is prohibited to fulfil vows if they entail disobedience to Allah. Instead, the one who made the vow must perform the expiation of an oath.

Relevance to tawḥeed and the subject of the chapter

This hadith proves the obligation to fulfil one's vow, so long as it does not entail disobedience to Allah. This means that fulfilling a vow is an act of worship, and dedicating an act of worship to other than Allah is shirk.

Chapter 13

Seeking refuge in other than Allah

13.1

*A*llah (ﷻ) says:

﴿وَأَنَّهُۥ كَانَ رِجَالٌ مِّنَ ٱلْإِنسِ يَعُوذُونَ بِرِجَالٍ مِّنَ ٱلْجِنِّ فَزَادُوهُمْ رَهَقًا ۝﴾

(سورة الجنّ: ٦)

❝There were persons among humankind who took shelter with persons among the jinn, but they [only] increased their sin and transgression.❞ *(Qur'an 72: 6)*

Allah, Most Glorified, informs us in this verse that there were people from among the human race who turned to people from among the jinn. The humans sought protection with them, but their pleas to them only caused the jinn's pride and injustice to increase, and this caused the jinn to increase the fear and misguidance already felt by humankind.

Benefits derived from this verse

1. It is prohibited to seek protection with others in place of Allah.
2. Whoever seeks protection from other than Allah will be disappointed, and such people will be guilty of injustice against the ones they called upon.

3. This verse confirms the existence of the jinn and there being men and women who interact with them.

Relevance to the topic of the chapter

This Qur'anic verse proves the prohibition of seeking shelter or protection with other than Allah because doing so is an act of worship. Dedicating worship to other than Allah is shirk.

Important note

If we understand from Allah's words ⟨they [only] increased their sin and transgression⟩ that 'they' refers to the humans, then this means that the supplication of the humans only increased the jinn's own arrogance and oppression. However, if we understand from the verse that 'they' refers to the jinn, then it would mean that the jinn increased humankind's fear and misguidance.

13.2

It is reported that Khawlah bint Ḥakeem (مَ) heard Allah's Messenger (ﷺ) say: «If someone visits a place and says, 'I seek refuge in the most perfect Words of my Lord, from the evil of what He has created,' then no harm shall befall him until he departs from that place.» (recorded by Muslim)

Khawlah bint Ḥakeem informs us that the Prophet (ﷺ) has approved it as a Sunnah for Muslims that when they visit a dwelling, they should seek protection with Allah, rather than with the jinn or others. Muslims should seek protection with Allah from the evil of His creation. The Prophet (ﷺ) informed us that whoever seeks refuge and shelter in the most complete and perfect Words of Allah, which are free from every defect, then Allah will be sufficient protection for that person from every evil present in His creation, until the person leaves that place.

Benefits derived from this hadith

1. The hadith is evidence of the blessing of this particular supplication.
2. The Qur'an was revealed, not created.[46]
3. Protection is not sought with other than Allah.
4. Seeking shelter with Allah is prescribed by the religion.
5. This hadith is evidence of the completeness and perfection of the Qur'an because, being the Word of Allah, it is necessarily perfect and complete.

Relevance to the topic of the chapter

This hadith proves that seeking protection with other than Allah, or with one of His attributes, is not permissible because seeking shelter or protection is an act of worship and dedicating an act of worship to other than Allah is shirk.

---

[46] This is because the Qur'an is the Word of Allah, and as such, it cannot be created.

Chapter 14

Seeking aid from other than Allah

14.1

*A*llah (ﷻ) says:

﴿وَلَا تَدْعُ مِن دُونِ ٱللَّهِ مَا لَا يَنفَعُكَ وَلَا يَضُرُّكَ فَإِن فَعَلْتَ فَإِنَّكَ إِذَا مِّنَ ٱلظَّٰلِمِينَ ۝﴾

(سورة يُونس: ١٠٦)

﴿Nor call on any besides Allah, such can neither profit you, nor hurt you. If you do, then you will surely be one of the unjust wrongdoers.﴾

(Qur'an 10: 106)

In this verse, Allah, Most Glorified, forbids His Prophet, Muhammad (ﷺ) — and the forbiddance applies to the whole Ummah — from performing acts of worship, in particular, supplication, for any other besides Allah. No one besides Allah possesses power to benefit or harm. Then Allah informs His Prophet (ﷺ) that calling upon others than Allah makes a person one of the wrongdoers and one of the polytheists.

Benefits derived from this verse

1. Bestowment of benefit and protection from harm are only from Allah, the All-Mighty, the All-Powerful.
2. Those who call upon other than Allah, believing that the other

possesses the power to benefit or harm them without Allah, has committed an act of shirk.

3. Shirk is referred to here as a form of injustice.

Relevance to tawheed and the subject of the chapter

This Qur'anic verse proves that invoking anything other than Allah is futile since only Allah grants benefit or provides protection from harm. Supplication is worship, and worship must only be directed purely and sincerely to Allah.

14.2

Allah (﷽), says:

﴿وَإِن يَمْسَسْكَ ٱللَّهُ بِضُرٍّ فَلَا كَاشِفَ لَهُۥٓ إِلَّا هُوَۖ وَإِن يُرِدْكَ بِخَيْرٍ فَلَا رَآدَّ لِفَضْلِهِۦۚ يُصِيبُ بِهِۦ مَن يَشَآءُ مِنْ عِبَادِهِۦۚ وَهُوَ ٱلْغَفُورُ ٱلرَّحِيمُ ۝﴾

(سورة يُونس: ١٠٧)

❲If Allah touches you with adversity, there is none who can remove it but He. If He designs some benefit for you, there is none who can keep back His favour; He causes it to reach whomever of His slaves He wills, and He is the Most Forgiving, Most Merciful.❳

(Qur'an 10: 107)

In this verse, Allah, Most Glorified, informs His Prophet, Muhammad (ﷺ), that both good and evil are determined by Allah, the All-Mighty, the All-Powerful. None of His created beings — whoever it may be — has the power to lift harm or prevent benefit coming to any person since all power of disposal is in Allah's Hands. In His wisdom, He forbids to whom He wills, and He gives to whom He wills from His bounty. He is Oft-forgiving to whoever turns in repentance to Him, even to the one who has committed shirk. Allah is full of mercy.

Benefits derived from this verse

1. All goodness and evil is at Allah's disposal.
2. This verse confirms Allah's divine attribute of wish or decree.[47]
3. It also confirms Allah's divine attribute of will.[48]
4. Allah's dominion and sovereignty is total and all-encompassing.
5. This verse mentions two of Allah's names: *Al-Ghafoor* (the Most Forgiving) and *Ar-Raheem* (the Most Merciful to all in this world and to the believers in the hereafter). Each of these names encompasses the meaning of the other.

Relevance to tawheed and the subject of the chapter

This Qur'anic verse proves that preventing or removing harm and the granting of benefit come only from Allah, the All-Mighty, the All-Powerful. Seeking them from other than Allah is an act of shirk.

14.3

Allah (ﷻ) says:

﴿إِنَّمَا تَعْبُدُونَ مِن دُونِ ٱللَّهِ أَوْثَٰنًا وَتَخْلُقُونَ إِفْكًا إِنَّ ٱلَّذِينَ تَعْبُدُونَ مِن دُونِ ٱللَّهِ لَا يَمْلِكُونَ لَكُمْ رِزْقًا فَٱبْتَغُوا۟ عِندَ ٱللَّهِ ٱلرِّزْقَ وَٱعْبُدُوهُ وَٱشْكُرُوا۟ لَهُۥٓ إِلَيْهِ تُرْجَعُونَ ١٧﴾ (سورة العنكبوت: ١٧)

---

[47] divine wish or decree: *irâdah*

[48] divine will: *mashee'ah*

❨You do naught but worship idols besides Allah, and you invent falsehood. The things that you worship besides Allah have no power to give you sustenance. So seek sustenance from Allah, worship Him and be grateful to Him; to Him will you return.❩ *(Qur'an 29: 17)*

In this verse, Allah, Most Glorified, tells us about Prophet Ibrâheem (ﷺ) and how he made clear to his people the truth concerning the idols which they worshipped. Those idols possessed no power to harm or to benefit, and Ibrâheem's people had made up a lie by attributing such powers to them. Goodness may only be sought from Allah, and from none other. Allah alone is the One Who has the right to be worshipped and praised. It is Allah Who deserves our gratitude. All individuals created by Allah will return to Him when they die. Then, they will be resurrected, and they will receive the recompense of their deeds.

Benefits derived from this verse

1. The original religion of all the prophets is tawḥeed.
2. The worship of idols is utter falseness.
3. All goodness and evil is within Allah's power.
4. It is an obligation to worship Allah and be grateful to Him.
5. The verse confirms the coming of the Day of Resurrection.

Relevance to tawḥeed and the subject of the chapter

This Qur'anic verse proves that provision must not be sought except from Allah because supplicating for provision from other than Allah is an act of shirk.

14.4

Allah (ﷻ) says:

وَمَنْ أَضَلُّ مِمَّن يَدْعُواْ مِن دُونِ ٱللَّهِ مَن لَّا يَسْتَجِيبُ لَهُۥٓ إِلَىٰ يَوْمِ ٱلْقِيَٰمَةِ وَهُمْ عَن دُعَآئِهِمْ غَٰفِلُونَ ۝ وَإِذَا حُشِرَ ٱلنَّاسُ كَانُواْ لَهُمْ أَعْدَآءً وَكَانُواْ بِعِبَادَتِهِمْ كَٰفِرِينَ ۝

(سورة الأحقاف : ٥-٦)

❨Who is more astray than one who calls upon other than Allah, such as will not answer him until the Day of Resurrection, and who are [even] unaware of their calls to them. When humankind is gathered [on the Day of Resurrection], they [the false deities] will become enemies to them and will deny their worship.❩ *(Qur'an 46: 5-6)*

Allah, Most Glorified, informs us in this verse that none is further astray nor more ignorant than the one who rejects the worship of the All-Hearing, the One Who answers. Instead, such a person worships things which are unable to answer the person's supplications, neither now nor until the Hour comes. They cannot answer either because they themselves are slaves of Allah, who are bound to worship Him, such as the angels, the prophets and the righteous, or because they are inanimate objects, such as idols. Then Allah makes clear to us that humankind will be gathered together on the Day of Resurrection. Then, those who worshipped other than Allah will be shown the uselessness of their deeds. Their objects of worship will declare themselves innocent of them and their actions; indeed they will become their enemies, rejecting them and all that they did.

Benefits derived from these verses

1. The most ignorant and farthest astray of all people are those who call upon other than Allah.
2. Their false objects of worship are ignorant of them and cannot answer them.
3. Supplication is a kind of worship.

4. On the Day of Resurrection, false gods will have enmity towards those who worshipped them.

5. On the Day of Resurrection, these false objects of worship will declare themselves innocent of their worshipers.

Relevance to the topic of the chapter

These Qur'anic verses prove that there is none more ignorant, none farther astray than the one who calls upon other than Allah. Supplication is an act of worship, and dedicating an act of worship to other than Allah is shirk.

The rejection by those animate objects of worship that include the angels, the prophets, and the righteous, will be by their mouths, obviously. As for the inanimate objects that were worshipped, such as idols, trees, and stones, it has been said that Allah will create for them the power of speech, and they will speak to denounce their worshipers and the worshipers' deeds. It has also been said that inanimate idols will reject their worshippers by their silence, lifelessness, and inability to do anything.

14.5

Allah (ﷻ) says:

وَأَمَّن يُجِيبُ ٱلْمُضْطَرَّ إِذَا دَعَاهُ وَيَكْشِفُ ٱلسُّوٓءَ وَيَجْعَلُكُمْ خُلَفَآءَ ٱلْأَرْضِ أَءِلَـٰهٌ مَّعَ ٱللَّهِ قَلِيـلًا مَّا تَذَكَّرُونَ ۝

(سورة النَّمل: ٦٢)

❝Is not He Who responds to the distressed one, when he calls Him, and Who removes the evil, and makes you inheritors of the earth, generation after generation, [better than your false gods]? Is there any [other] deity with Allah? Little it is that you bear in mind [the warning].❞

(Qur'an 27: 62)

Allah, Most Glorified, defines some of the Attributes which are purely for Him, and nobody else. It is Allah Who responds to those in dire straits, lifts harm from them, and protects humankind. Then Allah makes it clear that those who will not accept this warning, nor fear the consequences, and will not worship only Allah, will not heed any warning.

Benefits derived from this verse

1. Making one's supplications purely for Allah will ensure their acceptance.
2. This verse confirms the blessing of supplication.
3. Allah's power is all-encompassing over goodness and evil.
4. The Oneness of Allah's Lordship is proof for the tawheed of worship.
5. Allah answers the supplications of the distressed and the oppressed.
6. Knowledge of Allah is part of the human being's fitrah, or natural state.

Relevance to tawheed and the subject of the chapter

This Qur'anic verse proves that none can answer the oppressed or the distressed except Allah, the Exalted, because supplication is a form of worship and dedicating an act of worship to other than Allah is shirk.

14.6

«In the time of the Prophet (ﷺ) there was a hypocrite[49] who used to harm the believers, and some of them said: Come, let us seek aid from the Messenger of Allah (ﷺ) against this hypocrite. But the

---

[49] It is likely that the hypocrite referred to here is 'Abdullâh ibn Ubayy.

Prophet (ﷺ) answered: Aid must not be sought from me; aid must only be sought from Allah.» (recorded by aṭ-Ṭabarâni)

This hadith informs us that a man from amongst the hypocrites used to harm the Companions (may Allah be pleased with them) in any way he could. So some of the Companions went to the Prophet (ﷺ) to seek his aid putting an end to this harm. Even though the Prophet (ﷺ) was able to assist them, he forbade them from seeking help from him. Instead, he (ﷺ) guided them towards that which was better for them — to seek aid from Allah, to ask Him to alleviate their distress and protect them from their enemies, in accordance with the dictates of tawḥeed.

Benefits derived from this hadith

1. This hadith is evidence that the hypocrites used to do their utmost to harm the Muslims.
2. In those things which are beyond a people's power, it is prohibited to seek help from other than Allah.

Relevance to tawḥeed and the subject of the chapter

This hadith proves the forbiddance of seeking aid from other than Allah in those things which are beyond the capabilities of all but Him. Seeking aid is an act of worship, and dedicating acts of worship to other than Allah is shirk.

There is no contradiction between this hadith and the Words of Allah, the Exalted: ﴾And the man from amongst his own people appealed to him for aid.﴿ [50] *(Qur'an 28: 15)*

---

[50] This verse refers to the story of Moosâ (عليه السلام) in which a man from his own people called to him to help him against an Egyptian. Moosâ (عليه السلام) did help him, and in the course of the struggle, Moosâ (عليه السلام) struck the man and unintentionally killed him.

This verse tells us that it is permissible to seek aid from another of Allah's created beings in those things which are within the person's power to change. The hadith does not prohibit that, but the Messenger of Allah (ﷺ) guided them to that which is better — that is to seek aid from Allah, the All-Mighty, the All-Powerful; for Allah says: ﴾When my slaves ask you [O Muhammad] about me, [inform them that] verily, I am near [in My Knowledge, My Hearing, and My Seeing]. I answer the request of every supplicant when he calls upon Me.﴿ *(Qur'an 2: 186)*

Chapter 15

Only Allah can grant benefit or remove harm

15.1

*A*llah (ﷻ) says:

﴿ ... أَيُشْرِكُونَ مَا لَا يَخْلُقُ شَيْئًا وَهُمْ يُخْلَقُونَ ۝ وَلَا يَسْتَطِيعُونَ لَهُمْ نَصْرًا ۝ ﴾

(سورة الأعرَاف: ١٩١–١٩٢)

﴿Will they associate [with Me] those that do not create, but are [themselves] created — those that can bring them no victory?...﴾

(Qur'an 7: 191-192)

In this verse, Allah rejects and censures the polytheists from among the Arabs and the non-Arabs and those false gods which they worship besides Him, which cannot bring into being anything. These false gods were themselves created by Allah from nothing. They cannot help those who worship them. In fact, they cannot even help themselves should some misfortune befall them, and this is the ultimate in weakness and powerlessness.

Benefits derived from these verses

1. These verses are evidence of the ignorance of the polytheists.
2. All that is worshipped besides Allah is weak and powerless; therefore, logically, it is not fit to be worshipped.

Relevance to tawḥeed and the subject of the chapter

These Qur'anic verses prove the negation of all worship except that of Allah. Worship of other than Allah is false and rejected, and this includes everything to which people turn besides Allah, such as graves, trees, and the like. Thus, turning towards other than Allah in order to obtain some benefit or protection from harm is an act of shirk.

Important note

The warning here is against worshipping those who are blessed with the power of thinking and logic, though there are also many objects of worship which are inanimate.

15.2

Allah (ﷻ) says:

﴿يُولِجُ ٱلَّيْلَ فِي ٱلنَّهَارِ وَيُولِجُ ٱلنَّهَارَ فِي ٱلَّيْلِ وَسَخَّرَ ٱلشَّمْسَ وَٱلْقَمَرَ كُلٌّ يَجْرِى لِأَجَلٍ مُّسَمًّى ذَٰلِكُمُ ٱللَّهُ رَبُّكُمْ لَهُ ٱلْمُلْكُ وَٱلَّذِينَ تَدْعُونَ مِن دُونِهِۦ مَا يَمْلِكُونَ مِن قِطْمِيرٍ ۝ إِن تَدْعُوهُمْ لَا يَسْمَعُوا۟ دُعَآءَكُمْ وَلَوْ سَمِعُوا۟ مَا ٱسْتَجَابُوا۟ لَكُمْ وَيَوْمَ ٱلْقِيَٰمَةِ يَكْفُرُونَ بِشِرْكِكُمْ وَلَا يُنَبِّئُكَ مِثْلُ خَبِيرٍ ۝﴾

(سورة فاطر: ١٣-١٤)

﴾He merges the night into the day [by decreasing the hours of the night and adding them to the hours of the day] and He merges the day into the night [by decreasing the hours of the day and adding them to the hours of the night]. He has subjected the sun and the moon; each runs its course for a term appointed. Such is Allah, your Lord; His is the dominion. Those whom you call upon instead of Him do not own not even a *qitmeer* [the thin membrane covering a date-stone]. If you call upon them, they hear not your call, and even were they to hear, they could not grant [your request] to you. On the Day of Resurrection, they will disown your ascribing them as partners [with Allah]. And none can inform you [O Muhammad] like He [who is the All-knowing].❯ *(Qur'an 35: 13-14)*

Allah (﷾) informs us in these verses that He decreases the hours of the night and adds them to the hours of daylight, and vice versa, according to the changing seasons, by His will and in accordance with His divine decree. He has subjected the sun and the moon; these two lights bring innumerable benefits to humankind, by Allah's will. Thus, He Who is Able to do all things has the exclusive right of Lordship and the right to be worshipped alone, without partners. How could it be otherwise, when His is the Dominion over all created things and everything that is worshipped besides Him possesses nothing, not even the covering of a date-stone, nor do they hear the supplication of those who call upon them? Even if they were able to hear, they would be incapable of responding. Indeed, on the Day of Resurrection, they will reject those who worshipped them and reject the act of shirk in that worship. In addition, there is no one who can inform the Messenger (ﷺ) of the truth of these matters and their outcome like Allah, the All-Knowing, does.

Benefits derived from these verses

1. The sun and moon move in their orbits and are not stationary.
2. Idols do not possess any power to benefit or harm those who worship them, either in this world or in the hereafter.
3. Shirk will be the cause of enmity between the worshipers and the worshipped.
4. Knowledge should be taken from its original source — in this case, Allah, Who is the source of all knowledge.

Relevance to tawḥeed and the subject of the chapter

These Qur'anic verses reject and condemn the idea that those deities worshipped besides Allah have any power to benefit or harm the worshipers. The verses prove that supplicating to other than Allah is shirk.

15.3

It is authentically reported, on the authority of Anas (رضي الله عنه): «The Prophet (ﷺ) was struck during the battle of Uḥud, and one of his molar teeth was broken, at which he said: How can a people ever be successful, when they strike their Prophet? So Allah revealed: ﴾The matter is not for your decision, whether He turns in mercy to them or punishes them; for verily, they are the wrongdoers.﴿ *(Qur'an 3: 128)*» (recorded by Muslim)

In this hadith, Anas ibn Mâlik (رضي الله عنه) informs us that during the Battle of Uḥud, the Prophet (ﷺ) received an injury to his head, which bled, and one of his teeth was broken. The Prophet (ﷺ) became despondent of the prospect of their accepting Islam because of their outrage against the personage of Allah's chosen Messenger and the enmity which they showed him. Then Allah revealed this verse: ﴾The matter is not for your decision...﴿ So it became clear to the Prophet (ﷺ) the path that he must follow and that forgiveness or punishment for the polytheists rests with Allah, the Exalted, alone and with no other.

Benefits derived from this hadith

1. The prophets are subject to illness and injury, and this is proof of their humanity and a rejection of those who ascribe divine attributes to them.[51]

---

[51] Such as certain Jews who claimed that 'Uzayr (عليه السلام) was the son of God;=

2. The prophets are unable to do anything, except what Allah wills for them; so how about other lesser created beings?

3. No one knows what a person's last actions will be, except Allah.

4. Turning to Allah in sincere repentance wipes out all previous sins.

5. Wrongdoing, especially shirk, will be punished.

Relevance to tawḥeed and the subject of the chapter

This hadith proves that the prophets, who are the best of people, do not possess any power to benefit or harm. If the prophets do not have this ability, then surely those who are less than the prophets do not have the ability either. This hadith proves that benefit or harm comes only from Allah, and requesting it from other than Him is shirk.

15.4

It is reported on the authority of Ibn 'Umar (may Allah be pleased with them both): «I heard the Messenger of Allah (ﷺ) saying, as he raised his head from bowing in the second unit of the dawn prayer: 'O Allah! Curse so-and-so and so-and-so' after saying *'Sami' Allâhu liman ḥamidah'* and *'Rabbanâ wa lak al-ḥamd'*. Then, Allah revealed: ❴The matter is not for your decision...❵.» (recorded by Bukhari) [52]

In another narration, it is reported that the Prophet (ﷺ) made supplications against Ṣafwân ibn Umayyah, Suhayl ibn 'Amr, and Al-Ḥârith ibn Hishâm, and so this verse was revealed: ❴The matter is not for your decision...❵ (recorded by Aḥmad)

=and most Christians, who claim that 'Eesâ is the son of God; and the deviant Braillawis, who ascribe divine attributes to the Prophet Muhammad (ﷺ)

[52] Reported by an-Neesâboori in *The Reasons for Revelation*; he said that it was narrated by Bukhari and Muslim.

'Abdullâh ibn 'Umar (may Allah be pleased with both of them) informs us in this hadith that the Prophet (ﷺ), while straightening up from bowing in the second unit of the dawn prayer, said: "Allah hears the one who praises Him," and "Our Lord! To You is due all praise." He (ﷺ) followed this by invoking Allah's curse on the heads of a number of the pagans of Quraysh. Then Allah revealed to him a verse prohibiting him from doing so, and this was because of Allah's knowledge of what the future held for some of them, who would eventually embrace Islam and become good Muslims.

Benefits derived from this hadith

1. In the prayer, the Imam recites 'Sami' Allâhu liman ḥamidah' as well as 'Rabbanâ wa lak al-ḥamd' aloud.
2. It is lawful to invoke Allah upon someone in times of need.
3. The hadith is proof that the Qur'an is revealed, not created.
4. The prophets do not possess any power to benefit or harm anyone, nor do they have knowledge of the unseen.

Relevance to tawḥeed and the subject of the chapter

This hadith proves that the prophets, though they are the best of people, do not have power to benefit or harm. If the prophets do not have this ability, then surely those who are less than the prophets do not have the ability either. This hadith proves that benefit and harm are in Allah's power only, and so seeking them from other than Him is an act of shirk.

Important note

It has been authenticated that the three persons mentioned in the hadith, Ṣafwân ibn Umayyah, Al-Ḥârith ibn Hishâm, and Suhayl ibn 'Amr, all later embraced Islam.

15.5

It is reported on the authority of Abu Hurayrah (رضي الله عنه): «When the verse ﴾And warn your nearest kinsmen﴿ *(Qur'an 26: 214)* was revealed, Allah's Messenger (ﷺ) stood up and said: You people of Quraysh (or something similar)! Save your own souls! I possess nothing with which to protect you from Allah. 'Abbâs ibn 'Abdil Muttalib! I possess nothing with which to protect you from Allah. Safiyyah, aunt of the Messenger of Allah! I possess nothing with which to protect you from Allah. Fâtimah bint Muhammad! Ask of me of what I have, anything you wish, but I possess nothing with which to protect you from Allah.» (recorded by Bukhari and Muslim)

Abu Hurayrah (رضي الله عنه) informs us in this hadith that when the Words of Allah ﴾warn your nearest kinsmen﴿ were revealed, the Messenger of Allah (ﷺ) stood amongst them and addressed them, and requested them to save themselves from the punishment of Allah by obeying Him and His Messenger (ﷺ). He told them that he could not save them or protect them from Allah's severe chastisement. Then he addressed some of his close family members, one at a time, so that they should not be proud or conceited and depend upon their relationship to him.

Benefits derived from this hadith

1. The Qur'an is revealed, not created.
2. Nothing can benefit a person except his or her good deeds.
3. Relying on one's ancestry or family ties for salvation from Allah's punishment, rather than good deeds, is falseness.
4. Those closest to Allah's Messenger (ﷺ) are those who obey him, not those who claim close family ties.
5. It was permissible to ask the Messenger of Allah (ﷺ) for that which was in his power, while he was alive.

Relevance to tawheed and the subject of the chapter

This hadith proves that the prophets do not have control over the benefits which will reach a person, nor the harm, so how could any lesser person? The hadith proves that bringing benefit or harm is the special prerogative of Allah alone, and therefore seeking them from other than Him is an act of shirk.

There is no contradiction between this hadith and the hadiths which confirm the Prophet's intercession because the latter inform us that he will intercede for the believers after Allah allows him to do so, while the former hadith rejects the idea that he can save us by his own power.

Chapter 16

The position of the Angels

16.1

*A*llah (ﷻ) says:

﴿وَلَا تَنفَعُ ٱلشَّفَٰعَةُ عِندَهُۥ إِلَّا لِمَنۡ أَذِنَ لَهُۥ حَتَّىٰٓ إِذَا فُزِّعَ عَن قُلُوبِهِمۡ قَالُواْ مَاذَا قَالَ رَبُّكُمۡ قَالُواْ ٱلۡحَقَّ وَهُوَ ٱلۡعَلِىُّ ٱلۡكَبِيرُ ٢٣﴾ (سورة سبإ: ٢٣)

❪No intercession can avail with Him, except for those whom He allows. So much so that, when terror is removed from their hearts, they will say: What is it that your Lord has said? They will say: The Truth; and He is the Most High, the Most Great.❫ *(Qur'an 34: 23)*

Allah, Most Glorified, informs us in this verse that none can intercede on behalf of another on the Day of Judgement — whoever that might be — unless Allah, the All-Mighty, the All-Powerful, permits it. All, including the angels, will be prostrate due to their fear of Him. Then when the fear is removed from the angels' hearts, they will begin to ask one another about what Allah has said and what He has revealed. Some of them will answer that Allah has said nothing but the Truth, and He is the Most High, the Most Great.

Benefits derived from this verse

1. No one may intercede unless Allah wills it.

2. The verse confirms the greatness of Allah and the fear His greatness elicits among His slaves.

3. The verse confirms Allah's divine attribute of speech.

4. The words of Allah are free from all falseness.

5. Allah is above all of His creation — in His Self and in His attributes.

6. The verse is a confirmation of two of His names: *Al-'Aliyy* (the Exalted) and *Al-Kabeer* (the Most Great).

Relevance to tawḥeed and the subject of the chapter

This Qur'anic verse proves that even the angels fear Allah and are humbled before Him. As the angels themselves fear their Lord, how can anyone call upon them instead of Allah? Since such acts of worship of the angels are rejected, whether it is direct worship or an appeal for them to be intercessors with Allah, then what must be said about worshipping others, such as the inhabitants of graves who have even less right to be worshipped?

16.2

It is authentically reported from Abu Hurayrah (رضي الله عنه) that the Prophet (ﷺ) said: «When Allah orders a matter in the heavens, the angels beat their wings in humility and submission to His words. The sound of that is like the sound of a chain on smooth rocks, and they continue to do so until it enters their hearts. Then, when fear has been removed from their hearts, some of the angels ask: What has your Lord said? The others reply: The Truth, and He is the Exalted, the Most Great. The listening thieves (from the jinn) hear, one above another — and Sufyân, one of the narrators, described it by spreading out his fingers — and the thief hears the words and transmits them to the one below him, and he transmits it to the one below, and so on, until it reaches the tongue of the magician or the fortune-teller.

Sometimes a meteorite strikes the thief before he can convey the news. Sometimes he conveys it before he is struck, and then he adds a hundred lies to what he hears, and it is said: Did not the fortune-teller tell us such-and-such on such-and-such a day? Then the fortune-teller is believed because of these Words which were overheard from the heaven.» (recorded by Bukhari)

Allah's Messenger (ﷺ) informs us in this hadith that when Allah, the Exalted, decrees a matter in heaven, the angels fall prostrate in fear of Him and in glorification of Him. Then, when the fear is removed from their hearts, they begin to ask one another about what the Lord, All-Mighty, All-powerful, has said. One of them, probably Jibreel (Gabriel) (ﷺ),[53] replies that Allah has spoken the uncompromising Truth, of which there is no doubt. Sometimes a listening thief, who is a devil, overhears what is said and transmits it to the awaiting magician or the fortune-teller. A meteorite might strike the devil and incinerate him before he has the chance to pass on what he has heard, or the information might be passed on before he is destroyed — all in accordance with Allah's Will. The devil, the magician, or the fortune-teller adds a hundred lies to what has been heard, and the people hear and believe ninety-nine lies because of this one scrap of Truth which was heard from the heaven.

Benefits derived from this hadith

1. The hadith is a confirmation of Allah's being above His creation.
2. The hadith is evidence of Allah's greatness.
3. The hadith confirms Allah's divine attribute of speech.
4. The devils overhear what the angels are saying in the heavens, and Allah has allowed them to do so, as a test and a trial for them.
5. It is permissible to use practical examples in order to explain abstract matters.

---

[53] since he is the leader of the angels and the greatest of them

6. Devils are the source of knowledge for both the magician and the fortune-teller.

7. Some souls are attached to that which is vain and futile.

8. Sorcerers and fortune-tellers are liars and cheats.

Relevance to tawḥeed and the subject of the chapter

This hadith shows the position of the angels and that they fear and revere their Lord. The angels themselves worship Allah. So, if it is not permissible to worship them, whether by worshipping them directly or calling upon them as intercessors, then it is eminently clear that calling upon other than them is even more obviously futile.

16.3

An-Nawwâs ibn Sam‘ân (ﷺ) reported that Allah's Messenger (ﷺ) said: «When Allah, the Exalted, wishes to reveal something, He speaks out the Revelation and the heavens begin to shake — or he said 'thunder heavily' — due to fear of Allah, the All-Mighty, the All-Powerful. When the inhabitants of the heavens hear it, they fall down in prostration to Allah. Jibreel (ﷺ) is the first to raise his head, and then Allah speaks to him and Allah gives him the Revelation, according to His will. Then Jibreel (ﷺ) passes by the angels, and every time he passes through a different heaven, its angels ask him: What has our Lord revealed, Jibreel? Jibreel (ﷺ) answers: He has spoken the Truth, and He is the Most High, the Most Great. They all repeat the same after him, and then Jibreel (ﷺ) proceeds to the destination commanded by Allah, the All-Mighty, the All-Powerful.» (reported by aṭ-Ṭabarâni with a sound chain)

Allah's Messenger (ﷺ) informs us in this hadith that when Allah speaks the Revelation, it causes the heavens to shake with thunder and convulsions and the angels to fall down prostrate, in fear of His Majesty. The first of them to recover and raise his head is the angel Jibreel (🕊). Allah then speaks to him as He wills, after which Jibreel (🕊) departs with the Revelation to wherever Allah commands him. Every time he passes through one of the heavens, its inhabitants from among the angels enquire of him about what the Lord, All-Mighty, All-Powerful has commanded. Each time he gives the same reply that Allah has spoken the evident Truth, and He is the Most High, above all His creation, the Most Great, without equal in greatness.

Benefits derived from this hadith

1. The hadith confirms Allah's divine attribute of *irâdah*.[54]
2. It also confirms Allah's divine attribute of speech[55] and that His speech is heard.
3. Allah's might is unparalleled.
4. All of the heavens are inhabited.
5. The hadith is proof of Jibreel's superiority over the rest of the angels.
6. The hadith confirms two of Allah's names: *Al-'Ali* (the Exalted) and *Al-Kabeer* (the Most Great).

Relevance to tawḥeed and the subject of the chapter

This hadith clearly shows the position of the angels. It proves that the angels, who are among Allah's finest creations, fear Allah. So worship of them by others is false and an act of shirk.

---

[54] *irâdah*: want, wish, will, decree

[55] It is not easy to adequately translate the words *qawl* and *kalâm* into English, but we may say that *qawl* is when we say, 'Such-and-such a person *said*:....', whereas *kalâm* refers to the 'text': the spoken words of Allah, which are spoken to whom He wills of the angels or prophets. Both attributes of Allah are confirmed here.

Chapter 17

Intercession

17.1

*A*llah (ﷻ) says:

﴿وَأَنذِرۡ بِهِ ٱلَّذِينَ يَخَافُونَ أَن يُحۡشَرُوٓاْ إِلَىٰ رَبِّهِمۡ لَيۡسَ لَهُم مِّن دُونِهِۦ وَلِيٌّ وَلَا شَفِيعٌ لَّعَلَّهُمۡ يَتَّقُونَ ٥١﴾

(سورة الأنعام: ٥١)

❁And warn by it those who fear to be gathered before their Lord that besides Him they will have neither protector nor intercessor, so that they may become pious, God-fearing.❁   *(Qur'an 6: 51)*

Allah, Most Glorified, commands His Prophet, Muhammad (ﷺ), in this verse to inform and strike fear into those who are convinced of the truth of the Day of Resurrection. They will stand before their Lord on that Day, and they will find no helper, nor intercessor, to intercede between them and Allah's punishment. Thus, it is hoped that they will heed this warning and fulfil the commands of Allah and abstain from that which He has forbidden.

Benefits derived from this verse

1. Warnings only benefit those who believe.
2. This verse confirmation the Resurrection.
3. There will be no intercession except and until its conditions have been fulfilled.

Relevance to tawheed and the subject of the chapter

This Qur'anic verse proves that no intercession will be accepted until its conditions have been met. The verse proves that no one can intercede on his or her own initiative; therefore, to seek such intercession from someone among Allah's creation is an act of major shirk. Likewise, seeking intercession from idols, whose worshippers claim can intercede with Allah on their behalf, is shirk.

17.2

Allah (رضي) says:

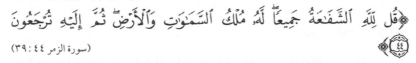

(سورة الزمر ٤٤ : ٣٩)

{Say: To Allah belongs all intercession. To Him belongs the dominion of the heavens and the earth, and to Him you will all return.}   *(Qur'an 39: 44)*

Allah, Most Glorified, commands His Prophet, Muhammad (صلى الله عليه وسلم), to inform the people, whatever their philosophy or creed, that the right to grant every manner of intercession is purely and solely for Allah, the All-Mighty, the All-powerful. None may contend with Him in it, nor can anyone intercede except by His permission. Then He affirms that He is the One and Only Disposer of Affairs in the heavens and the earth and all that they contain. There is no escaping a day when all of humankind will be returned to Allah. Then those who took others as intercessors will know the futility of their deeds.

Benefits derived from this verse

1. There are different types of intercession and to Allah belongs the rights of all intercession.

2. Intercession is the dominion of Allah and none may intercede unless He wills it and is pleased by the one for whom intercession is made.

3. This verse confirms the truth of the Resurrection.

Relevance to tawḥeed and the subject of the chapter

This Qur'anic verse proves that every kind of intercession is the dominion of Allah. Intercession will not be granted to anyone unless Allah permits it and is pleased by the one for whom intercession is sought. Therefore, seeking it from other than Allah is an act of major shirk, and that includes worshipping idols or other humans and claiming to do so in order to obtain their intercession.

Important note

Allah's Words ❴to Allah belongs all intercession❵ prove that intercession is of many different kinds, and the scholars have mentioned eight of them:

1. Major intercession: This will fall upon the shoulders of the Prophet Muhammad (ﷺ) after all the other prophets and Messengers have refused to accept it, on the Day of Resurrection. The people will ask all of the previous prophets and Messengers to intercede with Allah on their behalves, but they will refuse, saying: 'Myself! Myself!' Then they will come to the Messenger of Allah (ﷺ), and he will accept and go to his Lord and prostrate before Him for as long as Allah wills. Then he will be given permission to raise his head and intercede on behalf of the believing people, and no one other than he (ﷺ) shall be given this right and privilege.

2. Intercession for the people of paradise: This has been confirmed by the long hadith of Abu Hurayrah (ﷺ), narrated by Bukhari and Muslim, which mentions that the Prophet Muhammad (ﷺ)

will intercede with Allah on behalf of the People of paradise that its doors might be opened and they might be allowed to enter it.

3. Intercession for the disobedient Muslims: The Prophet Muhammad (ﷺ) will intercede with his Lord on behalf of those Muslims who have committed sins of disobedience to their Lord, All-Mighty, that they may not be placed in the Fire.

4. Intercession for the disobedient people of tawḥeed: He (ﷺ) will intercede with Allah on behalf of those Muslims who have entered hellfire because of their sins, that they may be removed from it. The authentic narrations concerning this have been widely reported and all of the Companions (may Allah be please with them) and the scholars who follow the Sunnah are agreed upon it.

5. Intercession for increasing the reward of the people of paradise: the Messenger of Allah (ﷺ) will intercede on behalf of a people from among the people of paradise that they may have their reward increased and their status elevated; and there is none who disputes this. (It is from a hadith recorded by Muslim.)

6. Intercession of the Prophet (ﷺ) for his uncle: He (ﷺ) will intercede on behalf of his uncle Abu Ṭâlib that his punishment in hellfire may be lightened. (This is from a hadith recorded by Bukhari and Muslim)

7. Intercession of children: Those children who died while still below the age of reason[56] will intercede on behalf of their believing parents. (This is from a hadith recorded by Muslim)

8. Intercession of some believers for others: It is authentically confirmed that some believers will intercede on behalf of other believers. (This is from a statement by Abu al-'Abbâs recorded by Bukhari.)

---

[56] defined in the Sharia as the age of puberty

17.3

Allah (جلجلاله) says:

﴿ٱللَّهُ لَآ إِلَٰهَ إِلَّا هُوَ ٱلۡحَيُّ ٱلۡقَيُّومُ لَا تَأۡخُذُهُۥ سِنَةٞ وَلَا نَوۡمٞ لَّهُۥ مَا فِى ٱلسَّمَٰوَٰتِ وَمَا فِى ٱلۡأَرۡضِ مَن ذَا ٱلَّذِى يَشۡفَعُ عِندَهُۥٓ إِلَّا بِإِذۡنِهِۦ يَعۡلَمُ مَا بَيۡنَ أَيۡدِيهِمۡ وَمَا خَلۡفَهُمۡ وَلَا يُحِيطُونَ بِشَىۡءٖ مِّنۡ عِلۡمِهِۦٓ إِلَّا بِمَا شَآءَ وَسِعَ كُرۡسِيُّهُ ٱلسَّمَٰوَٰتِ وَٱلۡأَرۡضَ وَلَا يَـُٔودُهُۥ حِفۡظُهُمَا وَهُوَ ٱلۡعَلِىُّ ٱلۡعَظِيمُ ﴿٢٥٥﴾ ﴾   (سورة البَقَرَة: ٢٥٥)

❴Allah! There is none who has the right to be worshipped but He, the Living, the Ever-lasting. Neither slumber nor sleep overtakes him. His are all things in the heavens and the earth. Who is it that can intercede in His presence, except as He permits? He knows what is before them and what is behind them, and they will not compass aught of His knowledge, except as He wills. His *kursi*[57] extends over the heavens and the earth and He feels no fatigue in guarding and preserving them, for He is the Most High, Most Great.❵

(Qur'an 2: 255)

Allah (جلجلاله), informs us in this verse that nothing has the right to be worshipped besides Him, because He is the Living, Whose life is complete and without beginning or end, Who gives life to His creation, but is in no need of anything and is afflicted by nothing which affects His slaves, such as tiredness, sleep, or hunger. His Lordship is complete and all-encompassing. His is the dominion of the heavens and the earth and all that is in them, and no one can say anything to Him concerning them, including in the matter of intercession. No one possesses power to intercede except as He wills and permits, and then only if Allah is pleased to allow that intercession.

---

[57] *kursi*: the resting place of the Feet of Allah, the Beneficent, and it is the largest of all created things after the *'arsh* (throne)

Allah informs us that no one encompasses anything of His knowledge except those whom He blesses and gives knowledge, whether revelation or other wisdom. He tells us that His kursi extends over all of the heavens and the earth and that guarding and protecting them causes Him no fatigue or discomfort, for He is the Most High, above all of His creation, and He is the Most Great, greater than all others who claim greatness.

Benefits derived from this verse

1. This verse affirms five of Allah's names:
    (i) Allah;
    (ii) *Al-Ḥayy* (the Living);
    (iii) *Al-Qayyoom* (the Ever-lasting);
    (iv) *Al-'Ali* (the Most High); and
    (v) *Al-'Adheem* (the Most Great).
2. Allah does not succumb to slumber or sleep, for He has no need of them. Those are attributes of His created beings and indicate their imperfection. Allah is far above any imperfection.
3. No one may intercede with Allah on his or her own initiative, only as Allah permits it.
4. The verse is evidence of Allah's will.
5. The verse is a confirmation of intercession after Allah permits it.
6. The verse includes proof of the existence of Allah's kursi.
7. Allah has complete power and knowledge.
8. Allah has the divine attribute of 'being above', both literally and metaphorically.
9. Allah's greatness is far above that of any created thing.

Relevance to tawḥeed and the subject of the chapter

This Qur'anic verse negates any intercession by Allah's created beings on their own initiative without His permission.

Therefore, seeking such intercession from other than Allah is an act of major shirk. That includes any worshipped thing, whose worshipers claim can intercede with Allah on their behalf.

Important note

This blessed verse has been described in authentic hadith as the greatest verse in the Qur'an. It is reported that whoever recites it in the evening will be protected from Satan until waking in the morning and also that whoever recites it in the morning will be protected from Satan until the evening, in accordance with Allah's will.

17.4

Allah (ﷻ) says:

﴿ ۞ وَكَم مِّن مَّلَكٍ فِى ٱلسَّمَٰوَٰتِ لَا تُغْنِى شَفَٰعَتُهُمْ شَيْـًٔا إِلَّا مِنۢ بَعْدِ أَن يَأْذَنَ ٱللَّهُ لِمَن يَشَآءُ وَيَرْضَىٰٓ ۩ ﴾   (سورة النّجْم: ٢٦)

⦃And no matter how many angels are in the heavens, their intercession will avail nothing except after Allah has given leave for whom He wills and pleases.⦄   *(Qur'an 53: 26)*

Allah, Most Glorified, informs us in this verse that in the heavens there are hosts of angels; but in spite of their large numbers and their elevated status in the sight of Allah, they cannot benefit anyone, unless Allah grants them permission to intercede and is pleased with their intercession.

Benefits derived from this verse

1. All of the heavens are inhabited by angels.
2. Intercession will only be granted on two conditions:

   (i) Allah permits the intercession, and

   (ii) He is pleased with the one for whom intercession is sought —
   and Allah is not pleased with anyone except the people of
   tawḥeed, as is confirmed by the hadith: «On behalf of whom
   will your intercession be most pleasing (to Allah), O
   Messenger of Allah? He (ﷺ) replied: The person who says
   'There is no god but Allah' sincerely from the heart.»
   [Bukhari, on the authority of Abu Hurayrah (ﷺ)]

3. The verse confirms Allah's divine attribute of will.
4. The verse confirms Allah's divine attribute of pleasure.

Relevance to tawḥeed and the subject of the chapter

This Qur'anic verse proves the negation of intercession by
every created thing, unless two conditions are fulfilled: (i) Allah's
permission is granted to the intercessor, and (ii) Allah is pleased with
the one for whom intercession is sought. This proves that intercession
belongs to Allah alone. Therefore, seeking it from other than Him is
an act of major shirk, and this especially includes the worship of
idols, in the belief that they can intercede with Allah.

17·5

Allah (ﷻ) says:

﴿قُلِ ٱدْعُوا۟ ٱلَّذِينَ زَعَمْتُم مِّن دُونِ ٱللَّهِ لَا يَمْلِكُونَ مِثْقَالَ ذَرَّةٍ فِى
ٱلسَّمَـٰوَٰتِ وَلَا فِى ٱلْأَرْضِ وَمَا لَهُمْ فِيهِمَا مِن شِرْكٍ وَمَا لَهُۥ مِنْهُم مِّن ظَهِيرٍ ۝٢٢﴾

وَلَا تَنفَعُ ٱلشَّفَعَةُ عِندَهُۥٓ إِلَّا لِمَنْ أَذِنَ لَهُۥ حَتَّىٰٓ إِذَا فُزِّعَ عَن قُلُوبِهِمْ قَالُوا مَاذَا
قَالَ رَبُّكُمْ قَالُوا ٱلْحَقَّ وَهُوَ ٱلْعَلِيُّ ٱلْكَبِيرُ ﴿٢٣﴾   (سورة سَبَإٍ: ٢٢-٢٣)

❰Say [O Muhammad]: Call upon those whom you claim [as gods] besides Allah. They have no power, not the weight of an atom in the heavens or on the earth. No share have they therein, nor is any of them a helper to Allah. No intercession can avail with Him, except for those for whom He has granted permission. So much so that, when terror is removed from their hearts, they will say: What is it that your Lord has said? They say: That which is true and just; and He is the Most High, Most Great.❱   *(Qur'an 34: 22-23)*

In these verses, Allah, Most Glorified, challenges the polytheists to petition their objects of worship which they have set up as partners with Allah, for those objects of worship will not be able to grant any benefit or protect anyone from harm. Those who are worshipped as partners to Allah possess not an atom's weight of goodness or evil in the heavens or the earth, nor do they have any share in the heavens or the earth, nor are they helpers for Allah, nor intercessors. Not even the angels or any other of Allah's created beings possess the power to intercede on behalf of anyone, except by His permission. Then Allah makes it clear that the angels, who are the most powerful of Allah's created beings, fall down in fear and submission to Allah and His awe-inspiring Majesty. Then, when the fear is removed from their hearts, they ask one another about what their Lord, the All-Mighty, the All-Powerful has said; and some of them answer that it is the firm truth, and He is the Most High, the Most Great.

Benefits derived from these verses

1. The polytheists' claims regarding the idols they worship are all false. Their idols do not possess any power or dominion in the

heavens or the earth, nor do they have any share in that or in Allah's help, nor do they have the power of intercession with Allah.

2. Intercession happens only after Allah permits it, and it does not occur at all without His permission.

3. The verses are evidence of the awesomeness of Allah and His greatness.

4. They affirm Allah's divine attribute of speech.

5. The verses confirm two of Allah's names:

(i) *Al-'Aliyy* (the Most High) and

(ii) *Al-Kabeer* (the Most Great).

Relevance to tawḥeed and the subject of the chapter

These Qur'anic verses prove that Allah's created beings cannot intercede on their own initiative. Granting intercession is the exclusive right of Allah; and therefore, to seek it from other than Allah is an act of shirk. This includes the worship of idols, which their worshipers claim have the power of intercession.

Important notes

1. Abul 'Abbâs said:

Allah has negated all that the polytheists do in worship, such as the belief that any besides Allah possesses sovereignty or has any share in sovereignty or aid. Nothing remains except intercession, and He has made clear that intercession is not possible except by His permission for the intercessor. The hadith of major intercession also supports this, for in it is reported the words of Allah on the Day of Resurrection: «Raise your head and ask and it shall be given; intercede and it will be accepted.» (Bukhari and Muslim)

2. Intercession will not be accepted unless Allah is pleased with the one for whom intercession is sought, as is proven by the Words of Him, Most High: ﴿And they offer no intercession except for those with whom He is well-pleased.﴾ Allah is well-pleased only with the people of tawḥeed as evident in the hadith: «On behalf of whom will your intercession be most pleasing (to Allah), O Messenger of Allah? He (ﷺ) replied: The person who says, 'There is no god except Allah,' sincerely from the heart.»

Chapter 18

Allah guides whom He wills

18.1

$\mathscr{A}$llah (ﷻ) says:

﴿إِنَّكَ لَا تَهْدِى مَنْ أَحْبَبْتَ وَلَٰكِنَّ ٱللَّهَ يَهْدِى مَن يَشَآءُ وَهُوَ أَعْلَمُ بِٱلْمُهْتَدِينَ ۝﴾

(سورة القَصَص: ٥٦)

❴Verily, you will not guide everyone whom you love, but Allah guides whom He wills and He knows best those who receive guidance.❵ *(Qur'an 28: 56)*

Allah informs the Prophet (ﷺ) that his persistent efforts to call his uncle Abu Ṭâlib to Islam will be of no avail, for Allah knows all things — past, present, and future, and no one other than Allah has knowledge of the unseen. Abu Ṭâlib will not be guided. Then, He informs His Messenger (ﷺ) that He makes the guidance successful for whichever of His slaves He wills. That is because He knows best who deserves to be guided to success.

Benefits derived from this verse

1. An acceptance of guidance occurs only by the will of Allah.
2. People have a natural love for their disbelieving family members — as long as they do not fight against Islam — and this does not

conflict with true faith and belief.

3. The verse is a confirmation of Allah's divine attribute of will.

Relevance to tawḥeed and the subject of the chapter

This Qur'anic verse proves that the Prophet (ﷺ) alone cannot cause his guidance to be accepted in spite of the fact that he is the noblest of all humankind. If he cannot guide anyone he wills, then obviously, no lesser human being can do so. Successful guidance comes only from Allah, and therefore seeking it from other than Allah is shirk.

Important note

There is no contradiction between this verse and the words of Allah, Most High: ❨Verily, you do guide [men] to the Straight Path.❩ *(Qur'an 42: 52)* In the former verse, Allah is negating the ability of the Prophet (ﷺ) to compel people accept his guidance. The latter verse simply states that Allah's Messenger (ﷺ) calls people to the Straight Path, as he has been commanded to do.

18.2

It is authentically reported on the authority of Ibn al-Musayyib that his father said: «'Abdullâh ibn Abi Umayyah and Abu Jahl were with Abu Ṭâlib as death was approaching him. Allah's Messenger (ﷺ) came and said to his uncle Abu Ṭâlib: O Uncle, say, 'There is no god except Allah and nothing has the right to be worshipped but Him.' It is a word by which I will plead for you with Allah. But the others said: Will you reject the faith of 'Abdul Muṭṭalib? The Messenger of Allah (ﷺ) repeated his words, and again they repeated their question. So the dying testament of Abu Ṭâlib was that he remained upon the religion of 'Abdul Muṭṭalib, and he refused to say,

'There is no god but Allah.' The Messenger of Allah (ﷺ) said: I will continue to ask forgiveness for you until I am forbidden to do so. Then Allah revealed:

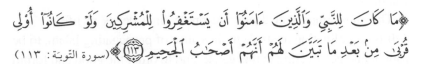

﴾It is not for the Prophet or those who believe with him to ask forgiveness for the polytheists, even though they be their close relatives, after it has been made plain to them that they are of the people of hellfire.﴿   *(Qur'an 9: 113)*

It was also concerning Abu Ṭâlib that Allah revealed: ﴾Verily, you will not guide everyone whom you love, but Allah guides whom He wills and He knows best those who will be guided.﴿ *(Qur'an 28: 56)*» (recorded by Bukhari)

Sa'eed ibn al-Musayyib (رضى الله عنه) informs us in this hadith that when Abu Ṭâlib was approaching death, the Prophet (ﷺ) asked him to pronounce the words of tawḥeed: 'There is no god except Allah.' The prophet (ﷺ) desired to be a witness for uncle's acceptance of Islam, but Abu Ṭâlib's two other visitors were wicked and aroused in him the passion of the days of ignorance. They reminded him of the religion of his ancestors. So Abu Ṭâlib refused to embrace Islam and died still following the false religion of his people. Immediately after his uncle's death, the Prophet (ﷺ) said that he would continue to ask forgiveness for him until Allah forbade him from doing so. This he did, until Allah revealed the above-mentioned verse.

Benefits derived from this hadith

1. It is permissible to visit sick polytheists when the purpose of doing so is the desire to call them to Islam.

2. Whoever says 'There is no god except Allah' at the time of death will be judged by appearances to be a Muslim, even though the person may never have done any good deeds or acts of worship in Islam.

3. The most important deeds are one's final deeds in life.

4. It is an obligation to strive in the cause of propagating Islam, to be patient and persevering in that cause, and to order the good and forbid the evil.

5. The hadith refutes of the claim of those who assert that 'Abdul Muṭṭalib and his ancestors were Muslims.

6. Evil people inflict harm upon good people.

7. It is forbidden to seek Allah's forgiveness for the disbelievers and polytheists, even though they may be close family members and even though they might perform services for Islam and the Muslims.

Relevance to tawḥeed and the subject of the chapter

This hadith proves that the success of guidance is not determined by the Prophet (ﷺ), and since he is the noblest of humankind, it stands to reason that no lesser mortal may be assured of success in efforts to guide others. The acceptance of guidance is from Allah alone, and therefore seeking it from other than Him is an act of shirk.

Chapter 19

Exaggerated praise
of the righteous

19.1

*A*llah (ﷻ) says:

﴿يَـٰٓأَهْلَ ٱلْكِتَـٰبِ لَا تَغْلُوا۟ فِى دِينِكُمْ وَلَا تَقُولُوا۟ عَلَى ٱللَّهِ إِلَّا ٱلْحَقَّ إِنَّمَا ٱلْمَسِيحُ عِيسَى ٱبْنُ مَرْيَمَ رَسُولُ ٱللَّهِ وَكَلِمَتُهُۥٓ أَلْقَىٰهَآ إِلَىٰ مَرْيَمَ وَرُوحٌ مِّنْهُ فَـَٔامِنُوا۟ بِٱللَّهِ وَرُسُلِهِۦ وَلَا تَقُولُوا۟ ثَلَـٰثَةٌ ٱنتَهُوا۟ خَيْرًا لَّكُمْ إِنَّمَا ٱللَّهُ إِلَـٰهٌ وَٰحِدٌ سُبْحَـٰنَهُۥٓ أَن يَكُونَ لَهُۥ وَلَدٌ لَّهُۥ مَا فِى ٱلسَّمَـٰوَٰتِ وَمَا فِى ٱلْأَرْضِ وَكَفَىٰ بِٱللَّهِ وَكِيلًا ۝﴾ (سورة النِّسَاء: ١٧١)

❰O People of the Book! Do not commit excesses in your religion, nor say of Allah anything but the truth. The Messiah, 'Eesâ the son of Maryam, is no more than a Messenger of Allah, and His Word which He bestowed upon Maryam, and a Spirit proceeding from Him. So believe in Allah and His Messengers. Say not 'Three' — desist! It will be better for you, for Allah is one God, glory be to Him. [Far exalted is He] above having a son. To Him belong all things in the heavens and on earth, and enough is Allah as a Disposer of affairs.❱

(Qur'an 4: 171)

In this verse, Allah, Most Glorified, forbids the Jews and Christians from exaggeration and excess in their religion, such as the deification 'Eesâ, the son of Maryam, by the Christians, while the Jews went to the opposite extreme and rejected him. Allah refutes the claims of both by describing 'Eesâ (﷽) as His Messenger and a Spirit from among the spirits created by Allah. Therefore they are obliged to believe truly in Allah alone, without attributing fathers, sons, wives, or companions to Him; and to believe in all of the Messengers and not to belie them or elevate them above their true status; and to reject the belief in the trinity; and to affirm their belief in Allah as the only God Who has the right to be worshipped. Allah is the only Lord, Owner, and Creator of the whole universe, and He is the sole Guardian of all creation.

Benefits derived from this verse

1. Excess in religion is forbidden.
2. It is prohibited to speak according to one's own opinion in matters of religion without evidence to support it.
3. The verse affirms the Prophethood and Messengership of 'Eesâ (﷽).
4. The verse refutes the claims of the Jews and Christians regarding the status of 'Eesâ (﷽).
5. The verse is an affirmation of Allah's divine attribute of speech.
6. The verse is evidence of the falseness of the belief in the trinity.
7. Every aspect of tawheed represents goodness.

Relevance to tawheed and the subject of the chapter

This Qur'anic verse shows what caused the People of the Book to belie and leave their religion. In the case of the Christians, it was their excessive praise and glorification of 'Eesâ (﷽) until they deified him and worshipped him as a partner with Allah. In the case of the Jews, it was their vilification of him.

19.2

Allah (ﷻ) says:

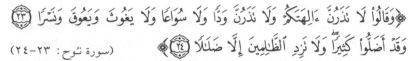

(سورة نُوح: ٢٣–٢٤)

❨They said: Do not abandon your gods. Do not abandon Wadd, or Suwâ', or Yaghooth, or Ya'ooq, or Nasr [all names of their idols]. — They have led many astray, and [O Allah!] do not increase the wrong-doers in aught save error.❩   *(Qur'an 71: 23-24)*

Allah, Most Glorified, informs us in these verses about polytheists. They are devoted to the worship of their idols as evidenced by their advising each other to worship them and not to abandon them, in particular, those mentioned in the verse. Then He (ﷻ), makes it clear that they have caused many to go astray by their false advice. They are described as wrong-doers who deserve their punishment and who are far astray from the Straight Path of Allah.

The names mentioned in the verse were the names of men who had been righteous. Their people became excessive in their love for them, so that when they died, Satan whispered to them that they should make images of them in order to remember them. Then later, after that generation died, the original purpose of the pictures was forgotten, and the succeeding generations began to worship them.

Benefits derived from these verses

1. Shirk was present among the former communities.
2. The five names mentioned in the verse are the names of the idols of the people of Nooḥ (Noah).
3. People who practice falsehood cooperate mutually in the perpetuation of that falsehood.

4. In general, it is permissible to supplicate to Allah against the unbelievers.

Relevance to tawḥeed and the subject of the chapter

These Qur'anic verses prove that exaggeration and excessive veneration of righteous people is an act of shirk because doing so means that one attributes to a created being what should only be attributed to Allah. Thus, they become worshipped as partners with Allah.

19.3

It is reported on the authority of 'Umar (رضي الله عنه) that the Messenger of Allah (ﷺ) said: «Do not praise me as the Christians extolled the son of Maryam. I am no more than a slave (of Allah), and so (instead) say that I am 'Allah's Slave and His Messenger'.» (recorded by Bukhari)

In this hadith, the Prophet (ﷺ) forbids his Ummah from praising him excessively in order that they may never raise him above the status in which Allah has placed him. Then he makes it plain that the correct way in which to speak of him is as a dependent, worshiping slave of Allah and His Messenger. Believing in him as Allah's Messenger entails believing him (ﷺ) in all that he says, obeying him in what he commands, abstaining from what he forbids, and knowing that Allah may not be worshipped except in accordance with the law which He has ordained.

Benefits derived from this hadith

1. It is forbidden to exceedingly praise the prophets and other righteous Muslims.

2. The Prophet (ﷺ) took great care to prevent any means that might lead to sin.

3. The Christians exaggerated in their praise of 'Eesâ (ﷺ).

4. The hadith refutes those who claim that Muhammad (ﷺ) was more than a Messenger.

Relevance to tawheed and the subject of the chapter

This hadith proves that excessive praise and glorification of the Prophet (ﷺ), who is the best of humankind, will lead the Muslims out of the fold of Islam, just as the Christians left their religion because of excessively extolling 'Eesâ (ﷺ). Excessive praise and glorification of Allah's creatures may lead to worship of them.

19.4

It is reported that the Messenger of Allah (ﷺ) said: «Beware of exaggerated praise, for it was only this which led those before you to destruction.» (recorded by Ahmad, an-Nasâ'i, and Ibn Mâjah)

In this hadith, the Prophet (ﷺ) forbids us from excess in religion and exaggerating the praises of Allah's created beings. This is so that we may not be destroyed like the communities that came before us when they practised excess in their religion and exceeded all bounds in worship.

Benefits derived from this hadith

1. It is forbidden to practice excess in religious matters.

2. Exaggeration in religious matters is a cause of destruction.

Relevance to tawheed and the subject of the chapter

This hadith proves that the reason for the destruction of former peoples was their exaggeration in matters of religion. Thus, excess in matters of religion or excessive praise and reverence of Allah's creatures removes a person from the legal bounds set by Allah. The ones who do so are following their own vain desires and elevating those desires to the level of partners with Allah. This is shirk because it is in contradiction with the pure Islamic concept of tawheed.

19.5

It is reported on the authority of Ibn Mas'ood (ﷺ) that the Messenger of Allah (ﷺ) said and repeated this statement three times: «Those who are extreme are destroyed.» (recorded by Muslim)

Because the Prophet (ﷺ) was sent to us with Allah's law, he warned us in his community against extremism and severity in all things, particularly in matters of religion which have been prescribed by Allah (ﷺ). He made clear for us the limits of our religion, and he repeated his words three times in order to emphasise their importance to the Companions who were listening so that they should understand and be warned of transgressing those limits.

Benefits derived from this hadith

1. Extremism in all matters is prohibited.
2. It is a virtue to stress important matters.
3. Islam is ease and flexibility, not extremism.

Relevance to tawheed and the subject of the chapter

This hadith proves that extremism in all matters, including reverence and praise of the righteous, is a cause of destruction. Extremism in religious matters, or excessive praising of righteous people, puts people beyond the limits imposed by Allah, and causes people to spends their lives in pursuit of their own vain desires, and this is shirk.

Chapter 20

Worshiping at the grave
of a righteous person

20.1

$\mathcal{I}$t is authentically reported on the authority of 'Â'ishah that Umm Salamah (may Allah be pleased with them both) told the Messenger of Allah (ﷺ) about a church she had seen in Abyssinia in which there were pictures. The Prophet (ﷺ) said: «Those people, when a righteous member of their group dies, or a pious slave (of Allah dies), they build a mosque over the grave and make images therein. In so doing, they combine two evils: (i) the evil of graves and (ii) the evil of images.» (recorded by Bukhari)

In this hadith, Umm Salamah (ﷺ) informed the Prophet (ﷺ) about a church in Abyssinia which she had seen when she migrated there with her husband to escape the persecution suffered by the early Muslims in Makkah. In the Abyssinian churches, there were images. The Prophet (ﷺ) explained to her the significance of what she had seen. When a pious person from among the Christians died, they would build an edifice over the grave and place the person's image in it, in order to remember the person and be inspired by the person's piety. The Prophet (ﷺ) added that these people were among the worst of people in the sight of Allah because they had combined two sins: (i) the sin of building over graves, which may lead eventually to the worship of their occupants; and (ii) the sin of making images of living beings, which may also lead to worship of those images, when the original purpose of their construction has been forgotten.

Benefits derived from this hadith

1. This hadith proves the acceptability of the evidence of a truthful woman.
2. Placing images in places of worship is among the evil deeds of the Christians.
3. It is forbidden to build mosques over graves.
4. It is prohibited to place images over graves.

Relevance to tawḥeed and the subject of the chapter

This hadith proves that building a place of worship over the grave of a righteous person is strongly condemned; therefore, how much worse it is for someone to actually worships the grave's occupant. It is forbidden to build mosques over graves because doing so entails glorification of their inhabitants and glorification is a form of worship. Dedicating worship to other than Allah is an act of shirk.

20.2

It is reported that 'Â'ishah (رضي الله عنها) said: «When the Messenger of Allah (ﷺ) was close to death, he covered his face with a cloth. Then, when it became difficult for him to breathe, he uncovered his face and said: May Allah curse the Jews and Christians who took the graves of their prophets as places of worship — do not imitate them. 'Â'ishah added: If it had not been for this, the Prophet's grave might have been raised above ground, but it was feared that it would be taken as a place of worship.» (recorded by Bukhari and Muslim)

'Â'ishah (ﷺ) informs us in this narration that when the Prophet (ﷺ) was near to death and in a state of delirium, he invoked Allah's curse on the Jews and Christians because they built places of worship over the graves of their prophets. Then 'Â'ishah explains that the Prophet (ﷺ) intended by his words to warn his Ummah against doing as the Jews and Christians had done. She made clear that the reason he forbade the Companions from burying him outside his house was to prevent them from taking his grave as a place of worship.

Benefits derived from this hadith

1. The hadith is evidence that the Prophet (ﷺ) was afflicted by the agonies of his illness.
2. The Prophet (ﷺ) cared deeply for his Ummah.
3. In general, it is permissible to invoke Allah's curse on the disbelievers.
4. There is a general prohibition of building over graves.
5. The hadith is a rebuttal to those who claim that building over graves — in particular those of Muslim scholars — is permissible.
6. Building over graves is a custom of the Jews and Christians.
7. This hadith is evidence of 'Â'ishah's knowledge and understanding in matters of Islamic jurisprudence.
8. This hadith gives a reason for burying the Prophet (ﷺ) in his house.

Relevance to tawheed and the subject of the chapter

This hadith proves that it is prohibited to build places of worship over graves or to worship Allah near graves. Therefore, how much worse it is to actually worship the occupant of the grave. It is forbidden to build places of worship over graves because this entails glorification of their inhabitants. Glorification is an act of worship, and directing such an act to other than Allah is shirk.

20.3

It is reported that Jundub ibn 'Abdullâh (ﷺ) said: «I heard the Prophet (ﷺ) say, five days before his death: Verily, I bear witness before Allah that I have taken none of you as my *khaleel* (a special, most beloved friend), for truly, Allah has taken me as His khaleel, just as He took Ibrâheem (ﷺ) as a khaleel. If I were to take any man from my Ummah as a khaleel, it would be Abu Bakr. Your predecessors used to take their prophets' graves as places of worship, but do not make graves into places of worship, for I have forbidden you to do this.» (recorded by Muslim)

Jundub ibn 'Abdullâh (ﷺ) informs us that the Prophet (ﷺ), shortly before his death, rejected that he had taken any man as his khaleel, and this was because his heart was completely filled with love for Allah as was the heart of his ancestor Ibrâheem (ﷺ). Then he said that, were he to take any man as his khaleel, the one with most right to be considered would be Abu Bakr aṣ-Ṣiddeeq (ﷺ) because of his many virtues, his unceasing efforts in the cause of Islam, and his help and support of the Prophet (ﷺ).

When the Prophet (ﷺ) knew that the Companions loved him and were influenced by him in everything they did, he began to fear that they might build an edifice over his grave for the purpose of worship, as the Jews and Christians had done with their prophets. So he explicitly forbade the building of places of worship over graves, especially his own.

Benefits derived from this hadith

1. The hadith confirms that the Prophet (ﷺ) is Allah's khaleel.
2. The hadith contains an affirmation of Allah's divine attribute of love.

3. The hadith also confirms that Ibrâheem is Allah's khaleel.

4. The hadith provides evidence of the virtue of Abu Bakr (ﷺ) and therefore of his right to be the first Caliph of the Muslims after the Prophet's death because the most loved of humankind in the eyes of the Prophet (ﷺ) naturally has more right than any other to be his successor.

5. Building places of worship over graves was the practice of the former nations.

6. It is prohibited to take graves as places of worship.

7. It is an obligation to take precautions against that which is undesirable.

Relevance to tawḥeed and the subject of the chapter

This hadith clearly prohibits the building of places of worship over graves because this entails glorification of their inhabitants. Glorification is a kind of worship, and directing acts of worship to other than Allah is shirk.

20.4

It is narrated by Ibn Mas'ood (ﷺ) that the Prophet (ﷺ) said: «Verily, the most wicked of people are those who, when the Hour overtakes them, are still alive, and those who take graves as places of worship.» (recorded by Aḥmad and Abu Ḥâtim)[58]

The Messenger of Allah (ﷺ) informs us in this hadith about the two categories of people upon whom the Hour, or Day of Judgment, will fall: (i) those who build places of worship over graves, and (ii) those who pray at those places of worship. This is

---

[58] Aḥmad narrates it with a good chain of narrators, and Abu Ḥâtim narrates it in his *Ṣaḥeeḥ* (collection of authentic hadiths).

implicit in the phrase 'taking the graves as places of worship'. Those who do so glorify the occupants of the graves, and deify them, and seek blessings from their graves. These actions are totally unacceptable to people who have uncorrupted souls and are still upon the fitrah. No people with an ounce of faith in their hearts can accept these actions because they conflict with all that is authentically reported in the Qur'an and the Sunnah.

Benefits derived from this hadith

1. It is a miracle that the Messenger's prophecy was fulfilled, as he predicted that some members of his Ummah would build places of worship over graves.
2. The Final Hour will not fall upon the believers.
3. The hadith confirms that the Hour will come.
4. It is prohibited to build places of worship over graves and to pray close to graves, even without building anything over them, because a place of worship does not have to be a building, but may be any place used for worship, even if it is outdoors.

Relevance to tawḥeed and the subject of the chapter

This hadith describes those who build places of worship over graves as the wickedest of people because their actions entail glorification of the graves' inhabitants. Glorification is a form of worship, and dedicating acts of worship to other than Allah is shirk. This hadith proves that building places of worship over graves is prohibited.

Important note

The rules of graves are four:

1. It is a favourable act for men to visit them, without undertaking a journey to do so, since the graves remind them of the hereafter.

2. Building over graves and burning lights over them is totally forbidden because it leads inevitably to shirk.

3. Taking the occupants of graves as intercessors or supplicating to them directly is an act of major shirk because supplication is a form of worship and directing it to other than Allah is shirk.

4. It is prohibited for women to visit graves, as the Prophet (ﷺ) said: «Allah has cursed those women who visit the graves.» (a reliable hadith recorded by Abu Dâwood)

What Shaykh al-Islam Ibn Taymiyah said concerning this matter:

The Messenger of Allah (ﷺ) forbade (building over graves) towards the end of his life and cursed whoever did so. Likewise he (ﷺ) forbade praying near them, even if no building is erected over them. This is the intended meaning here, since none of the Companions would have built a mosque over the grave of the Messenger of Allah (ﷺ), for every place where the intention for prayer is made is a place of worship. Indeed, every place which is used as a place of prayer may be classified as a mosque, as he (ﷺ) said: «The whole earth has been made for me a pure and clean mosque.» (an authentic, reliable hadith recorded by Abu Dâwood)

Chapter 21

Erecting structures over graves and adorning graves

21.1

*I*t is reported that the Messenger of Allah (ﷺ) said: «Oh, Allah! Do not let my grave become an idol that is worshiped. Allah's wrath is immense against those peoples who turned the graves of their prophets into mosques.» (a sound *mursal*[59] hadith recorded by Imam Mâlik in *Al-Muwaṭṭâ*)

The narrator informs us in this hadith that the Prophet (ﷺ) adjured his Lord to protect his grave from being taken as an object of worship besides Allah. Then he (ﷺ) made clear that Allah's wrath is upon all of His slaves who take the graves of the prophets as places of worship. Therefore, how much worse it is to actually take the graves' inhabitants as objects of worship.

Benefits derived from this hadith

1. Glorifying graves is worship and an act of shirk, however righteous the graves' inhabitants were.

---

[59] *Mursal* refers to a narration that a tâbi'ee ascribes to the Prophet (ﷺ) without mentioning the Companion that he took it from. (Editor)

2. This hadith confirms Allah's divine attribute of anger.

3. It is prohibited to build places of worship over graves.

4. It is forbidden to pray near graves even if there is no building erected over the grave.

Relevance to tawheed and the subject of the chapter

This hadith proves that graves will be taken as idols by some of this Ummah. That is why the Prophet (ﷺ) asked Allah to protect his grave from being taken as an object of worship. This hadith proves that taking graves as places of worship will lead to worship of their inhabitants, and this is an act of shirk.

21.2

In addition, according to Ibn Jareer, Sufyân narrated from Manṣoor that Mujâhid said regarding the statement of Allah, ﴾Have you seen *Al-Lât* and *Al-'Uzzâ* and another, *Manât*, the third [deity]?﴿ *(Qur'an 53: 19-20)*: "Al-Lât used to prepare special foods for the pilgrims, and when he died, the people began to sit at his grave." (recorded by Bukhari)

Relevance to tawheed and the subject of the chapter

This narration shows that Al-Lât was originally the name of a righteous man who used to prepare food for pilgrims. Then, after he died, the people began to exaggerate their praises of him, sitting at his grave and taking it as an object of worship besides Allah. For this reason, every grave whose inhabitant is praised in an exaggerated manner by the people is likely to become an object of worship, even though they may not refer to it as such.

21.3

It is reported that Ibn 'Abbâs (ﷺ) said: «Allah's Messenger (ﷺ) cursed those women who visit graves and the people who take them as places of worship and hang lights around them.» (a reliable hadith recorded by Abu Dâwood, at-Tirmidhi, and Ibn Mâjah)

In this hadith, the Prophet (ﷺ) cursed three groups:

(i) women who visit graves, because of the inherent weakness in them which may lead them to mourn the departed excessively;

(ii) those who take the graves as places of worship, because this leads to the glorification of the graves' inhabitants and worship of them; and

(iii) those who adorn the graves with lights, because this is a waste of wealth without purpose and it leads to the glorification of the graves' inhabitants, very similar to the glorification of idols by those who make them.

The hadith is a warning and an admonition to every person who would build places of worship over the graves of righteous persons or the graves of leaders. This leads the people to praise the deceased excessively and to experience a state of humility at the graves which they do not feel when they go to the mosques, the houses of Allah. Thus, this is among the greatest of sins. Indeed it is one of the major sins, which should be eradicated wherever it is found, as the Prophet (ﷺ) made this clear in this hadith, for he did not curse anyone except those who committed major sins.

Benefits derived from this hadith

1. In general, it is permissible to curse those who are corrupt.
2. Women are prohibited from visiting graves.

3. It is forbidden to take graves as places of worship or adorn graves with lights.

4. The wisdom of Islamic Law lies in its forbidding everything which may lead to shirk.

5. It is prohibited to spend and use up wealth without purpose.

Relevance to tawḥeed and the subject of the chapter

This hadith prohibits excessive praise and glorification of graves and their inhabitants, by building mosques or other places of worship over them or decorating them with lights, because this leads to them being taken as idols and worshiped.

Important notes

1. The purpose of prohibiting both the building of places of worship over graves and the adorning of them with lights is that these practices may lead to worship of the graves' inhabitants, not because graves are unclean.

2. There is no conflict between this hadith and the saying of the Prophet (ﷺ): «I had forbidden you to visit the graves, but (now I say) visit them» (narrated by Muslim), because the former is an exception for women from the general license granted by the latter.

Chapter 22

Protecting tawḥeed and blocking every path to shirk

22.1

*A*llah (ﷻ) says:

$$\text{﴿لَقَدْ جَآءَكُمْ رَسُولٌ مِّنْ أَنفُسِكُمْ عَزِيزٌ عَلَيْهِ مَا عَنِتُّمْ حَرِيصٌ عَلَيْكُم بِٱلْمُؤْمِنِينَ رَءُوفٌ رَّحِيمٌ ﴾}$$

(سورة التوبة ١٢٨: ٩)

❨Verily, there has come to you a Messenger from amongst yourselves. It grieves him that you should perish. He is ardently anxious over you; to the believers he is kind and merciful.❩

(Qur'an 9: 128)

In this verse, Allah has bestowed a great blessing upon humankind, in particular, the Arabs, because He sent to them a Messenger from amongst themselves, who spoke their language, whose lineage, nobility, and trustworthiness were well-known to them. Allah has described him as possessing certain divinely-given qualities, which make it incumbent upon all of us to follow him and believe in him. The Messenger (ﷺ) is troubled and grieved by whatever troubles and grieves his Ummah, and he ardently seeks that which is beneficial to them and earnestly desires that they be guided aright. He (ﷺ) is full of compassion for them.

Benefits derived from this verse

1. Allah has bestowed a great blessing upon humankind, particularly the Arabs, by sending a prophet to them from their own community, and through him, Allah saved them from the abyss of shirk and humiliation.
2. The Prophet cared ardently for his Ummah.

Relevance to tawḥeed and the subject of the chapter

This Qur'anic verse proves the care taken by the Prophet (ﷺ) for his Ummah, especially his protection of their tawḥeed and his great efforts to prevent them from falling into whatever might lead to shirk. This includes his prohibition of glorifying graves by building structures over them, and in particular, what he taught about his own grave — may Allah's peace and blessings be upon him.

22.2

It is reported that Abu Hurayrah (ﷺ) said: «Allah's Messenger (ﷺ) said: Do not make your homes into graves, nor make my grave into a place of celebration. Send your prayers and blessings upon me, for they will be conveyed to me wherever you may be.» (recorded by Abu Dâwood with a reliable chain)

Abu Hurayrah (ﷺ) tells us in this hadith that the Prophet (ﷺ) forbade us from abandoning our homes and making them into graves, where acts of worship are not performed and Allah's name is not mentioned. Then, he forbade us from taking his grave as a place of celebration, where people come to visit on a specific date or for a specific occasion. The Messenger of Allah (ﷺ) ordered us to send prayers and blessings upon him; and he informed us that the prayers and blessings of all Muslims, whoever they may be and wherever they may be, will be conveyed to him.

Benefits derived from this hadith

1. Abandoning worship in the home is forbidden.
2. It is prohibited to pray towards graves.
3. It is prohibited to visit the grave of the Prophet (ﷺ) on a special occasion or visit any grave in this manner.
4. It is an obligation to send prayers and blessings upon the Prophet (ﷺ).
5. Prayers and blessings upon the Prophet reach him (ﷺ) from wherever they are sent.
6. Those who are dead can benefit from the prayers and blessings of the living believers.

Relevance to tawḥeed and the subject of the chapter

This hadith proves that it is prohibited in Islam to take graves as places of celebration. This demonstrates the Prophet's protectiveness towards his Ummah from the danger of every path that might lead to shirk.

Important note

Some people have claimed that the Prophet's forbiddance of making his grave into a place of celebration necessitates that we should zealously cling to and visit his grave, as if he (ﷺ) had said: 'Do not make my grave an annual place of celebration, but visit it all the time.' However, this explanation is totally false and without substance, for the following reasons:

(i) This explanation is unclear and is therefore in contradiction to the established Islamic Law which is always clear.

(ii) Had the Prophet (ﷺ) intended what they claim, his family and Companions (may Allah be please with them) would have implemented it and ordered others to do likewise.

(iii) It has not been reported that the Companions (may Allah be pleased with them) ordered anyone to do this or that they did so themselves, and they were the most knowledgeable about the meaning of the Prophet's sayings.

22.3

It is reported that 'Ali ibn al-Ḥusayn saw a man approach a small niche near the grave of the Prophet (ﷺ) and go into the niche and begin to supplicate. So 'Ali prevented the man from doing so and said: «Shall I not tell you a hadith of the Prophet (ﷺ) which I heard from my father, who in turn heard it from my grandfather ['Ali ibn Abi Ṭâlib (ﷺ)], who reported that Allah's Messenger (ﷺ) said: Do not take my grave as a place of celebration, nor your homes as graves; send prayers and blessings upon me, for your salutations will reach me, wherever you may be.» (recorded by al-Maqdisi in *Al-Mukhtârah*)

'Ali ibn al-Ḥusayn informs us in this narration that he saw a man supplicating to Allah at the grave of the Prophet (ﷺ) and that he prevented him from doing so. He used as evidence a hadith which forbids taking the Prophet's grave as a place of celebratory visits and forbids abandoning worship of Allah in one's home. The Prophet (ﷺ) ordered us to send prayers and blessings upon him, saying that they would be conveyed to him, wherever the Muslim who sent them may be.

Benefits derived from this hadith

1. It is an obligation to reject wickedness.
2. Intentionally making supplication at the Prophet's grave, or any other grave, is prohibited.

3. Abandoning worship and remembrance of Allah in the home is prohibited.

4. It is forbidden to pray at graves.

5. The prayers and salutations which a Muslim sends upon the Prophet (ﷺ) will be conveyed to him whether the Muslim is near or far from his grave.

6. The dead believer can benefit from the supplications of the living believer.

Relevance to tawheed and the subject of the chapter

This hadith proves that it is forbidden to take the grave of the Prophet (ﷺ) as a place of celebration, in order to worship there. This shows the Prophet's protection of the purity of tawheed and his desire to close off every avenue that might lead to shirk.

Important note

Setting out on a journey, with the express intent of visiting the grave of the Prophet (ﷺ) is prohibited, because of his (ﷺ) words: «Do not saddle up your riding beasts, except to visit three mosques: the Sacred Mosque (in Makkah), this my mosque (in Madinah), and Al-Aqsâ Mosque (in Jerusalem).» (Bukhari and Muslim) In light of this, it is clear that whoever undertakes a journey in order to pray in the Prophet's Mosque is not guilty of any sin, while whoever does so in order to worship near the Prophet's grave has disobeyed the Prophet (ﷺ).

Chapter 23

Those of this Ummah who worship other than Allah

23.1

*A*llah (ﷻ) says:

﴿أَلَمْ تَرَ إِلَى ٱلَّذِينَ أُوتُواْ نَصِيبًا مِّنَ ٱلْكِتَٰبِ يُؤْمِنُونَ بِٱلْجِبْتِ وَٱلطَّٰغُوتِ وَيَقُولُونَ لِلَّذِينَ كَفَرُواْ هَٰٓؤُلَآءِ أَهْدَىٰ مِنَ ٱلَّذِينَ ءَامَنُواْ سَبِيلًا ٥١﴾

(سورة النساء ٥١: ٤)

❨Do you not see those who were given a portion of the Scriptures? They believe in *Jibt* and *ṭâghoot*[60] and say to the unbelievers that they are better guided than the believers!❩ *(Qur'an 4: 51)*

In this verse, Allah, Most Glorified, directs the attention of His Messenger, Muhammad (ﷺ), and that of all the Muslims, to the evil deeds of some of the Jews, who believed in the worship of other than Allah and preferred that to the believers' worship of their Lord. The Jews knew from their Scriptures that the religion of Islam was better than the worship of idols and that the Messenger of Allah (ﷺ) spoke

---

[60] *Jibt* and *tâghoot*: the name of a false idol and other things which were worshipped or obeyed in disobedience to Allah

the truth from his Lord, but their hatred and jealousy blinded them and prevented them from speaking the truth. Instead, their jealousy caused them to praise and flatter the unbelievers, but Allah will complete His light and guidance, even though the disbelievers detest it.

Benefits derived from this verse

1. The Jews had distorted the teachings of their revealed Scriptures.
2. False flattery in matters of religion and concealing the truth are among the characteristics of the Jews.
3. Shirk exists among the People of the Book.

Relevance to tawḥeed and the subject of the chapter

This Qur'anic verse proves the existence of shirk amongst the People of the Book. It has also been authentically reported from the Prophet (ﷺ) that the Muslims will imitate the People of the Book, and this includes committing shirk.

Important note

The reason for the revelation of this verse has been narrated by Imam Aḥmad, on the authority of Ibn 'Abbâs[61] (رضي الله عنهما), who said: «When Ka'b ibn al-Ashraf approached Makkah, the Quraysh said: Do you not see this orphan [meaning the Prophet Muhammad (ﷺ)], who is cut off from his family? He claims that he is better than us, while we are the patrons of the pilgrims and the Custodians [of the Sacred Mosque]. K'ab replied: You are better (than he). Then this verse was revealed: ﴾Verily, he who despises you will be cut off [from hope of mercy and forgiveness in the hereafter].﴿ *(Qur'an 108: 1)*»

---

[61] There is a sound chain of narrators all the way to him.

23.2

Allah (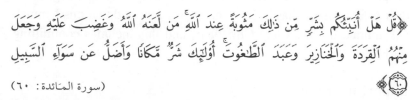) says:

﴿قُلْ هَلْ أُنَبِّئُكُم بِشَرٍّ مِّن ذَٰلِكَ مَثُوبَةً عِندَ ٱللَّهِ مَن لَّعَنَهُ ٱللَّهُ وَغَضِبَ عَلَيْهِ وَجَعَلَ مِنْهُمُ ٱلْقِرَدَةَ وَٱلْخَنَازِيرَ وَعَبَدَ ٱلطَّٰغُوتَ أُوْلَٰئِكَ شَرٌّ مَّكَانًا وَأَضَلُّ عَن سَوَآءِ ٱلسَّبِيلِ ۝﴾

(سورة المَائدة: ٦٠)

❨Say: Shall I inform you of something much worse than this [as judged] by the treatment received from Allah? [It is] those who incurred the curse of Allah and His wrath, those of whom some He transformed into apes and some into swine, those who worshipped ṭâghoot — they are worse in rank and far astray from the even Path.❩

(Qur'an 5: 60)

　　Allah addresses the Prophet (ﷺ) and tells him to say to these disbelievers from among the People of the Book: 'Shall I tell you about those who will receive the worst punishment on the Day of Resurrection? They are those of you whom Allah has banished from His mercy, those who have His wrath upon them, those whom He has turned into apes and swine, and those who worship idols.' Because of these evil attributes, Allah has informed us that they are the worst of people and the farthest astray.

Benefits derived from this verse

1. In general, it is permissible to curse the disbelievers.
2. This verse confirms of Allah's divine attribute of anger.
3. Allah has transformed some of the People of the Book into pigs and apes.
4. There exists shirk amongst the People of the Book.
5. Disobedience to Allah's will can result in chastisement in this world as it does in the hereafter.

Relevance to tawḥeed and the subject of the chapter

This Qur'anic verse proves the existence of shirk among the People of the Book, by their worship and obedience of things other than Allah. Also, it has been authentically reported that this Ummah will imitate the Jews and Christians, and this includes committing shirk.

Important note

Allah transformed some of the Jews into apes because the ape outwardly resembles the human being, although they are separate and distinct from them. Likewise, the Jews used to commit transgressions which, in some ways, outwardly appeared to be good deeds, while in fact, they were false.

23.3

Allah (ﷻ) says:

﴾وَكَذَٰلِكَ أَعْثَرْنَا عَلَيْهِمْ لِيَعْلَمُوٓا أَنَّ وَعْدَ ٱللَّهِ حَقٌّ وَأَنَّ ٱلسَّاعَةَ لَا رَيْبَ فِيهَآ إِذْ يَتَنَٰزَعُونَ بَيْنَهُمْ أَمْرَهُمْ فَقَالُوا ٱبْنُوا عَلَيْهِم بُنْيَٰنًا رَّبُّهُمْ أَعْلَمُ بِهِمْ قَالَ ٱلَّذِينَ غَلَبُوا عَلَىٰٓ أَمْرِهِمْ لَنَتَّخِذَنَّ عَلَيْهِم مَّسْجِدًا ﴿٢١﴾﴾

(سورة الكهف : ٢١)

﴾Thus did We make their case known to the people, that they might know that the Promise of Allah is true and that there can be no doubt about the Hour [of Judgement]. When they disputed among themselves about their affair, [some] said: Construct a building over them. — Their Lord knows best about them. Those who prevailed over their affair said: Indeed, we will build a place of worship over them.﴾   (*Qur'an 18: 21*)

Allah, Most Glorified, informs us in this verse that He drew the people's attention to the situation of the People of the Cave,[62] and the wisdom behind that was to prove to them that man can be resurrected after death. Then Allah, the Exalted, tells us about the dialogue which took place among the people. Some of them believed that they should build structures over the People of the Cave, although that which was incumbent upon them was for Allah to decide. Others preferred that they should build a place of worship over them.

Benefits derived from this verse

1. This verse tells about the story of the People of the Cave.
2. The verse confirms the truth of resurrection after death.
3. Making places of worship over graves was the practice of former peoples.

Relevance to tawḥeed and the subject of the chapter

This Qur'anic verse proves that the People of the Book used to build structures over graves. The Prophet (ﷺ) cursed them because of this, as their actions led to the worship of the graves' inhabitants. It has also been authentically reported that some of the people of this Ummah will imitate them and thus build mosques over graves and worship their inhabitants.

---

[62] People of the Cave: as told in the *Qur'an* (*18: 9-26*), these were a group of young men that Allah caused to fall asleep in a cave, where they remained sleeping for 309 (lunar) years until Allah awoke them.

23.4

It is reported that Abu Sa'eed al-Khudri (رضي الله عنه) said: «The Messenger of Allah (ﷺ) said: Surely, you will follow the ways of those before you, just as the flight of one arrow resembles another, so much so, that even if they entered the hole of a lizard, you would enter it. They (who were with him) asked: (Do you mean) the Jews and Christians? He (ﷺ) replied: If not them, then whom?» (recorded by Bukhari and Muslim)

Abu Sa'eed al-Khudri (رضي الله عنه) tells us in this hadith that the Messenger of Allah (ﷺ) informed the Companions (may Allah be pleased with them) that this Ummah will imitate the previous nations in their customs, their politics, and even their religion, indeed in all matters, as the flight of one arrow resembles another. Then he (ﷺ) further impressed upon us this fact, saying that even if those previous nations were to enter the hole of a lizard, the people of this Ummah would try to follow them. When the Companions (may Allah be pleased with them) asked him about the identity of those people, if they were the Jews and Christians, he (ﷺ) replied in the affirmative.

Benefits derived from this hadith

1. The hadith is evidence of a prophetic miracle, since the Messenger of Allah predicted correctly that the Muslims would one day imitate the Jews and Christians.
2. Making things clear by using powerful similes is an Islamic method of teaching.
3. It is forbidden to imitate the People of the Book.
4. It is permissible to ask questions of people of (religious) knowledge.

Relevance to tawheed and the subject of the chapter

This hadith proves that this Ummah will do as the People of the Book do; and among their actions is the worship of other than Allah.

23.5

Thawbân (ﷺ) reported: «The Messenger of Allah (ﷺ) said: Verily, Allah folded the earth for me, so much so that I saw its easts and its wests. The kingdom of my Ummah will reach as far as the earth was folded for me. The two treasures, both the red and the white, were given to me. I prayed to my Lord that He would not destroy my Ummah by a widespread drought and not give sovercignty over them to an enemy who annihilates them in large numbers, except from among themselves. Then verily, my Lord said: O, Muhammad! When I issue a decree, it is not withdrawn. I have promised your Ummah that I will not destroy it by a widespread drought and I shall not give sovereignty of them to an enemy who exterminates them in large numbers, even if they are stormed from all sides of the earth, except from among themselves. Only a portion of them will destroy another portion, and a portion will take another portion prisoner.» (recorded by Muslim)

In another hadith, the above was narrated by al-Barqâni with this additional saying of Allah's Messenger (ﷺ): «I fear for my Ummah that they will have leaders who will send them astray. When the sword is used among my people, it will not be withdrawn from them until the Day of Resurrection; and the Hour will not come until a tribe from among my Ummah attaches themselves to the polytheists and numbers of my people worship idols. There will be from among my Ummah thirty liars, each of them claiming that he is a prophet, though I am the Seal of the Prophets and no prophets will come after me. Still, some of my Ummah will continue to hold to the truth; and they will be victorious and they will not be harmed by those who oppose them until Allah's command comes.» (recorded by Muslim)

The Prophet (ﷺ) tells us in this hadith that Allah gathered together for him all of the earth, and he saw all that lay between the east and west. He saw that the kingdom of his people would stretch across all of the earth. Then he asked his Lord, the All-Mighty, All-Powerful, not to destroy his Ummah through drought or famine nor allow any foreign enemy to rule over them and slaughter them in large numbers. The Lord granted his request, but He, the Exalted, said that within the Ummah, they would quarrel amongst themselves and fight each other, and kill each other, and take each other prisoner.

Allah's Messenger (ﷺ) makes clear that the thing that he fears most for his Ummah is those leaders who will misguide the people, for the people will follow them and will be ruled by them, though these leaders have no knowledge. Thus, they will be astray themselves and will send others astray, and should the killing begin, it will not end until the Day of Resurrection. He (ﷺ) foresaw that a number of his Ummah would worship idols and that there would appear among them thirty liars who will claim to be prophets. Then, the Messenger of Allah (ﷺ) informs us that he is the Seal of the Prophets and that no other prophet will come after him. Finally, in order that we not despair, he (ﷺ) informs us that a number of his Ummah will hold fast to the true religion, and they will be aided by Allah and they will not be harmed by those who abandon them or those who plot against them, until the Command of Allah comes.[63]

---

[63] This would appear to be a reference to the wind which Allah will send, «...which will take away the souls of all the believers, so that when the Trumpet is sounded, there will be no one alive except the unbelievers.» (recorded by Muslim) — and Allah knows best.

Benefits derived from this hadith

1. It is a miracle of the Prophet (ﷺ) that he was able to predict what would happen to his Ummah in the future — some of which has come to pass and some of which has yet to happen.

2. Taking war booty is permissible for Muslims.

3. The Prophet cared for the fate of his Ummah.

4. The hadith confirms Allah's divine attribute of speech.

5. The cause of destruction of this Ummah will be quarrelling and warring within itself.

6. The danger to this community will come from misguided leaders, who will send their people astray.

7. Shirk will be present in this Ummah.

8. The hadith is a complete rejection of all those who claim to be prophets after Allah's Messenger Muhammad (ﷺ).

9. Muhammad (ﷺ) is the Seal of the Prophets.

10. There will be a continuation of the Truth among some of this Ummah, until the Command of Allah comes.

Relevance to tawḥeed and the subject of the chapter

This hadith proves that some of this Ummah will worship idols.

Chapter 24

Sorcery

24.1

*A*llah (﷾) says:

﴿وَٱتَّبَعُوا۟ مَا تَتْلُوا۟ ٱلشَّيَٰطِينُ عَلَىٰ مُلْكِ سُلَيْمَٰنَ وَمَا كَفَرَ سُلَيْمَٰنُ وَلَٰكِنَّ ٱلشَّيَٰطِينَ كَفَرُوا۟ يُعَلِّمُونَ ٱلنَّاسَ ٱلسِّحْرَ وَمَآ أُنزِلَ عَلَى ٱلْمَلَكَيْنِ بِبَابِلَ هَٰرُوتَ وَمَٰرُوتَ وَمَا يُعَلِّمَانِ مِنْ أَحَدٍ حَتَّىٰ يَقُولَآ إِنَّمَا نَحْنُ فِتْنَةٌ فَلَا تَكْفُرْ فَيَتَعَلَّمُونَ مِنْهُمَا مَا يُفَرِّقُونَ بِهِۦ بَيْنَ ٱلْمَرْءِ وَزَوْجِهِۦ وَمَا هُم بِضَآرِّينَ بِهِۦ مِنْ أَحَدٍ إِلَّا بِإِذْنِ ٱللَّهِ وَيَتَعَلَّمُونَ مَا يَضُرُّهُمْ وَلَا يَنفَعُهُمْ وَلَقَدْ عَلِمُوا۟ لَمَنِ ٱشْتَرَىٰهُ مَا لَهُۥ فِى ٱلْءَاخِرَةِ مِنْ خَلَٰقٍ وَلَبِئْسَ مَا شَرَوْا۟ بِهِۦٓ أَنفُسَهُمْ لَوْ كَانُوا۟ يَعْلَمُونَ ۝﴾ (سورة البَقَرَة: ١٠٢)

﴿They followed what the devils gave out against the power of Sulaymân [Solomon]: Sulaymân did not blaspheme, but the devils did blaspheme, teaching the people sorcery and such things as came down at Babylon to the two angels, Hâroot and Mâroot. But neither of these taught anyone [such things] without saying: "We are but a trial; so do not blaspheme." They learnt from them the means to sow discord between man and wife, but they could not thus harm anyone except by Allah's permission. They learned what harmed them, not what profited them, and they knew that the buyers [of magic] would have no share in the hereafter. Miserable was the price for which they sold their souls, if only they knew!⟩ *(Qur'an 2: 102)*

Allah, Most Glorified, informs us in this verse that the Jews and Christians turned away from the Book of Allah and instead devoted themselves to the study of sorcery, which the devils claimed was from the time of Sulaymân (﷽). They further falsely claimed that they had learned it from Sulaymân (﷽) himself, but Allah makes it clear that Prophet Sulaymân (﷽) did not commit acts of disbelief. It was the devils who blasphemed by teaching the people sorcery. Then Allah says that one of the objects of those who taught magic was to cause discord between men and their wives. Still, there can be no result from the machinations of the magician unless Allah permits it. Those who abandon the religion of Islam in favour of magic will have no reward on the Day of Resurrection, and wretched will be the lot which they have purchased for themselves by these actions, if they only knew it.

Benefits derived from this verse

1. Sorcery is one of the works of the devils.
2. Sulaymân (﷽) was innocent of practising magic.
3. Learning magic and teaching it are acts of disbelief.
4. Magic has no effect unless Allah wills it.
5. There is no benefit in magic.
6. The verse is proof of the vileness and wretchedness of the sorcerer.

Relevance to tawḥeed and the subject of the chapter

This Qur'anic verse proves that practising magic is an act of disbelief. This verse warns against practising magic, which cannot be performed without committing shirk, and shirk is a negation of tawḥeed.

Important notes

1. The Arabic word for magic is *sihr*. Linguistically, it means 'that whose cause is hidden'. In Islamic terms, it means the practice of writing spells on paper or tying knots which affect the heart and the body until the person becomes ill or dies, or it means to cause a rift between a man and his wife.

2. According to the Imams Aḥmad, Mâlik, and Abu Ḥaneefah, magic is an act of disbelief.

24.2

Allah (ﷻ) says:

﴿أَلَمۡ تَرَ إِلَى ٱلَّذِينَ أُوتُواْ نَصِيبًا مِّنَ ٱلۡكِتَٰبِ يُؤۡمِنُونَ بِٱلۡجِبۡتِ وَٱلطَّٰغُوتِ وَيَقُولُونَ لِلَّذِينَ كَفَرُواْ هَٰٓؤُلَآءِ أَهۡدَىٰ مِنَ ٱلَّذِينَ ءَامَنُواْ سَبِيلًا ٥١﴾

(سورة النِّسَاء: ٥١)

❨Do you not see those who were given a portion of the Book? They believe in Jibt and ṭâghoot and they say to the unbelievers that they are better guided than the believers!❩   *(Qur'an 4: 51)*

Allah directs the attention of the Muslims, in particular, the attention of His Messenger (ﷺ), to the practices of some of the People of the Book who deviated from the Truth by preferring magic and obedience to Satan over the Book of Allah and the knowledge and guidance it contains. They lied when they asserted that the polytheists are better than the Muslims and closer to the Straight Path.

Benefits derived from this verse

1. This verse is evidence that some of the People of the Book went astray.
2. The practice of magic was present among the People of the Book.
3. Flattery, lies, and hypocrisy are among the characteristics of the Jews.

Relevance to tawḥeed and the subject of the chapter

This Qur'anic verse proves the forbiddance of practising magic and censures those who do so. It proves that engaging in magic is an act of disbelief because its origin is in shirk.[64]

Important note

Muhammad ibn 'Abdil-Wahhâb noted that 'Umar (ﷺ) said that jibt (here) means magic and ṭâghoot means the devil. The Shaykh also said that Jâbir (ﷺ) defined the *tawâgheet*[65] as fortune-tellers, to whom the devils used to descend, one to every neighbourhood.[66]

24.3

It is reported on the authority of Abu Hurayrah (ﷺ): «The Messenger of Allah (ﷺ) said: Avoid the seven destroyers (destructive sins). The Companions (may Allah be pleased with them) asked: Messenger of Allah, what are they? He (ﷺ) replied:

---

[64] This is because the magicians do not place their faith in Allah but rather in the devils among the jinn to whom they supplicate in performing their magic.

[65] *tawâgheet*: plural of tâghoot

[66] reported in *Kanz al-'Ummâl*

Shirk or associating partners with Allah; sorcery; taking the life which has been prohibited by Allah, except in truth (in accordance with Islamic Law); devouring usury; consuming the property of orphans; running away on the day of battle; and making false charges against chaste, naive women.» (recorded by Bukhari and Muslim)

Because sins are the cause of loss and destruction, the Messenger of Allah (ﷺ) has commanded his followers to avoid the following major sins, which destroy those who commit them, both in this life and in the hereafter:

1. Shirk (associating partners with Allah) — This is because shirk ensnares people in that which debases them, which is the worship of other created beings.

2. Magic — This is because magic leads to many sicknesses in society, such as superstition and ignorance, fraud, swindling gullible people, and cheating people out of their money by lying and deception.

3. Taking the life which Allah has forbidden — This is because wilful murder leads to a state of chaos and disorder and breakdown of law and order and causes the people to exist in a state of fear and insecurity.

4. Devouring usury (*ribâ*) — This is because the presence of usury, or interest[67] in society causes loss of the peoples' wealth and property, as greedy and unscrupulous money-

---

[67] There is no difference between these two terms; the idea propagated by some Muslim 'modernists' that ribâ means excessive interest rates, and that moderate interest is therefore permissible, is totally without foundation and is in contradiction with the Qur'an, the Sunnah and the confirmed practices of the Companions (may Allah be please with them) who were the best people after the Prophet (ﷺ) in understanding the Sunnah and who used to avoid even those permissible transactions that in any way resembled ribâ.

lenders rook people of their honestly earned money, growing fat at the expense of hard-working people, with no benefit to the society, only to themselves.

5. Usurping the property of the orphan — This is because such behaviour constitutes injustice against one who is a minor, who has no one to help and support him or her except Allah.

6. Running away from the enemy without cause or reason — This is because it is an act of betrayal to one's fellow Muslims, and weakens their forces and breaks their morale.

7. Unjustly accusing chaste women of adultery — This is because slander destroys their reputations, results in loss of trust in them, and sows doubts concerning the paternity of their children.

Benefits derived from this verse

1. Sins cause destruction and loss to the perpetrator.

2. It is prohibited to associate partners with Allah, for it is the greatest sin against Allah.

3. It is forbidden to learn and teach magic.

4. It is prohibited to end a human life, except for what is legally sanctioned by Allah in Islamic Law.

5. It is forbidden to charge or accept interest on loans.

6. Illegally appropriating the property of an orphan is a major sin.

7. It is forbidden to run away from the field of battle, unless there is a valid reason, such as to deceive the enemy or to lend aid on another front.

8. It is prohibited to slander chaste women, whether they are married or unmarried women.

Relevance to tawḥeed and the subject of the chapter

This hadith proves the prohibition of learning and teaching magic. Magic is forbidden because it is based upon shirk.

24.4

It is reported that Jundub (ﷺ) learned from the Prophet (ﷺ): "The punishment for the magician is that he be struck (and beheaded) by the sword." (recorded by at-Tirmidhi)[68]

Magic is a serious problem for society, indeed a sickness, which results in corruption and evil, such as killing, stealing, cheating, fraud, and discord between spouses. Thus, Allah has provided a drastic cure for it, which is the execution by beheading of magicians, so that society may be freed from the evil which results from their actions.

Benefits derived from this hadith

1. It is prohibited to learn sorcery and to teach it.
2. The punishment for practising magic is death by beheading.

Relevance to tawḥeed and the subject of the chapter

This hadith proves that the punishment for sorcery is beheading, which clearly shows that it is forbidden. Learning and teaching magic are forbidden because magic is built upon a foundation of shirk.

---

[68] It is reported in marfoo' form and at-Tirmidhi stated, 'It is more correct to say that this hadith is *mawqoof* [in other words, a saying of Jundub, not a hadith of the Prophet (ﷺ)],' — and Allah knows best.

24.5

It is narrated that Bajâlah ibn 'Ubâdah said: "'Umar ibn al-Khaṭṭâb (رضى الله عنه) wrote: Execute every sorcerer and sorceress. So we executed three sorcerers." (recorded by Bukhari)

It is also reported authentically from Ḥafṣah (رضى الله عنها) that she ordered the execution of her female slave for practising magic upon her, and the slave was executed. Such an event has also been reported from Jundub (رضى الله عنه).

According to Imâm Aḥmad, the execution of sorcerers is authentically reported from three Companions: 'Umar, Ḥafṣah, and Jundub (may Allah be pleased with them all).

Relevance to the topic of the chapter

The author, Muhammad ibn 'Abdil-Wahhâb, has mentioned these narrations in order to make it clear that the opinion of the above-mentioned Companions (may Allah be pleased with them) was that magicians should be killed.

Chapter 25

Types of sorcery

25.1

*M*uhammad ibn Ja'far said on the authority of 'Awf ibn Ḥayyân ibn al-'Alâ': «Quṭun ibn Qabeeṣah informed us from his father that he heard the Prophet (ﷺ) say: Verily, *'iyâfah, ṭarq,* and *ṭiyarah* are all acts of sorcery.» (recorded by Aḥmad and Abu Dâwood with a reliable chain)

Because the Muslims at the beginning of Islam had recently come from the Days of Ignorance, they still carried with them many of the customs and superstitions of that time. Islam ordained for them freedom from such ignorant superstition, which revelation and common sense reject and for which no practical evidence can be produced. The hadith mentions three such beliefs and practices:

1. 'iyâfah — the belief that one's fortune is affected by the flights of birds, their species, or their cries;

2. ṭarq — drawing lines in the soil or sand and throwing stones in order to supposedly reveal secrets of the unseen;

3. ṭiyarah — the belief in omens and portents and their interpretation.

The Messenger of Allah (ﷺ) classified these three as acts of sorcery, and it is confirmed that practising magic, learning it, and teaching it are all prohibited. Therefore, it is incumbent upon every Muslim to avoid all types of sorcery and to disavow all connections with such beliefs and practices and their adherents.

Benefits derived from this hadith

1. This hadith is evidence that the actions of 'iyâfah, ṭarq, and ṭiyârah are all forms of sorcery, and they were practiced among some ignorant people.
2. Magic is prohibited.

Relevance to tawḥeed and the subject of the chapter

This hadith proves that the three above-mentioned practices are acts of sorcery and magic, and magic is built upon a foundation of shirk.

25.2

It is reported on the authority of Ibn 'Abbâs (ﷺ) that Allah's Messenger (ﷺ) said: «Whoever learns a part of astrology has learned a part of magic. Those who learn more accumulate more (sin).» (recorded by Aḥmad and Abu Dâwood with a sound chain)

Because knowledge of the unseen belongs to Allah alone, the Prophet (ﷺ) negated all attempts to uncover it, including astrology. Astrology is the belief that one can know the future by understanding the supposed influence produced by the movement of the stars and the planets on peoples' lives. Allah's Messenger (ﷺ) made it clear that learning such things is an act of sorcery and that the more a person learns, the more he or she is guilty of sin.

Benefits derived from this hadith

1. The hadith is evidence that the study of astrology is a kind of magic.
2. Magic is of more than one kind.

Relevance to tawḥeed and the subject of the chapter

This hadith proves that the study of astrology is a kind of magic and sorcery, and sorcery is founded upon shirk.

Important note

Attempting to uncover the secrets of the physical unknown using practical methods, such as studying the working of the universe, biology, and physics, is not considered an act of magic. Rather, these sciences are a fulfilment of the command of Allah and His Prophet (ﷺ) to seek knowledge.

25.3

It is reported on the authority of Abu Hurayrah (ﷺ) that Allah's Messenger said, "Whoever ties a knot and blows on it has committed an act of sorcery, and whoever commits an act of sorcery has committed an act of shirk, and whoever wears an amulet will be left to its control." (recorded by an-Nasâ'i)[69]

The Prophet (ﷺ) tells us in this hadith that anyone who makes knots in ropes and then blows upon them in order to ward off something or cause something to happen is guilty of practising magic. He (ﷺ) makes it clear that the person who practises magic has

---

[69] This hadith has a disconnected chain, and one of its narrators was known to be 'lenient'.

committed shirk. Likewise, a person who wears an amulet or talisman and believes that it will offer protection from harm will be abandoned to its protection, which is, of course, non-existent.

People who give their hearts to Allah and are filled with confidence in Him, the Most High, and depend upon Him alone, will find this is more than enough to suffice them. The believers have no need of sorcery and superstition while those who depend upon Allah's created beings — sorcerers and others — will attain only evil in this life and in the hereafter because they place their faith in other than Allah, while Allah is sufficient for His slaves.

Benefits derived from this hadith

1. It is forbidden to practise magic.
2. Blowing on knots is a form of magic.
3. The hadith is evidence that a sorcerer is one who practices shirk.
4. It is prohibited to wear anything as a means of protection or provision or for granting wishes.
5. Those who depend upon other than Allah will find themselves abandoned.
6. Those who depend upon Allah will find that Allah is sufficient for them.

Relevance to tawḥeed and the subject of the chapter

This hadith proves that wearing amulets and blowing upon knots are acts of sorcery. It is also proof that magic is shirk.

25.4

It is reported on the authority of Ibn Mas'ood (رضي الله عنه) that the Messenger of Allah (Blessings and peace be upon him) said: «Shall I not tell you what *'adhdhah*[70] is? It is *nameemah*.[71]» (recorded by Muslim)

In order to focus the attention of his Companions (may Allah be pleased with them) on what he was saying — because of the great love and affection that he had for them — the Prophet (ﷺ) used the form of a question, which he then proceeded to answer himself. He (ﷺ) asked them about '*adhdhah*. Then he explained to them that it is nameemah, which means to carry tales about someone behind his back, by quoting something he said about a person to that person, the result of which is to sow discord between those two people and to fill their hearts with enmity.

Benefits derived from this hadith

1. Asking questions is a part of the Islamic way of teaching.
2. Carrying tales is prohibited, and it is a major sin.

Relevance to tawḥeed and the subject of the chapter

This hadith proves that carrying tales is a kind of sorcery, because it produces the same effect as magic, or worse, by causing division among the people. Carrying tales is a kind of sorcery, and, as we have seen, sorcery is a form of shirk.

Important note

The person who is guilty of carrying tales is not considered a disbeliever, nor is it ordered that the person be killed, but the sorcerer is guilty of disbelief, because the sorcerer is depending upon other

---

[70] *'adhdhah*: literally, 'biting'

[71] *nameemah*: tale-bearing, such as saying: 'Such-and-such a person says you are untruthful.' Even if what that person says may be true, it is still considered to be carrying tales.

than Allah to fulfil wants and needs, while the tale-bearer is not. Still, because of its similarity in some respects to sorcery, it is incumbent upon every Muslim to avoid carrying tales, gossiping, and backbiting.

25.5

It is reported on the authority of Ibn 'Umar (ﷺ) that the Messenger of Allah (ﷺ) said: «Some eloquence (can be so beautiful), it constitutes sorcery.» (recorded by Bukhari and Muslim)

In this hadith, the Prophet (ﷺ) has compared excessive eloquence and expressiveness with words to magic, for the eloquent person may on occasion succeed in making the false appear true or vice versa. Eloquence can distort the truth by throwing dust in peoples' eyes and robbing them of some of their rights by deception and falsehood. The truth of this may be seen by anyone who visits a court of law and watches some lawyers at work.

Benefits derived from this hadith

1. Eloquence which attempts to make truth appear as falsehood and vice versa is forbidden.
2. Some types of eloquence have been derogatorily compared with magic.

Relevance to tawḥeed and the subject of the chapter

This hadith defines some eloquence as similar to sorcery because it deflects the heart as sorcery does; and as we have seen, sorcery is an act of shirk.

Important note

It is not to be understood from this hadith that the capacity of expressiveness with words constitutes disbelief, but since some forms of eloquence result in corruption and the usurpation of rights, it is in some ways comparable to sorcery. Therefore, it is incumbent upon us to abstain from it.

Chapter 26

Fortune-tellers and their like

26.1

𝒥t was narrated on the authority of Ḥafṣah (رضي الله عنها), one of the wives of the Prophet (ﷺ), that Allah's Prophet (ﷺ) said: «Whoever goes to a fortune-teller and asks about some matter (of the unseen) and believes the fortune-teller, will have his (or her) prayer rejected for forty days.» (recorded by Muslim)

The Prophet (ﷺ) informs us in this hadith that people who visit fortune-tellers, ask them about matters of the unseen — of which, in reality, only Allah possesses knowledge — and believe in what the fortune-tellers say will not have their prayers accepted by Allah for forty days, nor will they have any reward for them. This is a punishment for the major sin which they have committed.

Benefits derived from this hadith

1. Fortune-telling is prohibited.
2. It is forbidden to believe the prophesies of soothsayers and fortune-tellers.
3. A person may lose the reward of his or her prayers as a punishment for sins.

Relevance to tawḥeed and the subject of the chapter

This hadith proves the forbiddance of telling fortunes or believing in them. The Prophet (ﷺ) has condemned the people who visit fortune-tellers, for they have attempted to make fortune-tellers partners with Allah in possessing knowledge of the unseen.

Important note

It has been mentioned by the scholars (may Allah have mercy on them) that whoever believes in what the fortune-teller says does not have to repeat the prayers made during this period of forty days, but the person continues to have to perform them and receives no reward for them.

26.2

It is reported on the authority of Abu Hurayrah (ﷺ) that the Prophet (ﷺ) said: «Whoever goes to a fortune-teller and believes in what the fortune-teller says has disbelieved in what was revealed to Muhammad (ﷺ).» (recorded by Bukhari, Muslim, at-Tirmidhi, and an-Nasâ'i)[72]

The Prophet (ﷺ) informs us in this hadith that visiting a fortune-teller, asking the fortune-teller about the unseen, and believing his or her words are acts of disbelief in the Qur'an and the Sunnah because both of these revelations have belied fortune-telling. Allah is alone in His knowledge of the unseen.

---

[72] It was also narrated by al-Ḥâkim, who said that it is authentic according to the strict conditions of acceptance laid down by Bukhari and Muslim, and by Abu Ya'lâ with a good chain of narrators but in a mawqoof form.

Benefits derived from this hadith

1. Fortune-telling is forbidden.
2. Revelation is truth; thus, Allah's Messenger (ﷺ) accused the fortune-tellers of lying.
3. Believing the words of fortune-tellers is considered disbelief.[73]
4. The Qur'an is revealed, not created.

Relevance to tawḥeed and the subject of the chapter

This hadith proves clearly that the fortune-teller is a disbeliever and fortune-telling is disbelief. This is because the fortune-teller depends upon methods of shirk.

26.3

On the authority of 'Imrân ibn Ḥusayn (ﷺ) it is reported that the Prophet (ﷺ) taught: «Whoever practises the interpretation of omens and portents, or tells fortunes, or seeks advice from a fortune-teller, or practises magic, or asks another to do so, is not one of us; and whoever goes to a soothsayer and believes what he tells him has disbelieved in that which was revealed to Muhammad (ﷺ).» (recorded by al-Bazzâr with a reliable chain)[74]

---

[73] Based upon this hadith, it has been said by some scholars that one who believes the prophecies of a fortune-teller is a disbeliever. However, other scholars maintain that what is intended here is that the person who believes the words of a fortune-teller has committed an 'act of disbelief'. This is because, in the previous hadith, the Prophet (ﷺ) informed us that one who visits a fortune-teller and believes in what the fortune-teller says will have his or her prayers rejected for forty days, while if it were true that the person were a disbeliever, the person's prayers would not be accepted at all.

[74] Narrated by al-Bazzâr with a reliable chain of narrators in marfoo' form and by aṭ-Ṭabarâni in his book, *Al-Awsaṭ*, with a good chain of narrators but=

In this hadith, the Prophet (ﷺ) declares himself free and innocent from three kinds of people:

1. The one who seeks omens or has them interpreted;

2. The one who tells fortunes or seeks advice from fortune-tellers;

3. The one who practises magic or seeks the services of a magician.

Then the Prophet (ﷺ) adds, as an extra warning to the fortune-tellers and their clients, that whoever believes the words of fortune-tellers has disbelieved in the revelation given to him (ﷺ), namely the Qur'an and the Sunnah. This is because Allah and His Messenger (ﷺ) have informed us that knowledge of the unseen is only with Allah. Therefore, belief in fortune-tellers is a rejection of Allah's words and those of His Prophet (ﷺ).

Benefits derived from this hadith

1. Practicing sorcery, fortune-telling, and interpreting omens are all forbidden.
2. It is also forbidden to seek to have any of these three things done.
3. Believing the prophesies of a fortune-teller is disbelief in Islam.
4. The Qur'an is revelation, not created.

Relevance to tawḥeed and the subject of the chapter

This hadith proves, without doubt, that the fortune-teller is a disbeliever because the fortune-teller depends upon shirk in order to predict the future.

=without the words 'and whoever goes to a soothsayer' till the end.

26.4

The commentator of the Qur'an, Imam al-Baghawi, stated:

The 'seer' (*'arrâf*) who claims to know the unseen depends upon knowledge stolen [by the jinn, who overheard it from the lowest heaven] and falsehood and the like. It has been said that he is the same as the fortune-teller (*kâhin*), but the latter is, in fact, one who claims knowledge of the unseen events of the future. It has also been said that he is one who knows the secrets of the mind.

Ibn Taymiyah explained, "The 'seer' is a name for the fortune-teller, the astrologer, the thrower of sand, and all those who claim knowledge of these matters by such means."

Ibn 'Abbâs (رضي الله عنه) said, concerning people who practiced *abâjâd*[75] and astrology, "I do not consider that those who do this will have any share [of blessings or reward] with Allah."

---

[75] *abâjâd*: an ancient system of prediction based on use of the letters of the Arabic alphabet (*alif, bâ, jeem, dâl*, etc. — hence the name *abâjâd*)

Chapter 27

Counteracting magic with spells or incantations

27.1

$\mathcal{I}$t is reported on the authority of Jâbir (رضي الله عنه) that Allah's Messenger (ﷺ) was asked about *nushrah*, or counteracting magic with spells and incantation, and he said: «It is one of the works of Satan.» (recorded by Aḥmad with a reliable chain of narrators and by Abu Dâwood)[76]

Because curing magic with more magic spells or incantations was one of the actions of the Days of Ignorance, and the Companions (may Allah be pleased with them) had no desire or liking for the Days of Ignorance or its deeds, they asked the Prophet (ﷺ) about it. He (ﷺ) replied that it is one of the works of Satan, and it is well-known that Satan orders not except that which is corrupt and detestable to the believers. As for that which is permissible and not from the works of Satan, there is ruqyah, seeking refuge with Allah, and the use of all permissible medicines, which are those medicines which do not contain forbidden substances, such as alcohol or pork by-products.

---

[76] Abu Dâwood commented, 'Aḥmad was asked about these matters and he answered that Ibn Mas'ood detested all such things.'

Benefits derived from this hadith

1. It is prohibited to use methods which involve sorcery or shirk in order to counteract the effects of magic.
2. The works of Satan are all forbidden.

Relevance to tawḥeed and the subject of the chapter

This hadith proves the prohibition of counteracting magic with further magic, which was a practice from the Days of Ignorance and cannot be performed without committing shirk. The ones who perform magic to cure magic are themselves magicians.

27.2

«It is reported that Qatâdah said to Ibn al-Musayyib: A man is under the influence of a magic spell or is unable to have sexual relations with his wife; should we treat him with nushrah or use some other means to cure the spell? Ibn al-Musayyib replied: It is permissible (to use nushrah) since they intend by it restoration or mending. That which is beneficial is not prohibited.[77]» (recorded by Bukhari)

It is reported that al-Ḥasan al-Baṣri stated, "Magic is not counteracted by its like except by a magician."

Relevance to the topic of the chapter

This narration shows that al-Baṣri held that it is forbidden to counteract magic with magic and that the one who does so is a sorcerer.

---

[77] This is not a permission to use magic against magic. What is permitted=

27.3

Ibn al-Qayyim (may Allah have mercy on him) said that nushrah is counteracting the effects of magic, and there are two types of it:

1. Counteracting magic with its like, and this is the work of the devil;

2. Nushrah by means of ruqyah, seeking refuge with Allah, permissible medicines; and making supplications to Allah; and these are all permitted forms of nushrah.

Important note

It might be said, with some justification, that these words of Ibn al-Qayyim sum up the message of this chapter.

=here is the use of ruqyah, seeking refuge with Allah, and using permitted medicines, for how could Ibn al-Musayyib make permissible that which the Prophet (ﷺ) had forbidden?

Chapter 28

Believing in omens

28.1

*A*llah (ﷻ) says:

﴿فَإِذَا جَآءَتْهُمُ ٱلْحَسَنَةُ قَالُواْ لَنَا هَٰذِهِۦ وَإِن تُصِبْهُمْ سَيِّئَةٌ يَطَّيَّرُواْ بِمُوسَىٰ وَمَن مَّعَهُۥٓ أَلَآ إِنَّمَا طَٰٓئِرُهُمْ عِندَ ٱللَّهِ وَلَٰكِنَّ أَكْثَرَهُمْ لَا يَعْلَمُونَ ﴿١٣١﴾﴾

(سورة الأعراف ١٣١ : ٧)

❨When good came to them, they said: This is due to us. But when evil befell them, they ascribed it to omens connected with Moosâ and those with him! Verily, in truth the omens of evil are theirs in Allah's sight, but most of them understand not!❩ *(Qur'an 7: 131)*

In this verse, Allah, Most Glorified, describes the ways of Pharaoh and his people in their dealings with Moosâ (ﷺ) and his companions. When any good came to them, they would claim the credit for it themselves, not attributing it to Allah, but when any calamity befell them, they would blame it on the presence of Moosâ and his people. Then Allah makes plain the falseness of their claims. Allah confirms that whatever evil comes to them is from Him, and it is what they have earned by their disbelief and rejection of the Signs of Allah. Then He, the Exalted, explains the reason for their behaving in this manner; it is their ignorance and lack of knowledge that Allah is the One who ordains all good and evil.

Benefits derived from this verse

1. All good and evil are ordained by Allah.
2. It is prohibited to deny Allah's blessings.
3. It is forbidden to believe in omens.
4. Ignorance is the cause of all evil.

Relevance to tawḥeed and the subject of the chapter

This Qur'anic verse proves the prohibition of believing in omens. Belief in omens is a type of shirk because it is an attachment of the heart to other than Allah and a belief that the cause of events is other than He.

28.2

Allah (ﷻ) says:

﴿قَالُوا طَائِرُكُم مَّعَكُمْ أَئِن ذُكِّرْتُم بَلْ أَنتُمْ قَوْمٌ مُّسْرِفُونَ ۝﴾ (سورة يس: ٣٦)

❲They said: Your evil omens are with yourselves. If you are admonished [do you deem it an evil omen?] No! But you are a people transgressing all bounds.❳   *(Qur'an 36: 19)*

In this verse, Allah, Most Glorified, explains that the Messengers who came to their people with warnings and reminders were considered evil omens by them. However, those Messengers rejected this and told them that whatever afflicts the unbelievers is because of their disbelief and rejection of Allah's signs. The unbelievers were peoples who transgressed all decent limits and were estranged from the truth, preferring disbelief over faith, and that was the reason for the miserable end for the disbelievers.

Benefits derived from this verse

1. It is prohibited to believe in evil omens and have pessimism based upon those omens.
2. It is forbidden to exceed the limits ordained by Allah.
3. Exceeding Allah's prescribed limits is the cause of destruction and humiliation.

Relevance to tawḥeed and the subject of the chapter

This Qur'anic verse proves that it is forbidden to believe in evil omens. The verse rejects omens because they cause the heart to become attached to other than Allah, and this is shirk.

28.3

It is reported on the authority of Abu Hurayrah (رضي الله عنه) that the Messenger of Allah (ﷺ) said: «There are no *'adwâ*, no interpretation of omens, no *hâmah* and no *ṣafar*,» (recorded by Bukhari) «...and no *naw'* and no *ghoul*» are added in another version (recorded by Muslim).

In this hadith the Prophet (ﷺ) warned that there is no foundation to several beliefs and superstitions held by the Arabs of the time. They are false beliefs, which included:

1. 'Adwâ — infectious or contagious diseases, and the belief that these diseases have a will of their own and that they can be cause harm independent of Allah's decree;

2. Omens and portents and their interpretation;

3. Hâmah — the interpretation of omens based on the flight of a nocturnal bird;

4. Ṣafar — which some scholars said refers to parasites that infest the stomach and intestines of humans and cattle, while others said that it refers to the pagan belief that the arrival of the month of Safar in the Muslim calendar bodes ill, while the dictionary defines ṣafar as jaundice — and Allah knows best;

5. Naw' — the belief that the positions of the stars affect the climate;

6. Ghoul — the belief in ghosts and ghouls.

Benefits derived from this hadith

1. Illness cannot spread except by Allah's will.
2. It is utter falseness to believe in omens and their effect.
3. The beliefs of the Days of Ignorance regarding the flight of nocturnal birds are false.
4. It is false to have pessimism due to the approach of the month of Safar.
5. The beliefs of the Days of Ignorance regarding ghosts and ghouls are false.

Relevance to tawḥeed and the subject of the chapter

This hadith proves the falseness of belief in omens. A belief in omens causes an attachment of the heart to other than Allah, and this is shirk.

Important note

There is no conflict between this hadith, which states: «There is no 'adwâ...» and that in which the Prophet (Blessings and peace be upon him) said: «Flee from the leper as you would flee from a lion.» (recorded by Bukhari and Muslim) In the former hadith, what is intended is that no disease may affect us except by Allah's leave, while the latter hadith instructs us to undertake the necessary measures to ensure as best we can that we do not contract a disease. This is the true meaning of dependence on Allah: to do that which is in your power in order to attain your objective and then to depend upon Allah.

28.4

On the authority of Anas (ﷺ) it is reported that Allah's Messenger (ﷺ) said: «There is no 'adwâ and no interpretation of omens, but *fâl* (optimism) pleases me. They asked: What is fâl? He (ﷺ) replied: It is a good statement.» (recorded by Bukhari and Muslim)

Because good and evil are ordained by Allah, the Prophet (ﷺ) negated the idea that infectious disease of itself, may affect a person or that omens may affect us, either adversely or positively. Then he (ﷺ) endorsed and approved optimism because optimism means to think well of Allah and to be filled with positive zeal to achieve one's objectives, as opposed to pessimism, which produces lethargy and depression.

Benefits derived from this hadith

1. The hadith negates the belief that disease may affect us of itself, without Allah's leave.
2. It is absolute falseness to believe in omens.
3. It is desirable to be optimistic, rather than pessimistic.

Relevance to tawḥeed and the subject of the chapter

This hadith proves that belief in omens is false. The hadith rejects the belief in omens because such belief is a denial of Allah's divine preordination (*qadr*)[78] and because it causes the heart to become attached to other than Allah, and this is shirk.

28.5

It is authentically reported that 'Uqbah ibn 'Âmir (ﷺ) said: «Interpreting omens was mentioned in the presence of the Messenger of Allah (ﷺ) and he said: The best form of it is optimism (fâl), for it does not prevent a Muslim (from achieving his or her objective). Whenever any of you sees something he dislikes, he should say: 'O Allah! None but You brings good things. None but You can prevent evil things. There is no power and no strength except in You.'» (recorded by Abu Dâwood with a sound chain)

Because believing in omens is a sickness in society which held sway over peoples' souls in the Days of Ignorance, it was mentioned during a gathering in which the Prophet (ﷺ) was present. So he (ﷺ) informed the Companions (may Allah be pleased with them) that such beliefs were baseless and that while optimism, or seeing or believing something is a good sign, may be considered a form of belief in omens, it is much superior, because it necessitates thinking good of Allah and encourages positive thinking and hope for the good. He (ﷺ) informed them that signs which the ignorant people take as omens will not prevent any Muslims whose beliefs are correct from attaining their goals, nor weaken their resolve.

Then he (ﷺ) described an effective treatment for whoever is confronted by such supposed omens, which is to place the matter in Allah's Hands, so that the person may attract the good and repel the evil by Allah's leave and continue to depend only upon Allah in order to fulfil all of his or her goals.

---

[78] *qadr*: divine decree or divine preordination; meaning that all events — good and bad — were written and ordained by Allah, before their creation

Benefits derived from this hadith

1. Optimism is a permissible form of believing in omens.
2. It is desirable to be optimistic because it strengthens one's trust in Allah.
3. It is legislated to supplicate to Allah should any trace of the belief in omens take hold of one's heart.
4. Good and evil are ordained by Allah.

Relevance to tawḥeed and the subject of the chapter

This hadith proves the falseness of omens. It rejects the belief in omens because it negates belief in Allah's divine preordination and because it causes the heart to become attached to other than Allah, and this is shirk.

28.6

It is reported on the authority of Ibn Mas'ood (رضي الله عنه) that Allah's Messenger (ﷺ) said: «Belief in omens is shirk, belief in omens is shirk. There is none among us who is not afflicted by it, but Allah, by true dependence on Him, removes it from the heart.» (recorded by Abu Dâwood and at-Tirmidhi)[79]

Ibn Mas'ood informs us in this narration that the Prophet described the belief in omens as shirk, and he emphasised this by repeating it. Then he said that there is no one who is not afflicted by it to some degree at sometime or other, but that Allah will remove it from the hearts of those who place their complete trust in Him and depend upon Him alone.

---

[79] It is reported in marfoo' form. At-Tirmidhi said it is authentic but considered the last part of it to be Ibn Mas'ood's own statement.

Benefits derived from this hadith

1. Belief in omens is shirk.
2. It is desirable to emphasise important matters.
3. True dependence on Allah causes the belief in omens to be removed from the heart.

Relevance to tawḥeed and the subject of the chapter

This hadith rejects belief in omens because believing in omens necessitates a negation of belief in Allah's divine preordination and because it causes the heart to become attached to other than Allah, which is shirk.

28.7

It is reported on the authority of Ibn 'Amr (ﷺ): «The Prophet (ﷺ) said: Whoever is turned back from his objective by a bad omen has committed shirk. They asked: And what is the expiation for that? He (ﷺ) replied: It is to say, 'O Allah! There is no good except that which You bestow and there is no evil except that which You bestow, and nothing has the right to be worshipped but You.'» (a reliable hadith recorded by Aḥmad)

The Messenger of Allah (ﷺ) informs us in this hadith that those who allow themselves to feel pessimism due to a sign that might be taken as an omen and that causes them to deflect from their intentions has committed a form of shirk. When the Companions (may Allah be pleased with them) asked him what penance is due for committing this major sin, he (ﷺ) replied that it is to supplicate to Allah, rejecting the belief in good and evil omens and affirming their belief in Allah's divine preordination, His Oneness, and His sole right to be worshipped.

Benefits derived from this hadith

1. The hadith confirms the shirk of those who allow themselves to be guided by omens.
2. It shows that the repentance of those who commit shirk will be accepted.
3. The hadith offers guidance about what the one who succumbs to the temptation of omens should say and do as expiation.
4. All good and all evil occur in accordance with Allah's divine preordination.

Relevance to tawḥeed and the subject of the chapter

This hadith proves the shirk of those who allow themselves to be turned away from their goals by perceived omens.

28.8

The following is also narrated on the authority of Al-Faḍl ibn al-'Abbâs, "An omen is that which causes you to carry out some act or turns you away from some deed." (a weak hadith recorded by Aḥmad)

This is an excellent summing up of this chapter, for the kind of belief in omens which has been forbidden is that which determines our course of action or prompts us to abandon a course of action. Even optimism may fall under this category of prohibition if people rely upon optimism alone, without remembering dependence upon and trust in Allah, for then they are the same as those who depend upon omens of good or evil. Likewise, when a people hear or see something which they dislike and become pessimistic due to it, or allow it to determine their actions, they are also guilty of believing in omens.

Benefits derived from this hadith

1. It is forbidden to believe in an omen which causes one to take a certain course of action or deflects one from acting.

Relevance to tawḥeed and the subject of the chapter

This hadith proves the prohibition of believing in omens, when they cause us to alter our plans or to abandon them. The belief in omens is forbidden because it causes the heart to become attached to other than Allah and it negates belief in Allah's divine preordination, both of which amount to shirk.

Chapter 29

Astrology

29.1

Qatâdah (رضي الله عنه) said: «Allah created the stars for three reasons: (i) to adorn the heavens, (ii) as missiles against the devils, and (ii) as signs by which (the traveller) may be guided. So whoever claims more than this for them is in error and has lost his reward (on the Day of Resurrection) and taken upon himself that of which he has no knowledge.» (recorded by Bukhari)

In this narration, Qatâdah informs us that Allah, the Exalted, created the stars for only three purposes. The first is to beautify the night sky. The second is as projectiles against the devils, who approach the lowest heaven in order to overhear the angels speaking of the Commandments of Allah, which they then attempt to convey to the fortune-tellers and sooth-sayers.[80] The third is as guidance for the wayfarer at night, whether on land or at sea. He added that anyone who claims more than this for the stars, such as the claims of astrologers that the positions of the stars and planets exert an influence on our daily lives, is acting out of ignorance, has gone astray from the Straight Path, and will receive no reward from Allah on the Day of Judgement.

---

[80] This second part refers to meteorites, not stars, which are referred to in Arabic also as stars, as indeed they are in English (shooting stars, falling stars).

Benefits derived from this narration

1. There is wisdom in the creation of the stars.
2. It is falseness to claim that the creation of the stars has other meanings.
3. It is forbidden to believe in astrology.
4. A punishment is prescribed for those who practise or believe in astrology.

Relevance to tawḥeed and the subject of the chapter

This hadith informs us of the view of Qatâdah concerning astrology: that it is false and that it is forbidden. Qatâdah rejected that which the astrologers claim concerning the stars and knowledge of the unseen because it is an act of shirk to claim knowledge of the unseen, as such knowledge is only with Allah.

Important notes

1. Ḥarb informs us that while Qatâdah disliked the studying of the lunar phases, Ibn 'Uyaynah forbade it, and Aḥmad and Is-ḥâq permitted it.

2. Study of the stars is of three kinds:

   (i) A belief that takes one out of the fold of Islam, and that is the belief that the heavenly bodies of themselves decide the events of our daily lives.

   (ii) The belief that events may be predicted by studying the courses and relative positions of the stars and planets, which they claim is by Allah's ordainment and His will, and there is no doubt that this is forbidden and that this is a form of shirk.

   (iii) The study of the stars and the planets in order to have knowledge of their cycles for the purpose of aiding travellers, in order to know the direction of the *qiblah*,[81] and to know the time and seasons, and this is permissible.

3. Allah (ﷻ) says:

(سورة النّحل : ١٦)   ﴿وَعَلَـٰمَـٰتٍ ۚ وَبِٱلنَّجْمِ هُمْ يَهْتَدُونَ ۝﴾

﴿And marks and signs; and by the stars they are guided.﴾

(Qur'an 16: 16)

The suggestion that the words of Allah are an indication that astrology is permissible is totally false and baseless because its forbiddance has been reported in many authentic hadiths. Therefore, it is clear that the meaning of this verse is not as the ignorant and misguided have claimed, but that Allah has placed on the earth many natural signposts such as mountains, valleys, rivers, and trees, and in the sky there are stars to help the travellers find their way and help us know the time and the season.

29.2

On the authority of Abu Moosâ (ﺭ) it is reported that Allah's Messenger (ﷺ) said: «There are three who will not enter paradise: (i) the habitual wine drinker, (ii) the one who cuts family ties, and (iii) the one who believes in sorcery.» (recorded by Aḥmad)

The Messenger of Allah (ﷺ) informs us in this hadith that there are three categories of people who will not enter paradise because of the major sins which they committed, all of which are harmful to themselves and to the whole community. The first of them are the alcoholics because when they are under the influence of

---

[81] *qiblah*: the direction we face when we pray, the direction of the *Ka'bah* in Makkah

alcohol, their rationality and their inhibitions depart and they are likely to commit any number of sins. The second are those who break family ties because in so doing they cause strife, division, and enmity among members of their families. Their actions may result in the breakdown of the family unit, which is the basis of a healthy society. The third are the ones who believe in sorcery, which includes things like fortune-telling, astrology, and palm-reading, because this leads to cheating, fraud, and deception for the purpose of stealing the money of the innocent and the gullible.

Benefits derived from this hadith

1. Alcoholic drinks are prohibited.
2. It is an obligation to maintain family ties.
3. It is forbidden to believe in sorcery.

Relevance to tawheed and the subject of the chapter

This hadith proves that it is forbidden to believe in all kinds of sorcery, including astrology because belief in astrology necessitates the belief that someone other than Allah possesses knowledge of the unseen, and such a belief is shirk.

Chapter 30

Attributing rain to the movements of the stars

30.1

*A*llah () says:

(سورة الواقعة ٨٢: ٥٦) ﴿وَتَجْعَلُونَ رِزْقَكُمْ أَنَّكُمْ تُكَذِّبُونَ ۝﴾

❴And instead [of thanking Allah] for the provision He gives you, on the contrary, you deny [Him] by disbelief.❵   *(Qur'an 56: 82)*

Allah, Most Glorified, rebukes those who reject His blessings upon them, such as the rain which gives life to the land, causing the crops and fruits of the earth to grow. Instead, they attribute the rain to the movements of the moon and stars which have no power to either harm or benefit.

Benefits derived from this verse

1. All good and evil are ordained by Allah.
2. Rain is a blessing from Allah.
3. Attributing blessings to other than Allah is an act of disbelief in Him.

Relevance to tawḥeed and the subject of the chapter

This Qur'anic verse proves that whoever attributes blessings such as rain to the movements of the moon and stars is a disbeliever. The verse rejects the claims of those who attribute blessings to other than Allah because such a belief is shirk.

30.2

On the authority of Ibn Mâlik al-Ash'ari (ﷺ) it is reported that the Messenger of Allah (ﷺ) said: «There are four traits remaining from the Days of Ignorance to be found in my Ummah, which they will not (completely) abandon: (i) pride in the nobility of one's ancestors, (ii) defaming the ancestors of others, (iii) seeking rainfall from the stars, and (iv) excessive mourning and wailing for the dead.» Then he (ﷺ) added: «The wailing woman, if she does not repent before she dies, will be raised on the Day of Resurrection with a dress of liquid tar and a cloak of mange or scabies.» (recorded by Muslim)

Since the intention of Islam is to cut off every connection with the iniquitous customs of the Days of Ignorance, the Messenger of Allah (ﷺ) informs us in this hadith, in a spirit of censure and rebuke, that four customs of the Days of Ignorance will remain in this Ummah. The first is pride in the nobility of one's lineage, for this leads to slackness and idleness, as one rests on the laurels of one's forebears. The second is the disparagement of the ancestry of others, which leads to a situation in which people spend their time in seeking out weaknesses and defects in each others' backgrounds. This causes the reputation of Islam and the Muslims to suffer and results in division and enmity amongst the Muslims. The third is seeking rainfall from the stars because it causes the hearts to become attached to other than Allah and instead, the hearts become humble before His creations, which possess no power to benefit or harm. The fourth is excessive mourning and bewailing of the dead and eulogising them in loud voices, for this suggests a lack of acceptance of Allah's ordainments. It also adversely affects the deceased's family and spreads depression and despair. Because of this, the Prophet (ﷺ) stressed the punishment of such wailing women, should they not repent to Allah before they die.

Benefits derived from this hadith

1. The hadith refutes the evil customs practised during the Days of Ignorance.
2. It is prohibited to have pride in one's ancestry, to defame the lineage of others, and to mourn excessively and bewail the dead.
3. Those who seek rain from the stars and believe that they can, of their own accord, send rain are disbelievers, while those who believe that the stars are the cause of rain, but that Allah made them so, are guilty of an act of disbelief, without being considered disbelievers.
4. Repentance is accepted as long as it is before the death of the penitent.
5. This hadith confirms one miracle of the Prophet (ﷺ) since his prophesy has proven true in every respect.
6. The hadith also confirms the reality of the Resurrection and the Judgement.

Relevance to tawḥeed and the subject of the chapter

This hadith proves that it is forbidden to seek rain from the movements of the stars, as this necessitates requesting blessings from other than Allah, and that is shirk.

Important note

It is permissible to mention a person by a nickname such as 'the son of the tall one' or 'the son of the thin man' or 'the son of the lame one' and so on, even though the person so named may dislike it, if it is the only way in which the person can be identified.

30.3

It is narrated that Zayd ibn Khâlid al-Juhani (رضي الله عنه) said: «Allah's Messenger (ﷺ) prayed the morning prayer with us at Ḥudaybiyah after it had rained during the night, and when he had finished, he addressed the people, saying: Do you know what your Lord said? They answered: Allah and His Messenger know best! He (ﷺ) said: (Allah said:) Some of My slaves this morning are true believers in Me and others are disbelievers. As for those who say, 'We have received rain from the bounty of Allah and His mercy,' they are believers in Me and disbelievers in the stars, while those who say, 'We have received rain from the movements of such-and-such a star,' are disbelievers in Me and believers in the stars.» (recorded by Bukhari and Muslim)

Zayd ibn Khâlid (رضي الله عنه) tells us in this hadith that the Prophet (ﷺ) led the people in morning prayer in the area known as Ḥudaybiyah, after a night of rain. After the prayer, he (ﷺ) faced the people and addressed them, wishing to encourage them to do good and to increase their knowledge. He (ﷺ) told them that Allah had revealed to him that the people are divided into two categories regarding the rain: (i) those who thank Him and (ii) those who are ungrateful to Him. As for those who are grateful and believe in Him, they are the ones who attribute the blessing of rain to Allah. As for those who are ungrateful and disbelieve in Him, they are the ones who attribute the rainfall to the positions of the planets and stars.

Benefits derived from this hadith

1. The hadith shows the virtue of the Imam's addressing the congregation after finishing the prayer.
2. It is a virtue to impart knowledge by asking: 'Do you know..?'
3. The hadith confirms Allah's divine attribute of speech.
4. The correct manner of responding to a question in religious matters when one does not know the answer is 'Allah knows best'.
5. It is forbidden to reject the blessings of Allah.
6. The hadith confirms Allah's divine attribute of mercy.
7. Attributing Allah's blessings to other than Allah is an act of disbelief.
8. It is forbidden to say or think that rain has been received due to the position of the stars.

Relevance to tawheed and the subject of the chapter

This hadith proves that attributing rainfall to the movements or positions of stars is forbidden. Whoever attributes rainfall to the stars' movements is a disbeliever, because he or she has attributed blessings to other than Allah, Who is the source of all blessings.

30.4

A hadith carrying the same meaning as the previous hadith is reported on the authority of Ibn 'Abbâs (رضي الله عنه): «Some (people) said: The promise of rain of such-and-such a star has come true. Then Allah revealed the following verses:

﴿ ۞ فَلَا أُقۡسِمُ بِمَوَٰقِعِ ٱلنُّجُومِ ۞ وَإِنَّهُۥ لَقَسَمٌ لَّوۡ تَعۡلَمُونَ عَظِيمٌ ۞ إِنَّهُۥ لَقُرۡءَانٌ كَرِيمٌ ۞ فِى كِتَٰبٍ مَّكۡنُونٍ ۞ لَّا يَمَسُّهُۥٓ إِلَّا ٱلۡمُطَهَّرُونَ ۞ ﴾

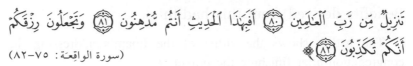

(سورة الواقعة: ٧٥-٨٢)

❨Furthermore, I call to witness the setting of the stars — and that is indeed a mighty oath, did you but know it — that this is indeed a Qur'an most honourable, in a Book well-guarded, which none has touched except the pure ones [such as the angels], a revelation from the Lord of the worlds. Is it such a Message as you would deny? And instead [of thanking Allah] for the provision He gives you, on the contrary, you deny [Him] by disbelief.❩   *(Qur'an 56: 75-82)*

In these verses, Allah, the Exalted, swears by the setting of the stars concerning the greatness of the Qur'an and its blessings, that it is preserved in a Book, which is in the hands of the angels, touched by none but the angels, and that it was revealed from the Owner of creation and the Director of its affairs, and that it is not, as the disbelievers claimed, poetry, or magic. Then Allah rebukes those who support the disbelievers and abet them by attributing to the stars that which is for Allah alone — the rain — for this is a denial of the Qur'an, which clearly states that it is Allah Who sends the rain.

Benefits derived from this hadith

1. It is for Allah to swear by anything He wills, but it is not permissible for His slaves to swear by anything except Allah or one of His divine attributes.
2. The verses confirm the greatness of Qur'an and that Allah has preserved it from all corruption and change.
3. The Qur'an was revealed, not created.
4. The verses are a confirmation of Allah's divine attribute of being above His creation.
5. It is forbidden to have friendly relations at the expense of religion.

6. It is prohibited to attribute the rain to the movements of the heavenly bodies.

Relevance to tawḥeed and the subject of the chapter

This hadith proves that whoever attributes blessings to other than Allah is a disbeliever. This includes attributing the rain to the movements of the stars and planets because to do so is to commit shirk.

Chapter 31

Loving other than Allah and His Messenger

31.1

$\mathcal{A}$llah (⬧) says:

﴿وَمِنَ ٱلنَّاسِ مَن يَتَّخِذُ مِن دُونِ ٱللَّهِ أَندَادًا يُحِبُّونَهُمْ كَحُبِّ ٱللَّهِ وَٱلَّذِينَ ءَامَنُوٓا۟ أَشَدُّ حُبًّا لِّلَّهِ وَلَوْ يَرَى ٱلَّذِينَ ظَلَمُوٓا۟ إِذْ يَرَوْنَ ٱلْعَذَابَ أَنَّ ٱلْقُوَّةَ لِلَّهِ جَمِيعًا وَأَنَّ ٱللَّهَ شَدِيدُ ٱلْعَذَابِ ۝﴾ (سورة البَقَرَة: ١٦٥)

❨Among the people are those who take [for worship] partners besides Allah; they love them as they should love Allah, but those of faith are greater in their love for Allah. If only the evil-doers could see. Behold! They would see the punishment. To Allah belongs all power, and Allah will strongly enforce the punishment.❩ *(Qur'an 2: 165)*

Allah, Most Glorified, informs us in this verse that some of the people set up partners with Allah, partners whom they love and glorify as they do Allah. Then Allah makes it clear that the believers love Allah more, for their love is a pure unadulterated love, which is only for Allah, while the love of the polytheists is corrupted and spoiled by their equal love of the other deities whom they have taken as partners with Allah. Then Allah warns that when those polytheists see the punishment that is theirs on the Day of Resurrection, they will know that all power belongs to Allah and that His punishment is deserved and appropriate.

Benefits derived from this verse

1. Love of Allah is a form of worship.
2. The love of the polytheists for Allah does not benefit them at all because of their shirk.
3. Shirk invalidates one's deeds.
4. Pure love for Allah is sign of true faith.
5. The verse confirms Allah's divine attribute of power.

Relevance to tawḥeed and the subject of the chapter

This Qur'anic verse proves that whoever loves someone or something as much as Allah has set up a partner with Allah, and this is an act of shirk.

Important note

In order that there should be no confusion in this matter, it is important to point out that love falls into two categories. The first is that which is pure, and that is worshipful love, which necessitates humility, submissiveness, exaltation, and complete obedience; none has the right to such love except Allah. The second kind of love is shared love. This includes natural love, such as the love of certain foods, certain aromas, the love of family, such as that of children for their parents and vice versa, and the love that a person may have for a friend. Such love may come and go, and strengthen and weaken, unlike the first category, for it is incumbent upon us to love Allah to the utmost of our ability.

31.2

Allah (ﷻ) says:

وَقُلْ إِن كَانَ ءَابَآؤُكُمْ وَأَبْنَآؤُكُمْ وَإِخْوَٰنُكُمْ وَأَزْوَٰجُكُمْ وَعَشِيرَتُكُمْ وَأَمْوَٰلٌ
ٱقْتَرَفْتُمُوهَا وَتِجَٰرَةٌ تَخْشَوْنَ كَسَادَهَا وَمَسَٰكِنُ تَرْضَوْنَهَآ أَحَبَّ إِلَيْكُم مِّنَ
ٱللَّهِ وَرَسُولِهِۦ وَجِهَادٍ فِي سَبِيلِهِۦ فَتَرَبَّصُوا۟ حَتَّىٰ يَأْتِيَ ٱللَّهُ بِأَمْرِهِۦۗ وَٱللَّهُ لَا
يَهْدِي ٱلْقَوْمَ ٱلْفَٰسِقِينَ ﴿٢٤﴾   (سورة التوبة: ٢٤)

❮Say [O Muhammad]: If it be that your fathers, your sons, your brothers, your wives, your kindred, the wealth that you have gained, the commerce in which you fear a decline, and the dwellings in which you delight are dearer to you than Allah and His Messenger, and striving hard, and fighting in His cause, then wait until Allah brings about His decision. Allah guides not the rebellious.❯ *(Qur'an 9: 24)*

In this verse, Allah, Most Glorified, commands His Prophet, Muhammad (ﷺ), to make it plain to the people that those who place love of worldly things above love of Allah, and His Prophet (ﷺ) and defence of His religion, will certainly see what awaits for them of chastisement from Allah. This is because Allah does not grant success to those who do not submit themselves to Him alone.

Benefits derived from this verse

1. It is forbidden to place one's love of worldly things above one's love of Allah.
2. It is permissible to have love for worldly things, as long as it does not interfere with one's love for Allah.
3. The love of Allah and His Messenger (ﷺ) are both obligatory, and love of one without the other is not acceptable.
4. The guidance of success comes only from Allah and no other.

Relevance to tawheed and the subject of the chapter

This Qur'anic verse proves the prohibition of placing one's love of worldly things above that of Allah. It proves the obligation to love Allah and His Messenger (ﷺ); and therefore, this kind of love is an act of worship. Directing worship to other than Allah is shirk.

31.3

On the authority of Anas (رضي الله عنه) it is reported that Allah's Messenger (ﷺ) said: «None of you truly believes until I am more beloved by him than his sons, his father, and all of humankind.» (recorded by Bukhari and Muslim)

Allah's Messenger (ﷺ) informs us in this hadith that no one has complete faith, nor can achieve the necessary level of faith to enter Paradise without punishment, until he or she places love of the Prophet (ﷺ) before love of parents, children, and all humankind. This is because love of the Messenger of Allah (ﷺ) means love of Allah, for the Messenger (ﷺ) is the one who brings to us Allah's revelation and guidance to His religion. Love of Allah and His Messenger (ﷺ) is not true unless it leads to the implementation of all of Allah's laws and abstinence from all that He has forbidden — and love of Allah's Messenger (ﷺ) is not demonstrated merely by singing his praises or by celebrating his birthday, which is a despicable innovation that was unknown to the Prophet (ﷺ) and his Companions (may Allah be pleased with them).

Benefits derived from this hadith

1. The negation of complete faith mentioned in this hadith does not necessitate exclusion from the fold of Islam.
2. Deeds are a part of faith, for love is an action of the heart.

3. It is an obligation to place one's love of the Messenger (ﷺ) before love of parents, love of children, and love of any other human.

Relevance to tawheed and the subject of the chapter

This hadith proves the obligation of placing one's love of Allah and His Messenger (ﷺ) before love of all others. This proves that love is an act of worship, and directing an act of worship to other than Allah is an act of shirk.

31.4

It is reported on the authority of Anas (ﷺ) that Allah's Messenger (ﷺ) said: «The one who possesses the following three qualities will have the sweetness of faith: (i) one to whom Allah and His Messenger are more loved than anything else; (ii) one who loves a person purely and solely for Allah's sake; and (iii) one who hates to return to disbelief after Allah has saved him, as he would hate to be thrown into the Fire.» In a nearly identical narration, Allah's Messenger (ﷺ) started by saying: «None of you will find the sweetness of faith until (i)...» (recorded by Bukhari and Muslim)

Allah's Messenger (ﷺ) informs us in this hadith that faith has a sweetness, and this sweetness will not be experienced by anyone except the person who places love of Allah and His Messenger (ﷺ) before that of all others. Such a person does not love anyone except for Allah's sake and hates disbelief and the idea of returning to it as much as he or she hates hellfire and would hate to be thrown into it.

Benefits derived from this hadith

1. This hadith confirms the sweetness of faith and that it is not achieved by every believer.

2. It is an obligation to place love of Allah and His Messenger (ﷺ) above love of all others.

3. It is permissible to refer to Allah and His Messenger (ﷺ) together.

4. Loving a person for Allah's sake is a part of faith.

5. It is an obligation to hate disbelief and its adherents.

Relevance to tawḥeed and the subject of the chapter

This hadith proves the obligation of loving Allah and His Messenger (ﷺ) more than all others. This shows that love is a form of worship, and directing an act of worship to other than Allah is shirk.

31.5

It is reported that Ibn 'Abbâs (رضي الله عنهما) said, "If someone has loved for Allah's sake, hated for Allah's sake, befriended for Allah's sake and showed enmity for Allah's sake will achieve by this Allah's friendship. The slave will not attain the real taste of faith, even though he may pray much and fast much, until he does all these things. Today, most people maintain relationships and love only for some worldly reason, but this will not profit them anything (on the Day of Judgement)." (recorded by Ibn Jareer aṭ-Ṭabari)

Relevance to tawḥeed and the subject of the chapter

This narration shows that Ibn 'Abbâs (رضي الله عنهما) considered love to be a form of worship and directing an act of worship to other than Allah to be shirk.

31.6

Ibn 'Abbâs (ﷺ) also said that the following words of Allah refer to the relations of love which are established other than for the sake of Allah:

(سورة البَقَرة: ١٦٦)   ❋ ... وَتَقَطَّعَتْ بِهِمُ ٱلْأَسْبَابُ ﴿١٦٦﴾ ❋

❲...And all relations between them would be cut off.❳

(Qur'an 2: 166)

Relevance to tawḥeed and the subject of the chapter

This narration shows that Ibn 'Abbâs (ﷺ) explained this verse to mean that if love is not for Allah's sake, it will be wasted; and on the Day of Judgement it will be a source of loss for the one who loved.

Chapter 32

Fearing other than Allah

32.1

$\mathscr{A}$llah (﷿) says:

﴿إِنَّمَا ذَٰلِكُمُ ٱلشَّيْطَٰنُ يُخَوِّفُ أَوْلِيَآءَهُۥ فَلَا تَخَافُوهُمْ وَخَافُونِ إِن كُنتُم مُّؤْمِنِينَ﴾

(سورة آل عِمرَان : ١٧٥)

﴿It is only Satan who suggests to you the fear of his supporters and friends. Do not fear them, but fear Me, if you are believers.﴾

(Qur'an 3: 175)

Fear of something worldly, from a person or another part of Allah's creation, sometimes causes Muslims to refrain from supporting and raising the flag of Islam. Allah, Most Glorified, informs us in this verse that any such fear which enters our hearts is only the deception of Satan and his followers, as Satan's deception takes many forms and spreads falsehood by various methods. Then Allah commands the Muslims to pay no heed to the whispers of these devils, but to fear Allah alone if they are truthful in their belief, for fear of Allah must take precedence over any other fears.

Benefits derived from this verse

1. It is forbidden to abandon one's obligations due to fear of another of Allah's created beings.

2. It is an obligation to fear Allah alone and fear Him sincerely.
3. Fear of Allah is a sign of faith.

Relevance to tawḥeed and the subject of the chapter

This Qur'anic verse proves the obligation of sincerely fearing Allah alone. Therefore, it is clear that fear is a form of worship, and directing an act of worship to other than Allah is shirk.

Important note

There are four kinds of fear:

1. Fear that someone other than Allah will cause one some form of illness, poverty, or other misfortune by that person's power and will, whether due to the feared one's claim of independent power or because of the feared one's supposed position as an intercessor with Allah — this kind of fear is forbidden, for it equates the one who is feared with Allah, which is an act of major shirk;

2. Fear of one of Allah's created beings which leads the one in fear to seek a solution from that which has been forbidden or to abandon that which is obligatory — this is forbidden;

3. Fear of Allah's promised recompense for the disobedient — this type of fear is the highest level of faith;

4. Natural fear, such as the fear of another of Allah's created beings, like fear of a lion or a snake — such fear is permissible.

32.2

Allah (ﷻ) says:

﴿إِنَّمَا يَعْمُرُ مَسَٰجِدَ ٱللَّهِ مَنْ ءَامَنَ بِٱللَّهِ وَٱلْيَوْمِ ٱلْأَخِرِ وَأَقَامَ ٱلصَّلَوٰةَ وَءَاتَى

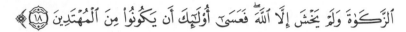

(سورة التوبة : ١٨)

❰The mosques of Allah shall be maintained only by those who believe in Allah and the Last Day, offer prayers perfectly, give zakâh and fear none but Allah. It is they who are most likely to be on true guidance.❱   *(Qur'an 9: 18)*

Allah, Most Glorified, tells us in this verse that, because the mosques are places of worship for the Muslims and centres of knowledge, leadership, and guidance, He has placed the responsibility of their building and maintenance in obedience to Allah and His Messenger (ﷺ) on the shoulders of the Muslims. He, the Exalted, adds that none should perform this duty except those who believe in the Oneness of Allah, believe in the Day of Recompense and Accounting, perform the obligations commanded by Allah in the prescribed manner, and do so purely for Him alone. Then Allah, All-Mighty, All-Powerful confirms that such people will be successful, by His will and His guidance.

Benefits derived from this verse

1. The building and maintenance of mosques for the purpose of worship is a sign of faith.
2. It is an obligation to perform the five prayers correctly.
3. It is an obligation to give zakâh to those who are entitled to it.
4. It is an obligation to fear and glorify Allah alone.

Relevance to tawḥeed and the subject of the chapter

This Qur'anic verse proves the obligation to fear and glorify Allah alone. Therefore fear and glorification is a form of worship, and to direct such worship to other than Allah is an act of shirk.

Important note

It has been said that building and maintaining mosques means being responsible for their planning, supervising their finances, and regularly organizing teaching and lectures by scholars there. It has also been said that what is intended is the physical construction, repair, maintenance, and cleaning of the mosques. It is more correct to say that the verse covers all of these meanings, since they do not contradict each other.

32.3

Allah, Most Glorified, says:

﴿وَمِنَ ٱلنَّاسِ مَن يَقُولُ ءَامَنَّا بِٱللَّهِ فَإِذَآ أُوذِىَ فِى ٱللَّهِ جَعَلَ فِتْنَةَ ٱلنَّاسِ كَعَذَابِ ٱللَّهِ وَلَئِن جَآءَ نَصْرٌ مِّن رَّبِّكَ لَيَقُولُنَّ إِنَّا كُنَّا مَعَكُمْ أَوَلَيْسَ ٱللَّهُ بِأَعْلَمَ بِمَا فِى صُدُورِ ٱلْعَٰلَمِينَ ﴿١٠﴾﴾ (سورة العنكبوت: ١٠)

﴿Then there are among people those who say: We believe in Allah. — But when they suffer affliction in Allah's cause, they treat human oppression as if it were the punishment of Allah! And if help comes to you [O Muhammad] from your Lord, they will surely say: We have [always] been with you! — Does not Allah know best all that is in the hearts of the worlds [of humankind and the jinn]?﴾

(Qur'an 29: 10)

Allah, Most Glorified, informs us in this verse that some of the people are hypocrites. By their words, they claim to believe, but when hurt comes to them from others because of their professed faith, they compare this temporary punishment of humankind to the lasting punishment of Allah and abandon their faith. Then, when Allah aids His followers and slaves from among the believers and blesses them with victory and spoils, they affect to believe once more, in order that they may receive a share of the spoils along with the believers. Allah warns them that He knows the hypocrisy that is in their hearts and that He will recompense them for it.

Benefits derived from this verse

1. Patience in the face of affliction borne for the sake of one's religion is a part of faith.
2. Hypocrisy is forbidden in religion.
3. It is the way of hypocrites to flee from the enemy in terror when the enemy advances, but to come forward in avarice and greed when the enemy is in retreat.

Relevance to tawḥeed and the subject of the chapter

This Qur'anic verse proves the obligation to place one's fear of Allah above fear of any of His creation. This shows that fear is a form of worship, and directing worship to other than Allah is shirk.

32.4

Abu Sa'eed al-Khudri (رضي الله عنه) said, "It is due to a lack of certainty (of faith) that a person pleases people and by so doing, invokes Allah's anger, and that he praises them for the livelihood which Allah has given him and that he blames them for the things not bestowed by Allah. Not even the avarice of the greediest of people can bring Allah's blessings, nor can the aversion of the one who hates it prevent it."

Abu Sa'eed informs us in this narration, which is attributable to the Prophet (صلى الله عليه وسلم), that it is weakness of faith and uncertainty which causes people to gratify others by their speech and actions at the expense of religious faith. They increase the people's pleasure with them at the same time as they decrease Allah's pleasure with them. They thank people for the blessings which Allah has given them and hold people to blame for those blessings which Allah does not ordain for them, forgetting that the One Who grants or withholds is Allah. Then Abu Sa'eed mentions that all bounty comes from Allah's Hand. Allah grants to whom He wills and He withholds from whom He wills. Unless Allah wills it, none of them can attract such bounty, even though they might be the greediest of people, nor can they withhold it from any, even though they may violently oppose the way Allah chooses to distribute it.

Benefits derived from this narration

1. Faith may increase and decrease, and strengthen and weaken.
2. Righteous deeds are a part of faith.
3. This narration confirms Allah's divine attribute of anger.
4. It is forbidden to thank people while believing that the blessing came from them independently, without Allah's having ordained it.
5. It is forbidden to blame people for what Allah has not ordained for us.
6. Good and evil are ordained by Allah.

Relevance to tawheed and the subject of the chapter

This narration proves the prohibition of abandoning an obligation due to fear of other humans. Such fear is a form of worship, and directing worship to other than Allah is shirk.

Important notes

1. This narration has some weakness in its chain of narrators, but other narrations strengthen and support it.

2. There is no contradiction between this narration and the hadith which states: «Whoever does not thank people does not thank Allah.» This latter hadith refers to thanking people for having done something which was within their power, such as giving financial aid. This is quite unlike thanking a person for making it rain or thanking a person for making the sun shine. Also, it is forbidden to thank a person for something in the belief that the person acted independently, without Allah's having ordained it.

32.5

On the authority of 'Â'ishah (﷿) it is reported that Allah's Messenger (ﷺ) said: «Whoever seeks Allah's pleasure at the expense of people's displeasure, will win Allah's pleasure and Allah will cause people to be pleased with him. Whoever seeks to please people at the expense of Allah's displeasure, will win the displeasure of Allah and Allah will cause people to be displeased with him.» (recorded by at-Tirmidhi; Ibn Ḥibbân and al-Albâni authenticated it)

The Prophet (ﷺ) informs us in this hadith that whoever seeks Allah's pleasure by obeying His commands and abstaining from all of that which He has prohibited, without caring whether or not doing so pleases others and without paying heed to their insults and oppression, will achieve Allah's pleasure. In addition, Allah will place love for that person in the hearts of humankind. As for the person who tried to please the people at the expense of his or her religion, such a person will incur the wrath of Allah, Most Glorified, Most High. Allah will place hatred of that person in the hearts of the people, as a punishment for the person's bad intentions — one only has to look at the present situation in the Muslim world to see the truth of this.

Benefits derived from this hadith

1. This hadith confirms Allah's divine attribute of pleasure.
2. Adhering strictly to the tenets of the religion will result in Allah's pleasure.
3. Hypocrisy in religious matters is forbidden.
4. The hadith confirms Allah's divine attribute of anger.
5. Hypocrisy in religious matters results in Allah's anger.
6. The love or hate in one's heart is in Allah's Hands.

Relevance to tawḥeed and the subject of the chapter

This hadith proves the forbiddance of abandoning obedience to Allah due to fear of others or seeking to please them. It proves the obligation to fear Allah alone. This shows that fear is a form of worship, and directing worship to other than Allah is shirk.

Chapter 33

Trusting in Allah

33.1

*A*llah's Words:

﴿قَالَ رَجُلَانِ مِنَ ٱلَّذِينَ يَخَافُونَ أَنْعَمَ ٱللَّهُ عَلَيْهِمَا ٱدْخُلُواْ عَلَيْهِمُ ٱلْبَابَ فَإِذَا دَخَلْتُمُوهُ فَإِنَّكُمْ غَٰلِبُونَّ وَعَلَى ٱللَّهِ فَتَوَكَّلُوٓاْ إِن كُنتُم مُّؤْمِنِينَ ٢٣﴾

(سورة المَائدة: ٢٣)

﴿Two men from among the God-fearing upon whom Allah had bestowed His grace said: Assault them [the enemy] from the [proper] gate. Once you are in, victory will be yours. And depend upon Allah, if you truly believe.﴾ *(Qur'an 5: 23)*

Allah, Most Glorified, informs us in this verse that two believing men of the Children of Israel advised their people and encouraged them to enter the city of Jerusalem, promising them that they would receive Allah's help if they did so. These two righteous men believed in Allah's promise which they had heard from the mouth of their Prophet, Moosâ (ﷺ). They asked their people to depend upon Allah and trust in[82] Him that He would fulfil His promise. They counselled their people not to be intimidated by the strength of the enemy forces, for victory is in Allah's Hands. Allah

---

[82] Dependence upon and trust in Allah is known as *tawakkul* in Arabic.

grants it to whom He wills and He withholds it from whom He wills, and He has promised the believers victory and He never breaks His promise.

Benefits derived from this verse

1. It is an obligation of members of the army to offer mutual advice and encouragement.
2. Faith and trust in Allah are the most important factors in attaining victory.
3. Trust in Allah is a condition of the acceptance of faith.
4. It is an obligation to trust in Allah and no other.

Relevance to tawḥeed and the subject of the chapter

This Qur'anic verse proves the obligation of sincere dependence on Allah and trust in Him alone. It shows that depending on Allah and trusting in Him is a form of worship, and directing an act of worship to other than Allah is shirk.

33.2

Allah (ﷻ) says:

﴿إِنَّمَا ٱلْمُؤْمِنُونَ ٱلَّذِينَ إِذَا ذُكِرَ ٱللَّهُ وَجِلَتْ قُلُوبُهُمْ وَإِذَا تُلِيَتْ عَلَيْهِمْ ءَايَـٰتُهُۥ زَادَتْهُمْ إِيمَـٰنًا وَعَلَىٰ رَبِّهِمْ يَتَوَكَّلُونَ ٢﴾   (سورة الأنفال: ٢)

❨Believers are those who, when Allah is mentioned, feel a tremor in their hearts and when His verses are recited to them, they [the verses] increase❩ their faith and they put their trust in their Lord, Alone.❩
(Qur'an 8: 2)

Allah, Most Glorified, informs us in this verse that the true believers are those who fear Allah and fear His punishment. As a result, they obey all of His commands and abstain from all that He has forbidden. When verses from the Noble Qur'an are recited to them, their faith and belief are increased, and they depend upon Allah and trust in Him alone. They entrust all matters to Him, doing all that is beneficial for them and abandoning that which is harmful for them.

Benefits derived from this verse

1. Fear of Allah and trust in Him are characteristics of the believers.
2. Faith increases and decreases.
3. It is an obligation to depend upon Allah and trust in Him alone.

Relevance to tawḥeed and the subject of the chapter

This Qur'anic verse proves the obligation to trust in Allah and depend upon Him alone. This confirms that trust and dependence are acts of worship, and directing worship to other than Allah is shirk.

33.3

Allah (﷾) says:

﴿يَٰٓأَيُّهَا ٱلنَّبِيُّ حَسْبُكَ ٱللَّهُ وَمَنِ ٱتَّبَعَكَ مِنَ ٱلْمُؤْمِنِينَ ۝﴾ (سورة الأنفال: ٦٤)

❲O Prophet! Sufficient for you is Allah, and for those who follow you among the believers.❳ *(Qur'an 8: 64)*

In this verse, Allah gives glad tidings to His Prophet, Muhammad (ﷺ), and his believing followers and promises them victory over their enemies. Allah commands them implicitly to trust in Him alone, for He is sufficient for them against their enemies.

Benefits derived from this verse

1. Allah is sufficient for those who trust in Him and depend upon Him alone.

2. Faith is an essential element in achieving victory.
3. It is an obligation of faith to love Allah alone.

Relevance to tawheed and the subject of the chapter

This Qur'anic verse proves the obligation of having faith, by loving Allah, which includes trust in Allah and no other. It shows that trust and dependence are forms of worship, and directing worship to other than Allah is shirk.

Important note

We have said that love includes trust and dependence because whoever has faith in Allah alone must, of a necessity, depend upon and trust in Him alone.

33.4

Allah (ﷻ) says:

﴿ ... وَمَن يَتَوَكَّلْ عَلَى اللَّهِ فَهُوَ حَسْبُهُۥٓ إِنَّ اللَّهَ بَٰلِغُ أَمْرِهِۦ قَدْ جَعَلَ اللَّهُ لِكُلِّ شَىْءٍ قَدْرًا ﴾

(سورة الطّلاق : ٣)

﴿...Whoever places his trust in Allah, sufficient is He for him, for Allah will surely accomplish His purpose, for verily, Allah has appointed for all things a due proportion.﴾   *(Qur'an 65: 3)*

Allah, Most Glorified, informs us in this verse that those who trust in Him and depend upon Him to fulfil their needs and wants will find that Allah is sufficient for them in every matter, whether worldly or religious. Truly, Allah will accomplish His purpose. Nothing escapes Him, and no request is difficult for Him. Then, so that those who ask Him do not become impatient, He informs us that He has appointed for everything a time and a place, which none can delay nor bring forward.

Benefits derived from this verse

1. This verse is evidence of the virtue of trust in Allah and dependence upon Him alone.
2. Trust and dependence are among the most important factors in achieving that which is beneficial and avoiding that which is harmful.
3. It is an obligation to believe in Allah's ordainment and His decree.
4. Allah's decree and His wisdom are perfect and complete.

Relevance to tawḥeed and the subject of the chapter

This Qur'anic verse proves the obligation of dependence upon Allah and trust in Him, for Allah protects His slaves and is sufficient for them when they depend upon their Lord. Thus, trust and dependence are forms of worship, and directing worship to other than Allah is an act of shirk.

33·5

Allah (﷾) says:

﴿ٱلَّذِينَ قَالَ لَهُمُ ٱلنَّاسُ إِنَّ ٱلنَّاسَ قَدْ جَمَعُواْ لَكُمْ فَٱخْشَوْهُمْ فَزَادَهُمْ إِيمَٰنًا وَقَالُواْ حَسْبُنَا ٱللَّهُ وَنِعْمَ ٱلْوَكِيلُ ۝﴾ (سورة آل عِمرَان: ١٧٣)

﴿[There were] those to whom people said: The people are gathering against you, so fear them. — But it only increased their faith. They said: For us Allah is sufficient and He is the best disposer of affairs.﴾

(Qur'an 3: 173)

When Abu Sufyân and his disbelieving people returned from the Battle of Uḥud, they began to gather an army from among them for another attack on the Muslims. On the road, they passed by a group of riders from Bani 'Abd al-Qays, and Abu Sufyân advised them to inform Prophet Muhammad (ﷺ) and his Companions (may Allah be pleased with them all) that the Quraysh were preparing to assault them with an overwhelming force. However, this threat did not discourage the Muslims. Instead, the believers were strengthened in their faith, and they trusted in Allah. They knew Allah was sufficient for them against their enemies, for He is the One Who is trusted above all others and He never fails the believers.

Benefits derived from this verse

1. One of the signs of true faith is steadfastness in the face of adversity.
2. Psychological warfare cannot harm the believers.
3. Faith increases and decreases.
4. It is recommended for the believers to say: '*Ḥasbunâ Allâhu wa ni'am al-wakeel*' (Allah is sufficient for us and He is the best disposer of affairs).
5. Taking whatever measures are required in order to achieve one's objectives is not in contradiction with trust in Allah and dependence upon Him; rather it is a requirement for that trust and dependence to be correct.

Relevance to tawḥeed and the subject of the chapter

This Qur'anic verse proves the obligation to trust in Allah, to depend upon Him alone, and to suffice oneself with Him. It proves that trust and dependence are forms of worship and directing worship to other than Allah is shirk.

Final words on this subject

It is reported that Ibn 'Abbâs (ﷺ) said: «❲Allah is sufficient for us and He is the best disposer of affairs.❳ *(Qur'an 3: 173)* — Prophet Ibrâheem (ﷺ) said it when he was thrown in the fire and Muhammad (ﷺ) said it when it was said to him: ❲The people are gathering against you, so fear them. — But it only increased their faith. They said: For us Allah is sufficient and He is the best disposer of affairs.❳ *(Qur'an 3: 173).*» (recorded by Bukhari and an-Nasâ'i)

Important note

Putting one's trust in Allah means the dependence of the heart on Allah and belief that He is sufficient against all others. Dependence and trust in Allah's creation is of three kinds:

1. Depending upon one of Allah's created beings to do something which no one is able to do except the Creator — this is major shirk;

2. Depending upon one of Allah's created beings to do something which is within the person's capabilities but in the belief that the person is able to do so independent of Allah's will — this is minor shirk;

3. Depending upon one of Allah's created beings to do something while knowing that it will only happen if Allah wills it — this is permissible, and an example would be depending upon people with whom you have business transactions to fulfil their side of the bargain.

Depending on Allah and trusting in Him is half of the religion, and the other half of it is turning in repentance to Allah. Dependence and trust does not negate taking precautions; instead, taking the necessary actions is a requirement for the dependence and trust to be accepted and for one's faith to be complete.

Chapter 34

Feeling secure against the plan of Allah

34.1

*A*llah (ﷻ) says:

﴿أَفَأَمِنُوا۟ مَكْرَ ٱللَّهِ فَلَا يَأْمَنُ مَكْرَ ٱللَّهِ إِلَّا ٱلْقَوْمُ ٱلْخَـٰسِرُونَ ٩٩﴾

(سورة الأعرَاف : ٩٩)

❴Did they then feel secure against the plan of Allah? None can feel secure against the plan of Allah except those who are lost.❵

(Qur'an 7: 99)

In this verse, Allah, Most Glorified, rebukes the people of the towns and cities to whom Guidance was sent, and people everywhere who behave as they did, because they did not give Allah the esteem which is His right, nor did they fear Him, though it was from Him that they received all blessings. Rather, they increased in their disobedience until Allah's wrath descended upon them and His punishment overwhelmed them. Then Allah, the Exalted, explains that no one behaves as they did except those who are doomed and will have no success in the hereafter.

Benefits derived from this verse

1. It is an obligation to fear Allah's plan.
2. It is permissible to describe Allah as planning, as a comparison.
3. A belief in security from Allah's plan results in destruction.

Relevance to tawḥeed and the subject of the chapter

This Qur'anic verse proves that it is obligatory to fear Allah's plan. It is forbidden to believe that one is secure from Allah's plan because this would necessitate a lack in Allah's completeness and this is in contradiction with a belief in pure Islamic monotheism.

34.2

Allah (ﷻ) says:

﴿ ... وَمَن يَقْنَطُ مِن رَّحْمَةِ رَبِّهِ إِلَّا ٱلضَّآلُّونَ ﴾ (٥٦) (سورة الحِجر : ٥٦)

◆...And who despairs of the mercy of his Lord except those who are astray?◆ *(Qur'an 15: 56)*

Because the mercy of Allah, Most Glorified, covers all things, and because the prophets were the most knowledgeable of people concerning Allah's mercy and His generosity, Ibrâheem (ﷺ) said that he did not doubt the news of the impending birth of a son to him, even though he and his wife were advanced in years, for he did not despair of the mercy and bounty of his Lord. His question to the angels, ◆Do you give me glad tidings [of a son] when old age has seized me?◆ merely reflected his surprise that he should have a son, bearing in mind his old age and that of his wife. Then he (ﷺ) asked rhetorically: ◆And who despairs of the mercy of his Lord except those who are astray?◆.

Benefits derived from this verse

1. It is forbidden to despair of Allah's mercy.
2. The verse confirms Allah's divine attribute of mercy, in a manner befitting His Majesty.
3. Despair of Allah's mercy is a sign of ignorance and being astray.

Relevance to tawḥeed and the subject of the chapter

This Qur'anic verse proves that it is forbidden to despair of Allah's mercy because this suggests a lack in Allah's most perfect generosity and this is in contradiction with a belief in pure Islamic monotheism.

34·3

It is reported on the authority Ibn 'Abbâs (رضي الله عنهما) that the Messenger of Allah (ﷺ) was asked what the major sins were, and he (ﷺ) replied: «Associating partners with Allah (by committing shirk), despairing of Allah's mercy, and believing that one is safe from Allah's plan.» (a reliable hadith recorded by al-Bazzâr and aṭ-Ṭabarâni)

Because obedience to Allah and His Messenger (ﷺ) was of the utmost importance to the Companions of the Prophet (ﷺ) and the overriding goal of their lives, they asked the Messenger of Allah (ﷺ) about the major sins in order that they might refrain from them. So he (ﷺ) informed them about some of the worst of them. The first which he mentioned, and the worst of all, was shirk, or associating partners with Allah, because no deeds are accepted where shirk is involved, no matter how praiseworthy those deeds might be. Then he (ﷺ) mentioned both despair of Allah's mercy and believing that one is safe from Allah's plan, for the Muslim should be in a state between hope and fear. A believer does not despair of Allah's mercy and compassion, which are without limit, for to do so would be to think ill of the Most Generous of all; nor does a believer depend totally on Allah's mercy, to the extent of abandoning those righteous deeds for which humankind was created, namely the worship of Allah.

Benefits derived from this hadith

1. Sins are categorized as major or minor.
2. All manner of shirk, of despair of Allah's mercy and compassion, and of believing oneself safe from Allah's plan are forbidden, and all these are major sins.
3. It is an obligation to both fear Allah and hope for His mercy.
4. The hadith confirms Allah's divine attribute of mercy, in a manner befitting His Majesty.
5. It is permissible to describe Allah's plan in comparison with the plans of His creatures.
6. It is an obligation to think well of Allah, All-Mighty, All-Powerful.

Relevance to tawheed and the subject of the chapter

This hadith proves the obligation of fearing Allah while at the same time hoping for His mercy because this is confirmation of Allah's completeness and perfection, belief in which is a necessary requisite for correct tawheed.

Important note

Scholars have said that it is incumbent upon every Muslim to come to Allah in a state of fear and hope, like a bird on its wings, but that hope should predominate at the time when death approaches.

34·4

It is reported that Ibn Mas'ood (ﷺ) said, "The most heinous of all the major sins are: shirk; believing that one is safe from Allah's plan; despairing of Allah's mercy; and losing hope of Allah's relief." (an authentic narration recorded by aṭ-Ṭabarâni)[83]

Ibn Mas'ood (ﷺ) informs us in this narration that sins are major and minor. Of the major sins, some are more serious than others. The worst of all major sins is shirk, or associating partners with Allah, for no deed will be accepted if it is accompanied by shirk. After mentioning shirk, he goes on to inform us of another of the worst major sins, which is believing that one is safe from Allah's plan or that Allah will not punish the disobedient. This erroneous belief springs from complete dependence on Allah's mercy, without fearing His punishment, and it leads to abandoning the righteous deeds for which we were all created. Then Ibn Mas'ood (ﷺ) mentions another of the worst major sins, which is despairing of Allah's mercy and compassion and losing all hope of His relief. This is a major sin because this belief entails thinking ill of Allah, the All-Mighty, All-Powerful.

Benefits derived from this narration

1. All forms of shirk, of believing oneself safe from Allah's plan, of despairing of Allah's mercy and compassion, and of losing all hope of His relief are forbidden, and all of these are major sins.
2. Sins are categorized as minor, major, and the worst major sins.

---

[83] also reported by Abdur-Razzâq in *Al-Musannif*, vol. 10, p. 459 and graded authentic by al-Haythami and Ibn Katheer; its chain of transmission is authentic. Some have said it is a *mawqoof* hadith.

3. It is permissible to describe Allah's plan in comparison with those of His creatures.

4. This narration confirms Allah's divine attribute of mercy, in a manner befitting His Majesty.

5. It is an obligation to be fair and just in all matters.

Relevance to tawḥeed and the subject of the chapter

This narration proves the obligation of fearing Allah's punishment, while hoping for His mercy. Fear and hope of Allah are necessary for one's tawḥeed to be complete.

Chapter 35

Patience in the face of adversity

35.1

$\mathcal{A}$llah (﷾) says:

﴿وَمَآ أَصَابَ مِن مُّصِيبَةٍ إِلَّا بِإِذْنِ ٱللَّهِ وَمَن يُؤْمِنۢ بِٱللَّهِ يَهْدِ قَلْبَهُۥ وَٱللَّهُ بِكُلِّ شَىْءٍ عَلِيمٌ ١١﴾ (سورة التغابن: ١١)

◈No kind of calamity occurs except by Allah's leave. And whoever believes in Allah, Allah will guide his heart [aright], for Allah knows all things.◈ *(Qur'an 64: 11)*

Allah, Most Glorified, informs us in this verse that no calamity, whether loss of wealth, loved ones, or other things, occurs unless Allah has written it and ordained it. Whoever truly believes this will most assuredly be guided by Allah so that he or she accepts and bears with equanimity the trials and tribulations of life and acknowledges Allah's wisdom, for Allah knows what is best for His slaves, and He is Most Kind, Most Merciful.

Benefits derived from this verse

1. Evil, like good, is ordained by Allah.
2. The verse is evidence of the blessing of faith, and that it results in right guidance of the heart and an upright character.
3. Allah's knowledge is of an all-encompassing nature.

4. The reward of goodness is goodness.

5. The guidance of success comes only from Allah, Most High.

Relevance to tawḥeed and the subject of the chapter

This Qur'anic verse proves that patience and composure in the face of Allah's ordainments are signs of faith in Allah.

Important notes

1. The Arabic word for patience is *ṣabr*. Linguistically speaking, it means prevention, while in religious parlance, it means preventing or restraining oneself from succumbing to depression or anxiety, guarding the tongue from complaint and angry words, and guarding the limbs from forbidden deeds, such as slapping the cheeks, tugging at the hair, and tearing the clothes.

2. Ṣabr may be divided into three categories: (i) patiently persevering in observing obedience to Allah's commands; (ii) refraining from what Allah has forbidden; and (iii) patiently forbearing in the face of calamities which Allah may ordain for us.

35.2

'Alqamah said, "The person referred to in the verse (quoted above) is the one who, when calamity strikes him, knows that it is from his Lord and accepts it with equanimity and submits (himself to Allah's will)."

Relevance of this narration
to the subject of the chapter

This narration shows that 'Alqamah (رضي الله عنه) considered patience and calm acceptance in the face of calamity to be signs of faith.

35·3

It is reported on the authority of Abu Hurayrah (ﷺ) that Allah's Messenger (ﷺ) said: «Two habits found in people are signs of disbelief: defaming a person's lineage and bewailing the deceased.» (recorded by Muslim)

Because Islam came to abolish vile customs which are incompatible with its lofty principles, the Prophet (ﷺ) informed the Companions (may Allah be pleased with them) that defaming another's ancestors and excessive mourning of the dead are traits of disbelief from the Days of Ignorance, which will remain among some of the Muslims. This is a warning to us, for these two traits cause evil to the individual and to the community. Slandering another's ancestors is bound to cause hurt to that person and unjustified distress. As for bewailing the deceased, this provokes renewed grief and fear on the part of the bereaved and shows lack of acceptance of Allah's decree. Bewailing is often accompanied by lying, as the wailers indulge in exaggerated eulogies of the deceased and raise the person above his or her true station.

Benefits derived from this hadith

1. It is forbidden to slander another's ancestors or bewail the dead.
2. These two traits will remain in this Ummah.
3. A person may possess some of these traits of disbelief without being a disbeliever.
4. Islam has prohibited everything that might lead to division in society.

Relevance to tawheed and the subject of the chapter

This hadith proves the forbiddance of bewailing the dead, for this connotes a lack of forbearance and a lack of acceptance of Allah's decree, both of which are necessary requisites of the true believer.

35.4

It is narrated on the authority of Ibn Mas'ood (رضي الله عنه) that the Messenger of Allah (ﷺ) taught: «He who slaps his cheeks and tears his clothes and makes supplications of the Days of Ignorance is not one of us.» (recorded by Bukhari and Muslim)

Because Islam preaches the noblest of ideals and because it ennobles the soul, it has forbidden all manner of excessive mourning of the dead, such as slapping the cheeks, tearing the clothes, and making the supplications made during the Days of Ignorance.[84] It is made clear to us that such actions are completely un-Islamic because they cause unnecessary and prolonged grief to the bereaved, reflect a lack of acceptance of Allah's decree, and keep alive the evil customs of the Days of Ignorance, which Islam came to destroy.

Benefits derived from this hadith

1. It is forbidden to slap one's cheeks and tear one's clothes in anguish over the death of a loved one.
2. Many of the customs of the Days of Ignorance were false and futile, except those which conformed to Islamic Law and were confirmed by the Qur'an or the Sunnah, such as hospitality to the guest and the like.

---

[84] such as: 'Woe to me!' or 'May I be destroyed!'

Relevance to tawḥeed and the subject of the chapter

This hadith it proves that it is forbidden to slap one's cheeks and tear one's clothes and make the supplications of the Days of Ignorance.

Important note

It is permissible to weep for the dead if it is due to genuine feelings of sadness and compassion, but that weeping should be free from all traces of anger and hysteria.

35·5

On the authority of Anas it is reported that the Prophet (ﷺ) said: «When Allah wills good for His slave, He hastens to punish him in this life; and when He wills evil for His slave, He withholds punishing him for his sins until he comes before Him on the Day of Resurrection.» (recorded by at-Tirmidhi and al-Bayhaqi; graded as 'reliable but odd')[85]

Allah's Messenger informs us in this hadith, that sometimes Allah afflicts people with calamities in order to purify them of their sins, which otherwise, might cause them to be punished in the hereafter, and in order that they might receive the record of their deeds in their right hands and be among the successful on the Day of Reckoning. Alternatively, Allah may withhold punishment from people, not because He loves them or honours them, but so that when they are called forth on the Day of Reckoning, they will bear a heavy burden of sins and they will receive the full punishment of those sins. Allah grants His favour to whom He wills and punishes whom He

---

[85] Something very similar to this was narrated by Imam Aḥmad on the authority of 'Abdullâh ibn Mughaffal.

wills with justice; and He will not be asked about what He does, but the people will be asked about what they did.

Benefits derived from this hadith

1. This hadith confirms Allah's divine attribute of will, in a manner befitting His Majesty.
2. Good and evil are from Allah's divine preordainment.
3. The trials and tribulations to which the believer is subjected are signs of goodness, so long as they are borne with patience and without resorting to forbidden acts or abandoning one's obligations.
4. It is incumbent upon the Muslims to fear the continuation of only blessings and good health, lest they be a sign that their sins will not be wiped out by trials in this life.
5. It is an obligation to think well of Allah concerning the calamities which He might ordain for us.
6. It does not necessarily follow that when Allah gives us something good, He is pleased with us.

Relevance to tawḥeed and the subject of the chapter

This hadith proves that those who truly believe in Allah will bear the trials and tribulations which Allah ordains for them with patience and self-control for they believe that they hold the promise of goodness for them.

35.6

It is reported that the Prophet (ﷺ) said: «Verily, the greatness of the reward is tied to the greatness of the trial. When Allah loves a people, he puts them to trial. Whoever accepts it will enjoy Allah's pleasure, and whoever is displeased with it will incur Allah's displeasure.» (a reliable hadith recorded by at-Tirmidhi and Ibn Mâjah)

The Prophet (ﷺ) informs us in this hadith that the believers may be afflicted by calamities in this world, such as loss of wealth and loved ones, but that Allah will reward them for these calamities, if they bear them patiently. He (ﷺ) tells us also that the more a people's trials and tribulations increase, the more their reward with Allah increases. Trials are a sign of Allah's love for the believers, not His anger, and Allah's ordainment and His decree will be implemented. Whoever patiently perseveres in the face of adversity and accepts it will incur Allah's pleasure and His reward, while whoever is angry at what Allah has ordained and dislikes it will incur Allah's displeasure and His punishment.

Benefits derived from this hadith

1. Afflictions wipe out sins, so long as the afflicted does not abandon his or her obligations or commit forbidden acts.
2. The hadith confirms Allah's divine attribute of love, in a manner befitting His Majesty.
3. The trials to which the believer is subjected are signs of faith.
4. The hadith confirms Allah's divine attribute of pleasure, in a manner befitting His Majesty.
5. It is a virtue to accept Allah's decree and His ordainments with patience and equanimity.
6. It is forbidden to have anger over Allah's decree and His ordainments.

Relevance to tawheed and the subject of the chapter

This hadith forbids anger and despair in the face of Allah's preordination, and this shows that patient perseverance in the face of trials and tribulations is a part of faith.

Chapter 36

Riyâ' (Showing off)

36.1

$\mathscr{A}$llah (ﷻ) says:

﴿قُل إِنَّمَآ أَنَا۠ بَشَرٌ مِّثْلُكُمْ يُوحَىٰٓ إِلَيَّ أَنَّمَآ إِلَٰهُكُمْ إِلَٰهٌ وَٰحِدٌ فَمَن كَانَ يَرْجُواْ لِقَآءَ رَبِّهِۦ فَلْيَعْمَلْ عَمَلًا صَٰلِحًا وَلَا يُشْرِكْ بِعِبَادَةِ رَبِّهِۦٓ أَحَدًا ۝﴾ (سورة الكهف ١١٠:١٨)

❰Say [O Muhammad]: I am but a man like you, [but] it has been revealed to me that your God is One God. So whoever desires to meet his Lord, let him do righteous deeds and let him not associate any partners with his Lord in his worship.❱ *(Qur'an 18: 11)*

In this verse, Allah commands His Prophet, Muhammad (ﷺ), to tell the people the plain truth about himself. He (ﷺ) is a mere mortal, like them, without any divine attributes or angelic characteristics, but Allah has distinguished him from them by inspiring him with revelation. From that revelation there is the command to worship Allah alone, without ascribing partners to Him in any aspect of His divinity. Those who fear the meeting with their Lord on the Day of Resurrection, and hope for His reward, should make their deeds purely and solely for Allah, and their deeds should be in conformity with what the Prophet (ﷺ) taught.

Benefits derived from this verse

1. This verse confirms the status of Muhammad (ﷺ) as a messenger of Allah and denies that he possesses any divine attributes or angelic characteristics.
2. In this verse is proof of the testimony of faith: There is no deity other than Allah, none has the right to be worshipped except Him, and Muhammad is the Messenger of Allah.
3. The tawḥeed which our Prophet, Muhammad (ﷺ), brought is that of worship, for even those who disbelieve in Islam accept the truth of Allah's Oneness of Lordship.
4. The acceptance of deeds is conditional upon their being performed purely and solely for Allah, without shirk, and riyâ' or showing off is a kind of shirk.

Relevance to tawḥeed and the subject of the chapter

This Qur'anic verse proves the invalidity of deeds which contain elements of shirk, and riyâ' is a form of shirk.

The meaning of riyâ'

Riyâ' is defined as the performance of a deed with the intention of pleasing other than Allah. The difference between riyâ' and *sum'ah* (about which some people are confused) is that while riyâ' is done in order to show off in front of people, such as ostentatiously giving charity or praying, the latter involves the performance of good deeds in order to be heard, such as mentioning Allah or reciting the Qur'an in a loud voice. Both are committed with the same intention to favourably impress people, rather than with the sole intention of pleasing Allah.

36.2

Abu Hurayrah (رضي الله عنه) reported the following *hadith qudsi:*[86] «Allah says: I am independent of all the partners (ascribed to Me). Whoever performs a deed while associating partners with Me, I will abandon him and his shirk.» (recorded by Muslim)

Allah, Most Glorified, informs us in this qudsi narration that He is free and independent of all those false partners which are associated with Him. Therefore, He does not accept any deed which includes shirk, and riyâ' is a form of shirk. Riyâ' contradicts the belief that Allah is independent; riyâ' is not befitting His nobility. This is the clearest warning to all those who allow themselves to be seduced by the devil into performing actions with the intention of impressing people, rather than with the sole intention of pleasing Allah, so that when they come forth on the Day of Resurrection, they will find no good deeds credited to them. Instead they will find Allah and His reckoning — and Allah is swift in reckoning!

Benefits derived from this hadith

1. This hadith confirms Allah's divine attribute of complete independence from all partners.
2. Allah does not accept deeds except those which are performed purely and solely for His sake.
3. Showing off invalidates good deeds.
4. The hadith confirms Allah's divine attribute of speech, in a manner befitting His Majesty.

---

[86] *hadith qudsi*: 'sacred hadith': a hadith communicated to Prophet Muhammad (ﷺ) by Allah, but that is not part of the Qur'an

Relevance to tawḥeed and the subject of the chapter

This hadith proves the invalidity of deeds which contain shirk, and riyâ' is a form of shirk.

Important notes

1. When the intention behind a deed is other than Allah's pleasure, then the deed is in vain.

2. When the intention behind a deed is to please Allah, but after making this intention a person starts to slip into riyâ' but catches himself and rejects it, then the deed would be acceptable. However, if the person continues to be guilty of riyâ' until the completion of the deed, then according to some scholars, the deed would be in vain, while other scholars said that the deed would still be accepted because of the original intention, and this seems the most correct saying — and Allah knows best.

36.3

On the authority of Abu Sa'eed al-Khudri, it is reported: «Allah's Messenger said: Shall I not tell you what I fear for you more than the *dajjâl* (antichrist)? [87] They replied: Yes. He (ﷺ) said: It is hidden shirk, such as when a person stands in prayer and he improves his prayer when he knows that others are watching.» (a reliable hadith recorded by Aḥmad [88] and Ibn Mâjah)

---

[87] The *dajjâl* is the antichrist or false messiah, who will deceive many people by performing apparent miracles, such as giving life to the dead. There are many authentic hadiths about him.

[88] in marfoo' form

Allah's Messenger (ﷺ) informs us in this hadith that he worries for his Ummah and fears for them the trials of the dajjâl, but more than this, he fears for them hidden shirk, which is riyâ'. This is because the danger of the dajjâl is confined to a specific time, while the danger of riyâ' is present at all times and in all places, and because riyâ' is hidden and its power of seduction is great.[89] It is difficult to free oneself from its grip. In addition, it leads to showy and ostentatious behaviour, self-glorification, and self-promotion, all of which appeal to the weaknesses in humans.

Benefits derived from this hadith

1. Asking questions is an Islamic style of teaching.
2. The Prophet (ﷺ) expressed care and compassion for his Ummah.
3. The great dangers of riyâ' are that it is hidden, it is a strong temptation for most people, and it is difficult to abstain from it.
4. The hadith is evidence of the danger of the dajjâl to this Ummah.

Relevance to tawheed and the subject of the chapter

The Prophet (ﷺ) feared more than anything that this Ummah would be seduced by riyâ'. Therefore, it is incumbent upon us to be very careful and do our utmost to abstain from it and warn others of it.

---

[89] It is a common human weakness to enjoy being praised and hearing good about oneself.

Chapter 37

Performing good deeds for only worldly reasons

37.1

$\mathcal{A}$llah (ﷻ) says:

﴿وَمَن كَانَ يُرِيدُ ٱلْحَيَوٰةَ ٱلدُّنْيَا وَزِينَتَهَا نُوَفِّ إِلَيْهِمْ أَعْمَٰلَهُمْ فِيهَا وَهُمْ فِيهَا لَا يُبْخَسُونَ ۝ أُوْلَٰٓئِكَ ٱلَّذِينَ لَيْسَ لَهُمْ فِي ٱلْأَخِرَةِ إِلَّا ٱلنَّارُ وَحَبِطَ مَا صَنَعُواْ فِيهَا ... ۝﴾

(سورة هُود: ١٥-١٦)

﴿To whomever desires the life of this world and its glitter, We shall pay [the price of] their deeds therein — without decrease. They are those for whom there is nothing in the hereafter except the Fire. Vain are their deeds therein...﴾ *(Qur'an 11: 15-16)*

Allah, Most Glorified, informs us in these verses that whoever performs righteous deeds in order to obtain some worldly benefit from them, such as people who fight in Allah's cause with the intention of acquiring a share of the spoils of war, Allah will reward them in this world with long life, good health, and wealth in accordance with their deeds and their desires. They will not suffer any loss, at least, in this world. However, in the hereafter, they will be entitled to nothing because they have already been rewarded in this life. Their deeds are without merit or value, since they did not perform them for Allah's sake.

Benefits derived from these verses

1. Allah, the Exalted, may reward even the disbelievers for their deeds in this world, as He might reward the one who acts for worldly gain, but none of them will have any reward in the hereafter.
2. Shirk invalidates good deeds.
3. Seeking the life of this world invalidates one's good deeds in the hereafter.
4. Every deed performed without the intention of pleasing Allah is invalid.

Relevance to tawheed and the subject of the chapter

These Qur'anic verses prove that seeking the life of this world through righteous deeds invalidates their reward in the hereafter.

Important note

Seeking the life of this world through righteous deeds may be divided into three categories:

1. To perform deeds purely for Allah's sake, but with the hope that Allah will reward one for them in this life, such as people who give charity hoping that Allah will protect them from loss — this is prohibited;
2. To perform deeds in order to be seen by the people (riyâ') or to be heard by them (sum'ah) — this is a form of shirk;
3. To do good deeds in order to attain some material benefit from people, such as the one who accompanies the pilgrims to Hajj in order to receive payment for doing so, not for Allah's sake, or the one who seeks a reputation for being pious and religious

in order to make a living or to obtain employment. As for the people who intend by their deeds only to achieve Allah's pleasure, but they are granted some worldly reward by Allah, they are not guilty of any sin, but they will be considered to have received the reward of that deed in this world and their recompense in the hereafter may be adjusted accordingly. This is the case with the one who fights in the way of Allah and receives a share of the spoils.

37.2

It is authentically reported on the authority of Abu Hurayrah (ﷺ) that Allah's Messenger (ﷺ) said: «Perish the slave of the *deenâr*, the *dirham*,[90] the *khameeṣah*,[91] and the *khameelah*.[92] If he is given these things, he is pleased and if he is not, he is displeased. May such a person perish and be of the losers. If he is pierced with a thorn, may he not find anyone to remove it. Felicity[93] is for the one who holds the reins of his horse to strive in Allah's cause, with his hair unkempt and his feet covered with dust. If he is placed in the vanguard, he will be found in the vanguard, and if he is placed in the rearguard, he will be found in the rearguard. If he asks for permission, it is not granted and if he intercedes, it is not accepted.» (recorded by Bukhari, at-Tirmidhi and Ibn Mâjah)

In this hadith, the Messenger (ﷺ) informs us that there are some people to whom the life of this world is all-important. It is all they know about and all they care about. Their first and last goals are wealth, luxury, and ease. Such people will be destroyed and lost. The

---

[90] *deenâr* and *dirham*: units of money in different currencies
[91] *khameeṣah*: expensive, luxurious clothing
[92] *khameelah*: richly embroidered garments
[93] or, according to some scholars, a tree in paradise

sign of these people is their absorption with all things material. When they are given something, they are pleased, but when they are not given it, they are angry.

However, there are other people who have no goal except Allah's pleasure and the life of the hereafter. These people do not covet fame or glory; their only goal in life is obedience to Allah and His Messenger (ﷺ). The sign of people like these is their simplicity and humility and their lowly position in society, so that whenever they request something from their leaders, they are refused, and whenever they intercede on behalf of another, their intercession is not accepted. Still, their final destination is paradise and the best of rewards.

Benefits derived from this hadith

1. It is permissible in general to supplicate against disobedient people.
2. Being absorbed with the life of this world is strongly criticised.
3. Those who make material gain their sole objective in life will be among the losers.
4. It is a virtue to prepare oneself for jihad in Allah's cause.
5. It is a virtue to participate in jihad in Allah's cause.
6. Military discipline is a form of Islamic training.
7. It is a virtue to be in the vanguard of the army.
8. People are judged by their actions, not by appearances.
9. It does not necessarily follow that a person whom Allah esteems will be held in high esteem by the people and vice versa.

Relevance to tawḥeed and the subject of the chapter

This hadith proves that those who make material gain their main goal and purpose in life are considered worshipers of those things, for they have taken them as partners beside Allah.

Chapter 38

Obeying a leader who changes the law of Allah

38.1

*I*bn 'Abbâs (ﷺ) said: "Stones are about to rain down upon you from the sky. I say to you, 'Allah's Messenger (ﷺ) said such and such,' and you reply, 'But Abu Bakr and 'Umar said such and such.'" [94]

Because obedience is a form of worship, it is not allowed to obey anyone — human or jinn — unless it conforms with obedience to Allah and His Messenger (ﷺ). This is why Ibn 'Abbâs (ﷺ) repudiated those who were informed about what the Prophet (ﷺ) had pronounced upon a matter and then objected that Abu Bakr aṣ-Ṣiddeeq and 'Umar ibn al-Khaṭṭâb (may Allah be pleased with them both) [95] had said something different. Thus, in effect, they preferred the opinions of these two pious Companions over the revelation of

---

[94] While according to a number of scholars of hadith, this is a weak narration, its meaning is correct.

[95] Abu Bakr aṣ-Ṣiddeeq and 'Umar ibn al-Khaṭṭâb: two close friends of the Prophet (ﷺ) and the first and second Caliphs respectively, after his death. They were among the most knowledgeable and pious of the Companions (may Allah be pleased with them).

Allah. This incident allegedly occurred during a discussion about Hajj in which Ibn 'Abbâs (رضي الله عنهما) mentioned something which he had heard from Muhammad (ﷺ), the Messenger of Allah. Ibn 'Abbâs (رضي الله عنهما) warned them of Allah's approaching punishment and His anger for those who preferred the opinions of Abu Bakr and 'Umar (may Allah be pleased with them) to the guidance of Allah's Messenger (ﷺ). In view of this, it is even more detestable to prefer the opinions of lesser men than these two over the Book of Allah and the Sunnah of His Prophet (ﷺ).[96]

Benefits derived from this narration

1. This narration is evidence of the virtue of Ibn 'Abbâs (رضي الله عنهما) and his excellent understanding of religious matters.
2. No opinion which contradicts the Qur'an and the Sunnah is to be given heed, no matter from whom it emanated.
3. It is an obligation to be angry for Allah and His Messenger's sake.

Relevance to tawheed and the subject of the chapter

This narration proves that Ibn 'Abbâs (رضي الله عنهما) held that it is forbidden to prefer the opinion of any of Allah's created beings over the Sunnah of the Messenger of Allah (ﷺ) since to do so is an act of shirk because it constitutes obedience to other than Allah.

38.2

Imam Ahmad ibn Hanbal stated:

---

[96] Such as those who, when confronted with an authentic statement by the Prophet (ﷺ), say: 'Yes, but our Shaykh says...' or 'Yes, but in our school of Islamic jurisprudence it says...'

I am amazed at those people who know that a hadith's chain of narrators is authentic and, in spite of this, they follow the opinion of Sufyân (or anyone else), for Allah, the Exalted, says:

$$ \text{... فَلْيَحْذَرِ ٱلَّذِينَ يُخَالِفُونَ عَنْ أَمْرِهِۦ أَن تُصِيبَهُمْ فِتْنَةٌ أَوْ يُصِيبَهُمْ عَذَابٌ أَلِيمٌ ۝ } $$

(سورة النُّور: ٦٣)

...Let those who oppose his [the Messenger's] commandment beware, lest some fitnah befall them or a painful torment be inflicted on them.   *(Qur'an 24: 63)*

Do you know what that fitnah is? That fitnah is shirk.[97] Maybe the rejection of some of his words would cause one to doubt and deviate in his heart and thereby be destroyed.

In this narration, Imam Aḥmad ibn Ḥanbal (may Allah have mercy on him) rejects those who abandon the Sunnah of the Prophet (ﷺ) after it has been made clear to them its authenticity and its meaning has been explained to them. They reject the Sunnah in favour of the opinion of Sufyân ath-Thawri[98] and other scholars, in spite of the scholars' human fallibility. Imam Aḥmad warns them against deviating through their rejection of Allah's Book or the Sunnah of His Prophet (ﷺ). This is because blind followers of the different schools of thought frequently change the meanings of Qur'anic verses and hadiths, or quote them out of context, or claim that they have been abrogated in order to make them conform with their particular views. Then the Imam supports his contention by mentioning the words of Allah, Most High. Let the Qur'an be sufficient proof for us all.

---

[97] *Fitnah* is usually translated as trial or tribulation, and shirk is the greatest type of trial or tribulation.

[98] Sufyân ibn Sa'eed ibn Masrooq ath-Thawri: a great scholar of Hadith and fiqh. He died in the year 61 A.H., aged 64 years.

Benefits derived from this narration

1. It is the opinion of Imam Aḥmad (may Allah have mercy on him) that it is forbidden to abandon the Sunnah of Allah's Messenger (ﷺ) in favour of the statement of any person, no matter how knowledgeable and pious the person may be.

2. Every commandment of the Prophet (ﷺ) is considered obligatory, unless there is some proof to indicate that it is only a preference or recommendation.

3. Rejecting the Law of Allah leads to destruction in this world and in the hereafter.

Relevance to tawḥeed and the subject of the chapter

This narration proves that Imam Aḥmad considered it a deviation to abandon the Sunnah of the Messenger of Allah (ﷺ) in favour of the sayings of others. Abandoning the Sunnah is shirk because it involves obedience to other than Allah and His Messenger (ﷺ), and the imam quotes from the Qur'an to prove his point.

38.3

'Adiyy ibn Ḥâtim (ﷺ) reported that he heard the Messenger of Allah (ﷺ) reciting this Qur'anic verse:

﴿اتَّخَذُوٓاْ أَحْبَارَهُمْ وَرُهْبَٰنَهُمْ أَرْبَابًا مِّن دُونِ ٱللَّهِ وَٱلْمَسِيحَ ٱبْنَ مَرْيَمَ وَمَآ أُمِرُوٓاْ إِلَّا لِيَعْبُدُوٓاْ إِلَٰهًا وَٰحِدًا لَّآ إِلَٰهَ إِلَّا هُوَ سُبْحَٰنَهُۥ عَمَّا يُشْرِكُونَ ۝﴾ (سورة التوبة: ٣١)

❨They have taken their rabbis and their monks as lords beside Allah and [they take as a lord] the Messiah, 'Eesâ, the son of Maryam, yet they were not commanded but to worship One God. None has the right to be worshipped but He — Praise and Glory to Him. [Far is He] from having the partners they associate [with Him].❭ *(Qur'an 9: 31)*

«Then I ('Adiyy ibn Ḥâtim) said to him (ﷺ): We don't worship them. He (ﷺ) said: Do they not forbid what Allah has permitted and do you not then forbid it (to yourselves); and do they not make permissible for you what Allah has forbidden and do you not then make it permissible (to yourselves)? I replied: Certainly! He (ﷺ) said: That is worshipping them.» (recorded by at-Tirmidhi, who graded it reliable)

'Adiyy ibn Ḥâtim (ﷺ) informs us in this hadith, that when he heard the Prophet (ﷺ) reciting Allah's words: ❬They have taken their rabbis and their monks as lords beside Allah. And [they take as their lord] the Messiah, 'Eesâ, the son of Maryam❭ *(Qur'an 9: 31)*, he contradicted the Prophet (ﷺ), saying that they do not worship them. In his mind, what was meant by worship was bowing, prostration, supplication, sacrifice, and the like, but the Prophet (ﷺ) informed him that their obedience to the rabbis and monks in forbidding the permissible and permitting the forbidden was a form of worship. They have thus made their rabbis and monks partners with Allah in obedience and in ordaining the Sharia.

Benefits derived from this hadith

1. The hadith is evidence that the rabbis and monks are astray.
2. The hadith confirms the shirk of the Jews and Christians.
3. The original Message of all the Messengers and Prophets was tawheed.
4. Obedience to any of Allah's created beings, if it entails disobedience to Allah, constitutes an act of worship.
5. It is an obligation to ask the people of knowledge about matters which one does not understand.

6. Blind obedience to any of Allah's created beings is rejected, for all except the prophets are fallible.

Relevance to tawḥeed and the subject of the chapter

This hadith proves that whoever obeys a religious scholar by making the permissible forbidden, or vice versa, has committed an act of shirk.

Chapter 39

Seeking judgement from other than Allah

39.1

$\mathcal{A}$llah's Words:

﴿أَلَمْ تَرَ إِلَى ٱلَّذِينَ يَزْعُمُونَ أَنَّهُمْ ءَامَنُوا۟ بِمَآ أُنزِلَ إِلَيْكَ وَمَآ أُنزِلَ مِن قَبْلِكَ يُرِيدُونَ أَن يَتَحَاكَمُوٓا۟ إِلَى ٱلطَّٰغُوتِ ... ۝﴾   (سورة النِّسَاء: ٦٠)

﴿Do you not see those who claim that they believe in what was revealed to you and to those before you? They wish to resort to ṭâghoot for judgement...﴾   *(Qur'an 4: 60)*

In this verse, Allah, Most Glorified, rebukes those hypocrites who pretend to believe in the revelations sent down to the Messengers (peace and blessings of Allah be upon all of them), but then make their hypocrisy clear by referring their disputes for judgement to other than Allah and His Messenger (ﷺ). They contradict their claims of faith, for they were ordered in the Last revelation to reject the judgement of all except Allah and His Messenger (ﷺ). Satan — may Allah curse him — makes their deviation from the law of Allah in favour of the opinions of men seem attractive to them, in order to lure them to that which is false and to lead them far astray from the Straight Path, after which, he abandons them to their fate.

Benefits derived from this verse

1. The Books of Allah are revealed, not created.
2. It is forbidden to seek judgement from other than the Book of Allah and the Sunnah of His Messenger (ﷺ).
3. Seeking judgement from other than the law of Allah is a sign of hypocrisy in belief.
4. Whoever judges by other than what Allah has revealed is a ṭâghoot, or leader of shirk. This includes all those who judge by man-made laws in contradiction to the Qur'an and the Sunnah.
5. Shunning Allah's law is the cause of the Muslims' problems and hardships in this day and age.
6. It is forbidden to separate Allah's religion from any aspect of life, including politics and law.

Relevance to tawḥeed and the subject of the chapter

This Qur'anic verse proves the hypocrisy of those who seek judgement from other than Allah and His Messenger (ﷺ). The verse rejects those who do not fulfil the obligations of the testimony of faith: there is no god but Allah and Muhammad is His Messenger. This testimony includes faith in the judgement of Allah's Messenger (ﷺ) and action in accordance with it.

39.2

Allah (ﷺ) says:

﴿وَلَا تُفْسِدُوا۟ فِى ٱلْأَرْضِ بَعْدَ إِصْلَـٰحِهَا وَٱدْعُوهُ خَوْفًا وَطَمَعًا إِنَّ رَحْمَتَ ٱللَّهِ قَرِيبٌ مِّنَ ٱلْمُحْسِنِينَ ۝﴾ (سورة الأعراف: ٥٦)

❮Do no mischief on the earth after it has been set in order, but call on Him with fear and longing for the Mercy of Allah is [always] near to those who do righteous deeds.❯ *(Qur'an 7: 56)*

Islam came to set right the world and set right Allah's slaves. For this reason, Allah, Most Glorified, forbids in this verse all manner of corruption and wanton destruction in the earth, such as cutting down trees, vandalising private property, violating the rights of others, murder, theft, rape, and so on. Allah has set the earth in order by sending Messengers with revealed scriptures full of wisdom, knowledge, and guidance for humankind and the jinn.

Then, Allah commands us to turn to Him in supplication in fear of His punishment, but also in hope of His mercy. So that worshipers might not lose hope if their prayers are not immediately answered, He, the Exalted, informs us that His mercy is near to the believers, who do righteous deeds in the best way, in the knowledge that though they do not see Allah, He is always watching them.

Benefits derived from this verse

1. It is forbidden to spread any manner of corruption in the earth, by any means that may be used.
2. Every kind of righteousness and goodness in the earth is the result of obedience to Allah and His Messenger (ﷺ).

Relevance to tawḥeed and the subject of the chapter

This Qur'anic verse forbids spreading corruption in the earth. This includes the prohibition of seeking judgement from other than Allah and His Messenger (ﷺ) because this conflicts with the testimony of the Muslim that nothing has the right to be worshipped except Allah and that Muhammad is the Messenger of Allah.

39·3

Allah (ﷻ) says:

(سورة البَقَرَة: ١١-١٢)

❮When it is said to them: Do not make mischief in the earth, they say: We are only peace-makers. Of a surety, they are the mischief-makers, but their [hearts] do not understand.❯ *(Qur'an 2: 11-12)*

Allah, Most Glorified, makes clear in these verses the depth of wickedness and foolishness of the hypocrites. When it is requested of them to cease their disobedience and their attempts to divide the Muslims, they reply that they want only to achieve peace between the Muslims and the People of the Book by their actions. However, Allah makes plain to us, in the second verse, that they themselves are the cause of the corruption and mischief. The reason for their wilful deception and misguidance is their ignorance of the fact that Allah will send down revelation to His Prophet (ﷺ) to expose them and reveal their hypocrisy.

Benefits derived from these verses

1. Disobedience causes corruption in the earth.
2. The hypocrites who dwell among the Muslims are a danger to them.
3. It is prohibited to act upon human opinions when they contradict the Qur'an and the Sunnah.
4. Attempting to justify acts of disobedience is an attribute of the hypocrites.

Relevance to tawheed and the subject of the chapter

These Qur'anic verses prove that it is forbidden to spread corruption in the earth, which includes abandoning the judgement of Allah and accepting the judgement of others instead.

39.4

Allah, the Exalted, says:

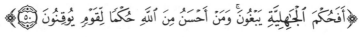

(سورة المائدة: ٥٠)

❲Do they then seek a judgement from the Days of Ignorance? But who, for a people who have firm faith, can give better judgement than Allah?❳

(Qur'an 5: 50)

In this verse, Allah rebukes those who abandon the judgement of Allah, whose wisdom, justice, and mercy are complete and incomparable, in favour of the flawed, ignorant, unjust, vain judgements of His created beings. Then He, Most Glorified, Most High, confirms a second time that His judgement is better and wiser than all other judgements, for He is the Creator of humankind and therefore knows best what is beneficial for them and what is harmful to them. There is general agreement among Muslim scholars that the Muslims will never be free from the serious problems which beset them until they return completely to the teachings of Islam. The truth of this is apparent when one compares the situation of Islam's enemies to that of the Muslims.

Benefits derived from this verse

1. Every judgement which does not come from the Book of Allah or the Sunnah of His Messenger (ﷺ) is of the Days of Ignorance.

2. Every judgement which does not concur with Allah's law is falseness.

3. It is forbidden to divorce the religion (of Islam) from the affairs of government.

Relevance to tawḥeed and the subject of the chapter

This Qur'anic verse proves the prohibition of abandoning the judgement of Allah in favour of the judgement of others, for this constitutes a negation of the testimony of faith that there is no god but Him.

39.5

It is reported on the authority of 'Abdullâh ibn 'Amr (﷽) that the Messenger of Allah (ﷺ) said: «None of you (truly) believes until his desires are in accordance with that which I have brought.» (a reliable hadith recorded by an-Nawawi)

Allah's Messenger (ﷺ) informs us in this hadith that the believers will not achieve the necessary completeness of faith until their words and deeds and their beliefs are in accordance with the Prophet's Sunnah.

Benefits derived from this hadith

1. Those whose desires conflict with that which Allah and His Messenger (ﷺ) love lack a completeness of faith.
2. It is forbidden to judge by other than that which Allah has revealed.
3. Every religious deed which does not conform to Islamic law is invalid.
4. Complete obedience is a part of complete faith.

Relevance to tawḥeed and the subject of the chapter

This hadith proves that it is forbidden to judge by other than Allah's law which was taught by Allah's Messenger (ﷺ) since doing so would invalidate the testimony of faith that there is no god except Allah and Muhammad is the Messenger of Allah.

39.6

Ash-Sha'bi said: «A dispute took place between a man from among the hypocrites and a man from among the Jews; and so the Jew said: Let us seek judgement from Muhammad. The Jew knew that he (ﷺ) did not accept bribes. But the hypocrite said: Let us seek judgement from the Jews. The hypocrite knew that they accepted bribes. So both of them agreed to take their case to a fortune-teller in Juhaynah and seek his judgement; then Allah revealed:

﴾أَلَمۡ تَرَ إِلَى ٱلَّذِينَ يَزۡعُمُونَ أَنَّهُمۡ ءَامَنُواْ بِمَآ أُنزِلَ إِلَيۡكَ وَمَآ أُنزِلَ مِن قَبۡلِكَ يُرِيدُونَ أَن يَتَحَاكَمُوٓاْ إِلَى ٱلطَّٰغُوتِ ... ﴿٦٠﴾﴾   (سورة النِّسَاء: ٦٠)

﴿Do you not see [O Muhammad,] those who claim to have faith in what was revealed to you and to those before you? They desire to resort for judgement to ṭâghoot...﴾   *(Qur'an 4: 60)*»

Ash-Sha'bi (ﷺ) informs us in this narration that a dispute took place between a man from among the Jews of Madinah and a man who outwardly affected to have embraced Islam, while retaining disbelief in his heart. So the Jew, knowing of the Messenger of Allah's impartiality, justice, honesty, and even-handedness, suggested that they refer their dispute to him (ﷺ). The hypocrite, also knowing this and fearing it, suggested that instead they refer their matter to the Jews, whom he knew could be bribed. In the end, they both agreed to refer their case to a fortune-teller from the village of Juhaynah. Then Allah revealed to His Messenger (ﷺ) the above verse, which exposed their wickedness, disgrace, and baseness to the world until the Day of Resurrection.

Benefits derived from this narration

1. One of the miracles of the Prophet (ﷺ) is that even his enemies testified to his honesty and justice.
2. It is forbidden to give or accept bribes.
3. One of the signs of hypocrisy is seeking judgement from other than Allah's law.
4. One of the characteristics of certain Jews is their acceptance of bribery.

Relevance to tawḥeed and the subject of the chapter

This narration proves that it is forbidden to seek judgement from other than Allah and His Messenger (ﷺ). It is hypocrisy to claim to believe in Allah and His Messenger (ﷺ) and yet seek judgement from others, for this is a negation of the testimony of faith.

39.7

Ibn 'Abbâs (رضي الله عنهما), the Prophet's Companion and one of the great commentators of the Qur'an, said that the previous verse was revealed with respect to two men who became involved in a dispute. One of them said, "Let us raise the matter with the Prophet (ﷺ)," while the other said, "Let us go to Ka'b ibn al-Ashraf." Then they went to 'Umar (رضي الله عنه), and one of them informed him of what had happened. 'Umar (رضي الله عنه) asked the one who had refused the judgement of the Messenger of Allah (ﷺ), "Is it so?" He replied, "Yes," upon which 'Umar (رضي الله عنه) struck him with his sword and killed him.[99]

The narrator informs us in this account, that the words of Allah, Most High: ❴Do you not see [O Muhammad] those who claim to have faith in what was revealed to you and to those before you?

---

[99] narrated by Ibn 'Abbâs and recorded in *Zâd al-Maseer*

They desire to resort for judgement to ṭâghoot *(Qur'an 4: 60)* were revealed concerning two men, one who was a Jew and the other a hypocrite, who fell into a dispute. The Jew suggested that they refer their dispute to the Messenger of Allah (ﷺ) because of his well-known sense of justice, fair play, and honesty, but the hypocrite suggested that they go instead to Ka'b ibn al-Ashraf, another Jewish man, because he knew that this man accepted bribes. In the end, they agreed to seek judgement from 'Umar ibn al-Khaṭṭâb (ﷺ), but when 'Umar heard that the hypocrite had rejected the judgement of Allah's Messenger (ﷺ), he slew him with his sword.

Benefits derived from this narration

1. It is a miracle of the Prophet (ﷺ) that even his enemies testified about his honesty and fairness.

2. Calling for judgement from other than the Book of Allah and the Sunnah of His Messenger (ﷺ) is a sign of hypocrisy.

3. It is permissible for the Islamic state to execute apostate Muslims-that is, those who declare openly their rejection of the judgement of the Prophet (ﷺ) or the Sharia.

4. It is an obligation to feel anger over a person who disrespects Allah, His religion, or His prophets.

5. It is an obligation to rebuke those who profane Islam.[100]

Relevance to tawḥeed and the subject of the chapter

This narration proves the prohibition of seeking judgement from other than Allah and His Messenger (ﷺ), because doing so invalidates the testimony of faith.

---

[100] It must not be understood from this narration that it is the right of every Muslim in an Islamic State to punish sinners or disbelievers. The position of 'Umar (ﷺ) due to his status as one of the foremost Companions and his=

Chapter 40

Denying Allah's names and attributes

40.1

*A*llah (ﷻ) says:

﴿ كَذَٰلِكَ أَرْسَلْنَٰكَ فِىٓ أُمَّةٍ قَدْ خَلَتْ مِن قَبْلِهَآ أُمَمٌ لِّتَتْلُوَاْ عَلَيْهِمُ ٱلَّذِىٓ أَوْحَيْنَآ إِلَيْكَ وَهُمْ يَكْفُرُونَ بِٱلرَّحْمَٰنِ قُلْ هُوَ رَبِّى لَآ إِلَٰهَ إِلَّا هُوَ عَلَيْهِ تَوَكَّلْتُ وَإِلَيْهِ مَتَابِ ﴿٣٠﴾ ﴾ (سورة الرّعد: ٣٠)

❲Thus, We have sent you among a people, [before whom] other peoples have passed away, in order that you might recite to them what We have revealed to you. But they reject [Allah,] the Most Gracious! Say: He is my Lord. There is none worthy of worship save Him. In Him I have placed my trust, and to Him I shall return.❳

(Qur'an 13: 30)

In this verse, Allah, Most Glorified, informs us that He has sent His Messenger, Muhammad (ﷺ), to this Ummah to lead them

---

=great knowledge and wisdom is not to be compared to that of any Muslim today. Were it to be permitted for every Muslim to take the law into his or her own hands, the situation in Muslim societies would rapidly descend into chaos.

from the darkness of ignorance and despair into the light of guidance and certainty, just as He sent to the previous nations Messengers with revelation. It is the responsibility of the Messenger (ﷺ) to impart to his people the Message that was revealed to him, even though the disbelievers may reject it and deny Allah's divine names and attributes. In addition, the Messenger (ﷺ) must remain steadfast in broadcasting the message of tawheed and firm in his dependence upon Allah in all matters. The Messenger (ﷺ), and all those who follow him, must turn to Allah in repentance and for guidance in every important affair.

Benefits derived from this verse

1. Rejection of any confirmed name or attribute of Allah is disbelief.
2. The verse confirms Allah's name: *Ar-Rahmân* (the Most Merciful to all His creatures in the life of this world).
3. It is an obligation to place one's trust and dependence in Allah, the Exalted, and no other.
4. It is an obligation to turn to Allah in repentance.

Relevance to tawheed and the subject of the chapter

This Qur'anic verse proves that rejecting any of Allah's names or His divine attributes is disbelief because it invalidates the belief in tawheed and the Oneness of Allah in His names and attributes.

40.2

It is reported that 'Ali (ﷺ) said, "Speak to the people in a way they will understand. Would you like that Allah and His Messenger be denied?" (recorded by Bukhari)

In this narration, the fourth Caliph, 'Ali ibn Abi Ṭâlib (ﷺ), commands the people of knowledge to guide others by speaking to them in a manner suited to their intellects and not to engage them in speech which is above their level of comprehension, in order that they may understand the message and not be misled. This would include caution with lengthy and involved explanations of Allah's names and attributes, for this might lead to misunderstanding and cause people to deny something from Allah's Book or the Sunnah of His Prophet (ﷺ) and this could cause them to be destroyed, without even knowing the reason.

Benefits derived from this narration

1. Whatever leads to the prohibited is itself prohibited.
2. It is not permissible to talk to people in a manner which they cannot understand, particularly in religious matters.

Relevance to tawḥeed and the subject of the chapter

This narration proves that it is forbidden to talk to people in a manner which they do not understand. This includes long and complex explanations of Allah's names and attributes, for that might lead to their rejecting something of His names and attributes, which would amount to disbelief because it entails negation of tawḥeed and negation of the Oneness of Allah in His names and attributes.

40.3

It is reported that Ibn 'Abbâs (ﷺ) saw a man spring to his feet in disapproval when he heard a hadith from the Prophet (ﷺ) about the divine attributes. Then Ibn 'Abbâs (ﷺ) said, "What kind of fear is it that these people have? They find that which they fear in the completely clear verses, which contain no ambiguity, and they are brought to ruin by those verses which are not entirely clear." (narrated by 'Abdur-Razzâq)[101]

'Abdullâh ibn 'Abbâs (&) informs us in this narration, that he saw a man rise to his feet in anger and disbelief when he heard a hadith of the Prophet (&) concerning Allah's divine attributes. Ibn 'Abbâs (&) rejected that man's action. He asked what such people feared from these verses, and why was it that they feared the clear, unambiguous Qur'anic verses, yet did not fear and reject those verses which are not entirely understood by them due to their limited knowledge.

Benefits derived from this narration

1. It is an obligation to reject the detestable.
2. It is an obligation to believe in all of Allah's names and attributes.
3. It is an obligation to believe in all of the divine revelation, the verses that are clear as well as those that are unclear.
4. It is permissible to discuss what relates to Allah's names and attributes from the Qur'an and the Sunnah in front of and for the benefit of laypersons.

Relevance to tawheed and the subject of the chapter

This narration proves the obligation of belief in all of Allah's names and attributes from the Qur'an and the Sunnah, and this is a necessary part of correct tawheed and the Oneness of Allah in His names and attributes.

---

[101] 'Abdur-Razzâq reports this on the authority of Ma'amar ibn Tâwoos who reported on the authority of his father that he heard it from Ibn 'Abbâs (&).

40.4

When the Quraysh heard Allah's Messenger mention Ar-Rahmân as a name of Allah, they rejected it, at which Allah revealed:

﴾ ... وَهُمۡ يَكۡفُرُونَ بِٱلرَّحۡمَٰنِ ... ۞﴿   (سورة الرّعد: ٣٠)

﴾...they reject Ar-Rahmân...﴿   *(Qur'an 13: 30)*

We are informed in this narration that when the Prophet (ﷺ) wished to include Allah's name Ar-Rahmân in the Treaty of Al-Hudaybiyyah, the pagans of Quraysh rejected it, saying that they did not know this name. About this incident, Allah revealed the verse: ﴾They reject Ar-Rahmân.﴿ *(Qur'an 13: 30)*

Benefits derived from this narration

1. The verse confirms one of Allah's names: Ar-Rahmân, which connotes the divine attribute of mercy and beneficence.
2. Whoever denies anything relating to Allah's names and divine attributes is a disbeliever and is destroyed.

Relevance to tawheed and the subject of the chapter

This narration proves the disbelief of one who denies anything of Allah's names and attributes because this is a negation of tawheed and the Oneness of Allah in His names and attributes.

Chapter 41

Denying the blessings of Allah

41.1

*A*llah's Words:

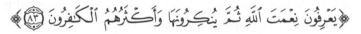

﴿يَعۡرِفُونَ نِعۡمَتَ ٱللَّهِ ثُمَّ يُنكِرُونَهَا وَأَكۡثَرُهُمُ ٱلۡكَٰفِرُونَ ۝﴾

(سورة النحل: ٨٣)

❨They know the favours of Allah, then they deny them; and most of them are ungrateful disbelievers.❩ *(Qur'an 16: 83)*

In this verse, Allah, Most Glorified, rejects all those who recognize in their hearts that all blessings are from Allah, and yet in spite of this, they deny them by their evil deeds. They worship other than Him, and they say that they achieved these blessings from Allah through the intercession of their idols, or they say that it is their inheritance from their fathers and their grandfathers, as if this is independent from the will of Allah. Allah, the Exalted, informs us that all those who do so are disbelievers in Allah and deniers of His Blessings.

Benefits derived from this verse

1. Even the pagans believed that Allah is the One Lord, the Creator and the Sustainer of the Universe.
2. Gratitude to Allah is not complete unless it is expressed in belief,

word, and deed.

3. Using the blessings of Allah for the purpose of disobedience to Him is to deny them.

Relevance to tawḥeed and the subject of the chapter

This Qur'anic verse proves that whoever attributes Allah's blessings to other than Him has denied the blessings. This is disbelief because in so doing they set up partners with Allah in the bestowal of blessings.

41.2

Mujâhid explained the meaning of the above-quoted verse as follows: "He (the one referred to in the verse) is the man who says: They (Allah's blessings) are mine, an inheritance from my fathers and my forefathers."

Relevance to tawḥeed and the subject of the chapter

This narration proves that Mujâhid considered the person who attributes Allah's blessings to other than Him to be a denier of those blessings and a disbeliever because to deny Allah's blessings is an act of shirk.

41.3

'Awn ibn 'Abdullâh said, "They say: If it were not for so-and-so, such-and-such an event would not have occurred."

'Awn ibn 'Abdullâh considered attributing events to any of Allah's created beings to be disbelief because this entails attributing benefit or harm to other than Allah, while in fact the creation possesses no power to harm or benefit except by Allah's will.

Relevance to tawheed and the subject of the chapter

This narration proves that 'Awn ibn 'Abdullâh held the view that believing that benefit or harm may occur due to the actions of other than Allah, independent of Allah's preordainment, is disbelief.

41.4

Ibn Qutaybah said: "They say: This is due to the intercession of our gods."

Ibn Qutaybah informs us in this narration that the polytheists attribute the blessings which they receive to be achieved through the power of intercession of their false gods. In doing so, they combine the sin of associating partners with Allah by worshipping idols with the sin of disbelief by attributing blessings to other than Him, the true granter of blessings.

Relevance of this narration to the subject of the chapter

This narration proves that Ibn Qutaybah considered attributing Allah's blessings to the intercession of idols to be disbelief.

41.5

Conerning the hadith of Zayd ibn Khâlid[102] in which Allah, the Exalted, said: «Some of My slaves this morning are true believers in Me and others are disbelievers...» Ibn Taymiyah explained:

Such commandments occur frequently in the Qur'an and the Sunnah. Allah condemns those who attribute His blessings to

---

[102] See 30.3 above for the complete text.

others whom they associate with Him. Some of the salaf have said that it is like the saying of some: 'The wind was favourable,' or 'The sailor was skilful,' and the statements of many people are like this.

The meaning of the above-mentioned narration is that when a ship is driven by a fair wind by Allah's command, they attribute this to the goodness of the wind or the skill of the sailor in sailing the ship. They forget their Lord, Who drove the ship on the sea, as a mercy to them. Attributing a speedy or safe voyage to the favour of the wind or the skill of the sailor is akin to crediting the rain to the movements of the stars and planets. Even if people do not intend by their words to suggest that the wind is the creator or instigator of these events along with Allah, that it is only the means by which the objective was achieved, it is still not fitting to include it beside Allah, the One. It does not befit Allah's favour that anyone should forget that it is He alone Who deserves gratitude and thanks, for all good is in His Hands and He is able to do all things. It is He Who grants all blessings in this world and in the hereafter. He is One, and He has no partners.

Benefits derived from this narration

1. Attributing blessings to any of Allah's creation is shirk in the Oneness of Lordship if it is believed that some part of the creation is the provider and instigator of those blessings. If it is believed that part of Allah's creation is the means by which the blessings were attained, then this is, at the very least, bad manners towards Allah, the true Provider of all blessings.

Relevance to tawheed and the subject of the chapter

This narration proves that Ibn Taymiyah considered attributing blessings to other than Allah to be shirk and a denial of those blessings.

Chapter 42

Ascribing partners to Allah in His Lordship

42.1

*A*llah's Words:

﴿يَٰٓأَيُّهَا ٱلنَّاسُ ٱعۡبُدُواْ رَبَّكُمُ ٱلَّذِى خَلَقَكُمۡ وَٱلَّذِينَ مِن قَبۡلِكُمۡ لَعَلَّكُمۡ تَتَّقُونَ ۝ ٱلَّذِى جَعَلَ لَكُمُ ٱلۡأَرۡضَ فِرَٰشًا وَٱلسَّمَآءَ بِنَآءً وَأَنزَلَ مِنَ ٱلسَّمَآءِ مَآءً فَأَخۡرَجَ بِهِۦ مِنَ ٱلثَّمَرَٰتِ رِزۡقًا لَّكُمۡۖ فَلَا تَجۡعَلُواْ لِلَّهِ أَندَادًا ... ۝﴾

(سورة البَقَرَة: ٢١-٢٢)

﴿O you people! Worship your Lord, Who created you all and those before you that you may become righteous, Who has made the earth a couch for you and the heavens a canopy and sent down rain from the heavens and brought forth therewith fruits for your subsistence; so do not set up rivals with Allah...﴾ *(Qur'an 2: 21-22)*

Allah, Most Glorified, commands people to worship Him Alone, in sincerity, because He is the One Who created them and those before them from nothing. Then He bestowed upon them innumerable blessings, such as the earth which He fixed that they may dwell upon it and the rain which He sends down in abundance, and from which they derive countless blessings, such as food to eat, water to drink, and trees for shade. Allah, Most Glorified, says that in spite of all that He provides for His slaves, they set up partners and equals with Him, though in reality, they know that He is their Creator and Provider. This is mere wilfulness on their part to commit disbelief, shirk, and other acts of disobedience.

Benefits derived from this verse

1. The verse is evidence of a number of Allah's blessings bestowed upon His creation.
2. The verse is evidence of tawḥeed: the Oneness of Worship through the Oneness of Lordship.
3. It is an obligation to worship Allah alone, without partners.

Relevance to tawḥeed and the subject of the chapter

This verse proves the obligation to abstain from obvious shirk and from hidden shirk. A type of hidden shirk includes saying things like 'Had it not been for the guard, the burglars would have come to us.'

42.2

Concerning this verse, Ibn 'Abbâs (ﷺ) said,

The word 'rivals' (in the above-quoted verse) means hidden shirk, which is less conspicuous than a black ant crawling on a black stone in the darkness of the night,[103] such as the saying 'By Allah and by your life,' or 'By your life,' or (people saying) 'If it had not been for this little dog, the

---

[103] This description of hidden shirk is from a hadith of the Prophet (ﷺ) narrated by Aḥmad.

burglars would have come to us,' or 'Had it not been for the duck in the house, the burglars would have come,' or like a man's saying to his companion, 'By Allah's will and your will' or 'As Allah and you will,' or a person saying, 'Had it not been for Allah and so-and-so...' — Do not mention anyone with Allah because all of this is shirk. (narrated by Ibn Abi Ḥâtim)

Relevance to tawḥeed and the subject of the chapter

This narration proves that Ibn 'Abbâs (رضي الله عنهما), one of the best and wisest of the Companions (may Allah be pleased with them) in understanding the religion, held the view that hidden shirk includes swearing by other than Allah, such as when people say things like 'By your life!' Likewise, it includes attributing benefit to the deeds of one of Allah's created beings, such as statement: 'Had it not been for the guard, the burglars would have stolen from us.' It also includes the attribution of benefit to the deeds of another alongside Allah, such as saying: 'Had it not been for Allah and so-and-so, the house would have burnt down.'

42.3

'Umar ibn al-Khaṭṭâb (رضي الله عنه) narrated that the Messenger of Allah (ﷺ) said: «Whoever swears by other than Allah has committed an act of disbelief or shirk.» (recorded by at-Tirmidhi and al-Ḥâkim)[104]

The Messenger of Allah (ﷺ) informs us in this hadith that swearing by other than Allah, Most Glorified, is tantamount to a denial of Allah, the One True God, and equivalent to associating

---

[104] At-Tirmidhi graded it as reliable, and al-Ḥâkim graded it as sound.

partners with Him. This is because the essence of swearing is glorification. It is not fitting that we should glorify anyone except Allah, the One True God and Lord, for to glorify something other than Allah is shirk.

Benefits derived from this hadith

1. Swearing by other than Allah is an act of major shirk. According to some scholars, it takes one out of the fold of Islam, while according to other scholars, it is a sinful act of shirk, which however does not necessitate one's becoming a disbeliever. It has also been said by others that it is an act of minor shirk, and Allah knows best.

2. There is no recompense for swearing by other than Allah, since it is an act of shirk. The culprit must instead turn in repentance to Allah and seek His Forgiveness.

Important notes

1. There is no contradiction between this hadith and the words of the Prophet (ﷺ): «By his father! He has succeeded,» and other similar hadiths, for it has been explained by scholars that (any such ruling derived from) this and other similar hadiths (would be) abrogated by the above hadith.

2. There is no recompense for swearing by other than Allah nor is it binding upon anyone to fulfil a promise made by swearing by other than Him. What is incumbent upon a person is to declare: '*Lâ ilâha illâ Allâhu waḥdahu lâ shareeka lahu*' (None is worthy of worship except Allah alone, without partners.) Then the person should spit[105] over the left shoulder three times and seek refuge with Allah, and the person should be determined never to repeat this act of shirk.

---

[105] a dry spitting that releases no spittle

42.4

Ibn Mas'ood (ﷺ) said, "That I should swear by Allah about a lie is more preferable to me than that I should swear by another about the truth." (recorded by aṭ-Ṭabarâni with a sound chain)

Ibn Mas'ood (ﷺ) informs us in this narration that it is sin to make any lie upon which Allah's name is invoked or make any truthful statement upon which the name of another is invoked. Still, the sin of swearing by Allah regarding a lie is lighter than the sin of swearing by someone or something other than Allah regarding the truth, because while swearing by Allah about a lie is a major sin, swearing by someone or something else is an act of shirk.

Benefits derived from this narration

1. It is forbidden to swear on the name of Allah when telling a lie.
2. It is permissible to swear by Allah upon the truth.
3. It is forbidden to swear by other than Allah, whether to the truth or to a lie.
4. If one is forced by circumstances to choose one of two undesirable courses of action, against one's will, one should do that which is less harmful.
5. Ibn Mas'ood (ﷺ) had a clear and precise understanding of Islamic teachings.
6. Swearing by other than Allah is a greater sin than swearing by Allah regarding a lie.

Relevance to tawḥeed and the subject of the chapter

This narration proves that Ibn Mas'ood (ﷺ) considered swearing by other than Allah to be forbidden because swearing by part of Allah's creation entails glorification of that person or thing and glorification is a form of worship. Directing an act of worship to other than Allah is shirk.

42.5

On the authority of Ḥudhayfah (رضي الله عنه), it is reported that the Prophet (ﷺ) said: «Do not say: 'As Allah wills and so-and-so wills,' but instead say: 'As Allah wills and then as so-and-so wills.'» (recorded by Abu Dâwood with a sound chain of narrators)

Ḥudhayfah (رضي الله عنه) informs us in this hadith that the Prophet (ﷺ) ordered his Companions (may Allah be pleased with them) not to equate the will of a human with the will of Allah, but to mention Allah's will first, then the will of others since this makes it clear that the will of human beings is subservient to the will of Allah. It is clear that if a person wills something but Allah does not will it, it can never happen, while if Allah wills something, even if the whole of humankind united to oppose it, it will, without any shadow of doubt, take place.

Benefits derived from this hadith

1. It is forbidden to equate the will of Allah's created beings with the will of Allah.
2. It is permissible to mentioning the will of a person after the will of Allah by saying 'then' as opposed to 'and'.
3. The hadith confirms Allah's divine attribute of will.

Relevance to tawheed and the subject of the chapter

This hadith proves the prohibition of equating the will of humans with the will of Allah by saying 'As Allah wills and so-and-so wills' because using the word 'and' suggests parity between the will of Allah and the will of a part of His creation, which amounts to shirk in matters of Lordship.

42.6

It is reported on the authority of Ibrâheem an-Nakhâ'i that he hated for anyone to say: 'I seek refuge in Allah and in you,' but he considered it permissible to say: 'I seek refuge in Allah and then in you.' Then he added that a person should say: 'If not for Allah, then so-and-so...' and he should not say: 'If not for Allah and so-and-so.'

Relevance to tawheed and the subject of the chapter

This narration proves that Ibrâheem an-Nakhâ'i held the view that it is forbidden to link seeking refuge in Allah with seeking refuge in one of His created beings. Likewise he considered it forbidden to link the actions of Allah with those of His creation, for do so is to set up a partner with Allah.

Chapter 43

Swearing an oath in Allah's name

43.1

$\mathcal{I}$t is reported on the authority of Ibn 'Umar (رضي الله عنه) that the Messenger of Allah (ﷺ) said: «Do not swear by your fathers. Whoever swears by Allah, let him speak the truth, and the one for whom the oath is taken in the name of Allah should be satisfied with it. Whoever is not satisfied with it, is not (one of the submissive slaves) of Allah.» (recorded by Ibn Mâjah with a reliable chain of narrators)

In this hadith, the Messenger of Allah (ﷺ) forbids the swearing of oaths in other than Allah's name because this entails glorifying Allah's created beings and excessively humbling oneself before them. Islam does not permit excessive humility towards other than Allah. Then the Prophet (ﷺ) commands those who swear in Allah's name to speak the truth because truth is a virtue at all times, even in ordinary speech; so clearly it is even more important to be truthful when speech is reinforced by an oath in Allah's name. Then he (ﷺ) orders the one to whom an oath in Allah's name is made to believe the fellow Muslim, unless it is proven that the person has not spoken the truth, for it is incumbent upon the Muslims to think well of their brothers and sisters in faith. Whoever does not do so, Allah has nothing to do with such a person.

Benefits derived from this hadith

1. It is forbidden to swear by other than Allah.
2. It is permissible to swear by Allah, so long as one is truthful.
3. Swearing by Allah when telling a lie is prohibited.
4. It is an obligation to accept the word of one who swears by Allah, unless it is proven that the person has lied.

Relevance to tawḥeed and the subject of the chapter

This hadith proves the obligation to accept the word of one who swears an oath by the name of Allah because by doing so one is glorifying Allah, and that is part of the completeness of tawḥeed.

Chapter 44

Saying: 'As Allah wills and you will'

44.1

$\mathcal{T}$he following incident is reported on the authority of Qateelah (رضى الله عنها): «A Jewish man came to the Prophet (ﷺ) and said to him: Verily, you (Muslims) commit shirk, for you say, 'As Allah wills and as you will,' and you say, 'By the Ka'bah!'[106] So the Prophet (ﷺ) ordered whoever wanted to swear to say, 'By the Lord of the Ka'bah!' and to say, 'As Allah wills, then as you will.'» (a sound hadith recorded by an-Nasâ'i)

Qateelah (رضى الله عنها) informs us in this hadith that a man from among the Jews of Madinah came to the Prophet (ﷺ) intending to malign Islam and the Muslims. He told the Prophet (ﷺ) that he and all the other Muslims were guilty of shirk. It is as if he wished to say, "You and your Qur'an say that we, the Jews, commit shirk; then what about you, when you swear by the Ka'bah and when you say: 'As Allah and you will.' Is this not also shirk?"

Thenceforth, the Messenger of Allah (ﷺ) forbade the Muslims from doing so, in order that their tawheed might be pure and unsullied and also so that there might not be even the slightest blemish upon the Muslims' religion which their enemies might

---

[106] *Ka'bah*: the House of Allah in Makkah, originally built by Prophets Ibrâheem and Ismâ'eel, and which Muslims face wherever they pray

exploit. He (ﷺ) guided them to the correct manner of swearing an oath, which is to swear by the Lord of the Ka'bah, not by the Ka'bah itself, for it is a created thing. He (ﷺ) also told them that if they wish to mention Allah's will along with the will of others, they should say: 'As Allah wills, then as you will,' because the use of the word 'then' does not imply parity between the will of Allah and the will of others, as does the use of the word 'and'.

Benefits derived from this hadith

1. Knowledgeable Jews know what minor shirk is.

2. A person's knowing the truth does not necessitate that he or she will become a believing Muslim.

3. Linking Allah's will with the will of others by using the word 'and' is minor shirk.

4. Swearing by other than Allah is shirk, no matter how elevated the status of the object upon which the oath is taken.

5. It is an obligation to accept the truth, no matter what its source.

6. The hadith confirms Allah's divine attribute of will.

7. The hadith confirms of the will of Allah's created beings, but in the knowledge that it is subordinate to the will of Allah.

8. It is permissible to link Allah's will with that of His creation by using the word 'then', as opposed to 'and'.

Relevance to tawḥeed and the subject of the chapter

This hadith proves that saying 'As Allah wills and you will' is an act of minor shirk.

44.2

On the authority of Ibn 'Abbâs (ﷺ), the following is reported: «A man came to the Prophet (ﷺ) and the man said: As Allah and you will. Upon hearing this, the Prophet (ﷺ) said: Would you set me up as a partner beside Allah? (Say:) As Allah Alone wills.» (recorded by an-Nasâ'i and Ibn Mâjah with a reliable chain)

Ibn 'Abbâs (ﷺ) informs us that a man came to Allah's Messenger (ﷺ) and consulted him about a certain matter. After hearing the Prophet's advice, he said: 'As Allah and you will, O Messenger of Allah!' The Prophet rebuked him for this statement and explained to him that placing his will on a par with the will of Allah was tantamount to ascribing him as a partner to Allah, which is prohibited to the Muslim. Then he (ﷺ) guided the man to the correct manner, which is to say: 'As Allah Alone wills.'

Benefits derived from this hadith

1. It is an obligation to reject that which is detestable.
2. An ignorant person is excused due to ignorance until the person becomes aware of the mistake.
3. Linking the will of Allah with that of His creation by using the word 'and' is an act of minor shirk.
4. The hadith confirms Allah's divine attribute of will.

Relevance to tawḥeed and the subject of the chapter

This hadith proves that saying 'As Allah and you will' is an act of minor shirk.

Important note

There is no contradiction between this hadith and the saying of the Prophet (ﷺ): «Say: 'As Allah wills, then as you will,'» because to do so is permissible, while to say: «'As Allah Alone wills'» is preferred.

44·3

It is reported that aṭ-Ṭufayl, 'Â'ishah's half-brother (may Allah be pleased with them both) on her mother's side, said: «I saw in a dream that I came upon a number of Jews and I said to them: You are indeed a good people, were it not that you claim that 'Uzayr (ﷺ) is the son of Allah. They replied: You too are good, were it not that you say 'As Allah wills and as Muhammad wills.' Then, I came upon a number of Christians and I said to them: You are indeed a good people, were it not that you claim that the Messiah ['Eesâ (ﷺ)] is the son of Allah. They replied: You are also good, were it not that you say 'As Allah wills and as Muhammad wills.' When I awoke, I told someone about this. Then I went to the Prophet (ﷺ) and repeated it to him. He asked me: Have you told anyone about this? I said: Yes. Then he went to the pulpit and, after praising Allah, he said: *Ammâ ba'd*[107] ...Aṭ-Ṭufayl had a dream which he has already communicated to some of you. You used to say something which I was prevented from forbidding to you until now. Henceforth, do not say: 'As Allah wills and as Muhammad wills,' but say: 'What Allah Alone wills.'» (recorded by Aḥmad, Ibn Mâjah and ad-Dârimi with a sound chain)

Aṭ-Ṭufayl (ﷺ) informs us that he had a dream in which he saw the Jews and Christians. He praised them both, except that he pointed out to them their shameful behaviour in elevating their prophets to the status of deities, claiming them to be sons of Allah. They replied by praising the Muslims, except that they pointed out a blot on the Muslims' character, in that they used to link the will of Allah with that of Muhammad (ﷺ). When aṭ-Ṭufayl awoke, he informed a number of people about what he had dreamt, and then he

---

[107] *Ammâ ba'd*: 'as for what follows'; this is traditionally said after praising Allah when ready to move on to the topic at hand.

went to the Prophet (ﷺ) and told him about it. The Prophet (ﷺ) then rose and addressed the Muslims in the mosque. After praising Allah, Most High, he ordered them to be strict in their implementation of tawḥeed, particularly in what concerns Allah's will. Then he (ﷺ) told them that he had previously hated this saying, but that he had not been ordered to forbid it until now. Thenceforth, he forbade the Muslims from saying this, without fear of the truth, regardless of its source.

Benefits derived from this hadith

1. The hadith shows the virtue of aṭ-Ṭufayl (﵁).
2. The hadith confirms Allah's divine attribute of will.
3. It is prohibited to link Allah's will with that of His creations, using the word 'and' because to do so is to commit minor shirk.
4. In the time of the Prophet (ﷺ), a dream might form the basis for a legal judgement.
5. The hadith shows the good character of the Prophet (ﷺ), who did not hide anything from people.
6. It is part of Islam to begin a speech by praising and thanking Allah.
7. It is part of Islam to address the people on important matters.
8. It is lawful to say, after praising Allah, '*Ammâ ba'd* (as for what follows).'
9. It is part of Islam to make sure of the truth of a matter and not make hasty decisions.
10. It is commanded to practise tawḥeed in the matter of Allah's will.

Relevance to tawḥeed and the subject of the chapter

This hadith proves the prohibition of linking the will of Allah's created beings with that of Him, Most High, using the word 'and', for this suggests parity between the two wills and thus leads to shirk.

Chapter 45

Whoever curses time wrongs Allah

45.1

*A*llah (ﷻ) says:

$$﴿وَقَالُوا مَا هِيَ إِلَّا حَيَاتُنَا ٱلدُّنْيَا نَمُوتُ وَنَحْيَا وَمَا يُهْلِكُنَا إِلَّا ٱلدَّهْرُ وَمَا لَهُم بِذَٰلِكَ مِنْ عِلْمٍ إِنْ هُمْ إِلَّا يَظُنُّونَ ٧٤﴾$$

(سورة الجَاثِيَة : ٢٤)

❲They say: There is nothing but our life in this world. We die and we live and nothing destroys us except time. — And they have no knowledge of it, they only conjecture.❳   *(Qur'an 45: 24)*

Allah, Most Glorified, informs us in this verse about the disbelievers and atheists — Arabs and others — who do not believe in any life except the life of this world. They deny the Lord and Creator, Allah, Most High. They believe that nothing causes death except the passage of time. Then Allah, Most Glorified, refutes them by saying that they have absolutely no evidence for what they claim, but instead, depend upon surmise and their own vain opinions.

Benefits derived from this verse

1. Attributing good or evil to the passage of time is a sign of atheism.
2. This verse is a confirmation of a life after death for humankind.
3. *Ad-dahr* (time) is not one of Allah's names.

Relevance to tawheed and the subject of the chapter

This Qur'anic verse rejects those who attribute events to time, for they commit a great wrong against Allah. They are ascribing a partner to Allah, for it is He alone Who decrees what will be and what will not be.

45.2

It is authentically reported on the authority of Abu Hurayrah (رضي الله عنه) that the Prophet (ﷺ) said: «Allah, Most Blessed, says: The son of Âdam wrongs Me. He curses time, though I am time. In My Hands are all things, and I cause the night to follow the day.» (recorded by Bukhari) In another narration, the Prophet (ﷺ) says: «Do not curse time, for verily, time is Allah.» (recorded by Muslim)

Allah, Most Glorified, informs us in this hadith qudsi that people commit a great wrong against Allah when they curse time and attributes the occurrence of events to it, for Allah is the Lord of time and the Disposer of affairs and it is by His decree that events take place. Therefore to curse time is to curse the Owner of time.

In the second narration, the Prophet (ﷺ) forbids us from cursing time, saying that Allah is the Owner of time and the Disposer of it and all events and affairs, and this is a confirmation of what was reported in the preceding hadith qudsi.

Benefits derived from these hadiths

1. It is forbidden to curse time.
2. No actions may be attributed to time.

Relevance to tawḥeed and the subject of the chapter

These hadiths prove that to curse time is to commit a great wrong against Allah because those who do so believe that it is time which causes events to take place; this is shirk in Allah's Oneness of Lordship, for it is Allah alone Who determines events.

Chapter 46

Using the title 'King of kings' and the like

46.1

*I*t is authentically reported on the authority of Abu Hurayrah (رضي الله عنه) that the Prophet (ﷺ) said: «Verily, the lowest name to Allah is that of a man who calls himself 'King of Kings', for there is no king except Allah.» (recorded by Bukhari) In another narration, the same is said, but with the introduction: «The man who angers Allah most on the Day of Resurrection and the vilest...» Sufyân added: "It is like the (Persian) title *Shâhinshâh* (which also means 'King of Kings')."

Allah's Messenger (ﷺ) informs us in this hadith that the vilest, most contemptible, most wretched human being in the sight of Allah is the one who calls himself 'King of Kings' or the like, or is so called by others and is pleased with that. In so doing, such a person has elevated himself to the position of Lord, comparing himself to Allah, the true King of Kings. Then the Prophet (ﷺ) makes clear that there is no king of the universe, except Allah, the All-Mighty, the All-Powerful. This is a warning to all those who take such names and titles for themselves or attribute them to others, without perhaps, fully understanding the meaning or being aware of the great sin which they commit in so doing.

Benefits derived from this hadith

1. It is forbidden to name oneself 'King of Kings' or any other name which carries the same meaning, such as 'Emperor of All', 'Judge of Judges', and so on.
2. It is an obligation to abstain from using reprehensible expressions.

Relevance to tawḥeed and the subject of the chapter

This hadith proves that it is forbidden to take or give a person the title 'King of Kings' or 'Judge of Judges' because this is shirk in Allah's Oneness of Lordship.

Chapter 47

Naming a person with one of Allah's names

47.1

It is reported on the authority of Abu Shurayḥ (ﷺ) that he used to be known as Abul Ḥakam, until the Prophet (ﷺ) said to him: «Allah is Al-Ḥakam and His judgement will prevail. Abu Shurayḥ (ﷺ) replied: When my people dispute in any matter, they come to me for adjudication; and when I judge between them, both parties are pleased with my judgement. The Prophet (ﷺ) said: How excellent this is! Do you have any children? He said: Yes, Shurayḥ, Muslim, and 'Abdullâh. Then the Prophet (ﷺ) asked: Who is the eldest? He answered: Shurayḥ. Then the Prophet (ﷺ) said: Then (from now on), you will be known as Abu Shurayḥ.» (an authentic hadith recorded by an-Nasâ'i and others)

Abu Shurayḥ (ﷺ), whose real name was Hâni ibn Yazeed al-Kindi, came to the Prophet (ﷺ) in a delegation from his tribe. His nickname at that time was 'Abul Ḥakam', which means 'Father of judgement',[108] but when the Prophet (ﷺ) heard his people addressing him thus, the Prophet (ﷺ) rejected it. He (ﷺ) informed

---

[108] It was, and continues to be, a practice among the Arabs, when they notice a certain trait in someone to name him (literally) father of that trait; thus, the Companion Abu Hurayrah (ﷺ) was called 'Father of the kitten' because he was so fond of kittens that he used to carry one around with him.

them that Al-Ḥakam is one of Allah's names, for His is the final judgement, from which there is no appeal. Abu Shurayḥ then explained to him that his people had given him this name because of his skill in arbitration, which in most cases, satisfied both parties. The Prophet (ﷺ) was pleased with what Abu Shurayḥ (ﷺ) told him, and he praised him for his wisdom and good judgement. Then he (ﷺ) asked him if he had any children. Abu Shurayḥ (ﷺ) stated that he had three sons, the eldest of whom was named Shurayḥ. At this, the Prophet (ﷺ) informed him that from that point onward, he would be known as Abu Shurayḥ.

Benefits derived from this hadith

1. Islam erases what came before it.
2. Ignorant people are excused of their faults until they are made aware of them.
3. It is an obligation to reject that which is detestable.
4. The hadith confirms one of Allah's names: Al-Ḥakam.
5. It is permissible to refer disputes to those who are capable of wise and fair judgement, even though they may not be appointed judges, and both parties should accept such judgement.
6. It is a virtue to accept a Muslim's excuse when it is sound.
7. It is permissible to give a person a nickname that mentions his or her parentage to the first-born daughter.
8. It is lawful to name oneself by a nickname that mentions one's parentage to one's eldest child.

Relevance to tawḥeed and the subject of the chapter

This hadith proves the obligation to change one's name if there is any similarity between it and the names of Allah. This is because to describe oneself by one of Allah's names or a name with the same meaning is shirk, for it is a negation of tawḥeed and the Oneness of Allah in His names and attributes.

Chapter 48

Making fun of something in the religion

48.1

*A*llah (ﷻ) says:

﴿وَلَئِن سَأَلْتَهُمْ لَيَقُولُنَّ إِنَّمَا كُنَّا نَخُوضُ وَنَلْعَبُ قُلْ أَبِاللَّهِ وَءَايَٰتِهِۦ وَرَسُولِهِۦ كُنتُمْ تَسْتَهْزِءُونَ ۝ لَا تَعْتَذِرُوا۟ قَدْ كَفَرْتُم بَعْدَ إِيمَٰنِكُمْ إِن نَّعْفُ عَن طَآئِفَةٍ مِّنكُمْ نُعَذِّبْ طَآئِفَةَۢ بِأَنَّهُمْ كَانُوا۟ مُجْرِمِينَ ۝﴾

(سورة التوبة: ٦٥-٦٦)

❴If you question them, they declare emphatically: We were only talking idly and joking. Say: Was it at Allah, His signs and verses, and His Messenger you were mocking? Make no excuses! You have rejected faith after you had accepted it. If We pardon some of you, We will punish others amongst you because they were sinners.❵

(Qur'an 9: 65-66)

In these two verses, Allah, Most Glorified, refers to an incident in which the hypocrites, having taken part in the Battle of Tabook with the Muslims, began to discredit and insult the Muslims and their religion. Allah, the Exalted, informs His Prophet (ﷺ) about the reply of those hypocrites, when they are questioned about their lack of faith, that they will put forward untruthful and invalid excuses for their behaviour. They will claim that the slander which issued from their mouths was spoken only in jest. Then He, Most Glorified, tells the Prophet (ﷺ) to say that their excuses are not acceptable, for they are guilty of mocking Allah, His revelation, His proofs, His signs, and His Messenger (ﷺ). Still, in spite of this, He, Most Merciful, does not close the door completely on the hope of forgiveness and mercy for those of them who cease their hypocrisy and turn sincerely in repentance to Him. Finally, He, Most Blessed, confirms the severe chastisement which awaits those of them who continue in their hypocrisy and disbelief.

Benefits derived from these verses

1. Making fun of Islam and the Muslims is an act of disbelief.
2. According to some scholars of the Hanbali school of jurisprudence, repentance is not accepted from anyone who makes fun of Islam and the Muslims, while others held the view that repentance for this deed is accepted.[109]

Relevance to tawheed and the subject of the chapter

These Qur'anic verses prove the disbelief of one who mocks Allah, His signs and verses, or His Messenger (ﷺ).

48.2

The following is reported on the authority of Ibn 'Umar, Muhammad ibn Ka'b, Zayd ibn Aslam and Qatâdah (may Allah be

---

[109] Some scholars of the school of thought based upon the teachings of the great scholar, Ahmad ibn Hanbal, held that there is no repentance for the one who mocks the religion of Allah, and they took as evidence the words of Allah: ﴾Make no excuses! You have rejected faith after you had accepted it.﴿ (*Qur'an* 9: 66). According to these scholars, the only alternative for such a=

pleased with them): «In the course of the Battle of Tabook, a man came up and declared: We have seen none greedier, none so untruthful, and none so cowardly as these (Qur'an) reciters of ours. [He was referring to Allah's Messenger (ﷺ) and the Companions (may Allah be pleased with them).] 'Awf ibn Mâlik replied: (In fact), you are the liar and a hypocrite, and I shall inform the Messenger of Allah (ﷺ) (about what you have said). So 'Awf went to Allah's Messenger (ﷺ) in order to inform him of what had occurred, but he found that revelation had already preceded him. Then that man came to the Messenger of Allah (ﷺ) when the Messenger was just starting out on a journey on his camel. The man pleaded: We were only joking and indulging in travellers' talk to pass the time. Ibn 'Umar (may Allah be pleased with both of them) said: It is as if I see him before me now, clinging to the saddle-belt of Allah's Messenger's camel; the rough stones were battering his legs as he ran, and he was saying: We were only talking idly and joking. The Messenger of Allah (ﷺ) replied: ﴾Was it at Allah, His signs and verses, and His Messenger you were mocking? Make no excuses! You have rejected faith after you had accepted it.﴿ The Messenger (ﷺ) did not look towards him, nor did he say anything further.»[110]

'Abdullâh ibn 'Umar and the other above-mentioned narrators (may Allah be pleased with them) inform us in this hadith that during the Tabook Campaign, a man from among the hypocrites began to malign the Messenger of Allah (ﷺ) and the Companions and mock them, claiming that they ate too much food and that they were liars

---

=person would be to embrace Islam anew, by testifying that none is worthy of worship except Allah and that Muhammad (ﷺ) is the Messenger of Allah.

[110] Although this hadith is found in several classical texts, such as *Zâd al-Ma'âd* and *Tafseer ibn Abi Hâtim*, its status is unknown. The oldest source in which it is mentioned is Ibn Taymiyyah's work, *As-Sârim al-Maslool*, vol. 1, p. 31, where he neither verified nor referenced it. (Editor)

and cowards in battle. When 'Awf ibn Mâlik (رضي الله عنه) heard these words, he became angry for Allah and His Messenger's sake. 'Awf refuted these words, branding the man a liar and a hypocrite, and warning him that he would inform the Prophet (ﷺ) about what he had said. When he got to the Messenger (ﷺ), he found that he already knew of the incident because Allah had informed him through revelation. The Qur'an had uncovered the baseness and deceit of the hypocrites for all to see, and the revelation cursed their disbelief. After this, the hypocrite came to the Messenger of Allah (ﷺ) to try to explain his behaviour with patently false excuses, but Allah's Messenger refused even to look in his direction. He (ﷺ) merely replied by quoting the verse which Allah had revealed to him concerning this man and all those like him.

Benefits derived from this verse

1. The hypocrites are a danger to Islam and the Muslims.
2. Maligning Islam is a sign of hypocrisy.
3. Hatred for the Muslims and disparaging them is an act of disbelief.
4. It is an obligation to refute immediately that which is evil.
5. The hadith shows the true faith of 'Awf ibn Mâlik (رضي الله عنه).
6. It is permissible to brand a person a hypocrite if the person exhibits unmistakable signs of hypocrisy.
7. The hadith confirms one miracle of the Prophet (ﷺ) in that he was informed by revelation of the incident before 'Awf came to him.
8. Vain excuses are not accepted.
9. It is an obligation to be severe with those who mock the religion.

Relevance to tawḥeed and the subject of the chapter

This hadith and the verse contained in it prove the disbelief of one who makes fun of Allah, His Book, or His Messenger (ﷺ).

Chapter 49

Ingratitude for Allah's blessings

49.1

*A*llah (ﷻ) says:

﴿وَلَئِنْ أَذَقْنَهُ رَحْمَةً مِّنَّا مِنْ بَعْدِ ضَرَّآءَ مَسَّتْهُ لَيَقُولَنَّ هَذَا لِى وَمَآ أَظُنُّ ٱلسَّاعَةَ قَآئِمَةً وَلَئِن رُّجِعْتُ إِلَى رَبِّىٓ إِنَّ لِى عِندَهُ لَلْحُسْنَىٰ فَلَنُنَبِّئَنَّ ٱلَّذِينَ كَفَرُواْ بِمَا عَمِلُواْ وَلَنُذِيقَنَّهُم مِّنْ عَذَابٍ غَلِيظٍ ﴾

(سورة فُصِّلَت: ٥٠)

⟨Truly, if We give him a taste of mercy from Us, after some adversity has touched him, he is sure to say: This is for me; I think not that the Hour will be established, but if I am brought back to my Lord, surely, there will be for me the best with Him. — Then verily, We will show to the disbelievers what they have done and We shall make them taste a severe torment.⟩

(Qur'an 41: 50)

In this verse, Allah, Most Glorified, informs us that when He blesses the disbelieving or doubtful people with health, well-being, and wealth, after having been afflicted with sickness, poverty, or loss, those people will not be thankful to Allah, their Lord, but instead will boast that it is their right upon Allah to receive those blessing. Then Allah, the Exalted, makes clear that the reason for this is their doubt in the reality of the Day of Judgement and all that it entails, including the Resurrection and the Gathering. In their ignorance and stupidity, they exceed even this, for they believe that should it prove that the hereafter is a reality, they will find great blessings with their Lord despite their ingratitude. Then Allah warns them that they will be shown their deeds and they will be held to account for them on that Day, and they will receive a terrible punishment.

Benefits derived from this verse

1. Good and evil are by Allah's decree.
2. It is an obligation to be thankful for Allah's blessings.
3. This verse confirms the establishment of the Hour.
4. Doubt concerning the truth of the resurrection is disbelief in Islam.
5. Belief in Allah is not sufficient without belief in the resurrection.
6. The verse confirms the reward and punishment on the Day of Judgement.

Relevance to tawheed and the subject of the chapter

This Qur'anic verse proves that attributing blessings to other than Allah is disbelief because to do so is to set up partners with Him in Lordship.

49.2

It is reported that Abu Hurayrah (رضي الله عنه) heard the Messenger of Allah (صلى الله عليه وسلم) say: «Indeed, three men from the people of Israel, a leper, a bald-headed man, and a blind man, were tested by Allah. Allah sent to them an angel, who came (first) to the leper and asked him: What thing would you like most? He replied: A good complexion and good skin and that (the leprosy) which causes the people to be averse to me should depart from me. The angel touched him and his disease was cured, and he was given a fair complexion and good skin. The angel then asked him: What kind of property do you prefer? The man replied: Camels (or: Cows. Is-ḥâq, the narrator is not sure which). So he was given a pregnant female camel (or cow) and the angel said to him: May Allah bless you with it.

Then the angel came to the bald man and asked to him: What is the thing most loved to you? The man replied: Good hair and that (the baldness) which causes the people to be averse to me should depart from me. So the angel touched him and his affliction was gone and he was given fine hair. Then the angel asked him: What kind of property would you like best? He replied: Cows — or Camels. The angel gave him a pregnant cow and said: May Allah bless you with it.

Then the angel went to the blind man and asked him: What thing would you like best of all? He said: I would like that Allah restore my sight to me so that I might see the people. So the angel touched him and Allah restored his sight to him. Then the angel asked him: What kind of property do you most prefer? He replied: Sheep. So the angel gave him a pregnant sheep.

Later, all three of the pregnant animals gave birth to young and multiplied until one of them had a valley full of camels, while another had a valley full of cows, and the third had a valley full of sheep. Then the angel, disguised as a leper, went to the man who had been a leper and said: I am a poor man who has lost all his means while on a journey, and there is none who can satisfy my needs today except Allah and then you. I ask you by the One Who gave you your fair complexion and your fine skin and granted you so much wealth in livestock to give me a camel so that I may reach my destination. The man replied: I have many obligations (so I cannot give you one). The angel said: I think I know you; were you not a leper to whom the people had a strong aversion? Were you not a poor man and then Allah gave you (all of this)? The man replied: (No,) I got this property by way of inheritance. The angel said: If you are lying, may Allah make you as you were before.

Then the angel, in the shape of a bald man, went to the man who had been bald and said to him the same as he had said to the first man, but he too answered as the first one had. The angel said to him: If you are lying, may Allah make you as you were before.

Then the angel, disguised as a blind man, went to the man who had been blind and said: I am a poor man and a traveller whose livelihood has been cut off during the journey. I have no one to help me except Allah and then you. I ask you by Him Who has given you back your sight to give me a sheep that I may, with its help, complete my journey. The man said: Without doubt, I was blind and Allah gave me back my sight, so take what you wish from my property. By Allah! I will not prevent you from taking anything of my property, which you may have for Allah's sake. The angel replied: Keep your property with you. You have (all) been tested and Allah is pleased with you and is angry with your two companions.» (recorded by Bukhari)

The Prophet (ﷺ) informs us in this hadith about the true story of three poor men from the Children of Israel: a leper, a bald man, and a blind man, whose faith Allah wished to test. Allah sent to them an angel who cured them of their afflictions, by His will, and gave them wealth in livestock. Later, the angel came back to them and asked each of them for material help, assuming in each case, the form of the man prior to his cure and reminding each of them of Allah's mercy and Beneficence when he was in need. As for the leper and the bald man, they were ungrateful to Allah and refused, while the blind man acceded gladly to the angel's request. As a result, the former two earned Allah's anger, while the third earned His pleasure and Allah allowed him to retain his wealth.

Benefits derived from this hadith

1. The hadith confirms one of the Prophetic miracles, as Allah granted the Prophet (ﷺ) something of the knowledge of former peoples.

2. Attributing blessings to other than Allah is disbelief and the cause of their loss.

3. Attributing blessings to Allah is to express gratitude to Him, and gratitude causes the blessings to continue.

4. The hadith confirms the human attribute of will and that it is subordinate to the will of Allah.

5. The hadith confirms Allah's divine attribute of pleasure.

6. It also confirms Allah's divine attribute of anger.

Relevance to tawheed and the subject of the chapter

This hadith proves that attributing blessings to other than Allah is an act of disbelief in Allah. It is thus prohibited because it is shirk in Allah's Oneness of Lordship.

Chapter 50

Ascribing the birth of a child to other than Allah

50.1

*A*llah (ﷻ) says:

﴿ ۞ هُوَ ٱلَّذِى خَلَقَكُم مِّن نَّفۡسٍ وَٰحِدَةٍ وَجَعَلَ مِنۡهَا زَوۡجَهَا لِيَسۡكُنَ إِلَيۡهَا ۖ
فَلَمَّا تَغَشَّىٰهَا حَمَلَتۡ حَمۡلًا خَفِيفًا فَمَرَّتۡ بِهِۦ ۖ فَلَمَّآ أَثۡقَلَت دَّعَوَا ٱللَّهَ رَبَّهُمَا لَئِنۡ
ءَاتَيۡتَنَا صَٰلِحًا لَّنَكُونَنَّ مِنَ ٱلشَّٰكِرِينَ ﴿١٨٩﴾ فَلَمَّآ ءَاتَىٰهُمَا صَٰلِحًا جَعَلَا لَهُۥ شُرَكَآءَ
فِيمَآ ءَاتَىٰهُمَا ۚ فَتَعَٰلَى ٱللَّهُ عَمَّا يُشۡرِكُونَ ﴿١٩٠﴾ ﴾   (سورة الأعراف : ١٨٩-١٩٠)

❨It is He Who created you from a single being and made from it its
mate, in order that he might dwell with her. When he united with her
[in intercourse], she bore a light burden [by becoming pregnant] and
she continued to carry it. When she grew heavy, they both prayed to
Allah, their Lord: If You give us a righteous child, good in every
respect, we vow we shall be of the grateful ones. — But when He
gave them a righteous child, they ascribed to others a share in that
which He had given them; but Allah is Exalted, High above the
partners they ascribe to Him.❩   *(Qur'an 7: 189-190)*

Allah, Most Glorified, informs us in these verses that He
created humankind from a single human being, Âdam (ﷺ), and that

He created from him a wife, Hawwâ',[111] in order that they might live together in peace and harmony. He created in them the desire for sexual intercourse and made it permissible to them, in order that they might enjoy complete stability and repose and that their progeny might continue to multiply. When she became pregnant, they both called upon Allah and asked Him to give them a healthy, strong, righteous child. They swore that if He did so, they would be eternally grateful to Him, but when Allah answered their supplications and gave them that which they had requested, they named the child 'Abdul Hârith.[112] Thus, they ascribed others as partners with Allah; and Allah is far above that which they attributed to Him.

Benefits derived from these verses

1. Man is superior to woman, in the sense that he was created before her.
2. Marriage is preferred over bachelorhood.
3. It is an obligation to abstain from naming one's children with detestable names.
4. The verses are evidence of the virtue of motherhood and of what a mother endures during pregnancy and childbirth.
5. Supplication is part of Islam, and the verses confirm its benefits.
6. Ascribing partners to Allah invalidates one's gratitude to Him.
7. It is an obligation to abstain from anthropomorphic concepts and ideas regarding Allah.

Relevance to tawheed and the subject of the chapter

These Qur'anic verses prove that submission to other than Allah by naming one's children as slaves of other than Allah is shirk, as was correctly stated by the Companion Ibn 'Abbâs (رضي الله عنهما).

---

[111] Hawwâ': Eve

[112] 'Abdul Hârith: (literally) slave or worshipper of the cultivator

50.2

On the authority of Ibn 'Abbâs (may Allah be pleased with them both) it is reported that he said: «When Âdam (ﷺ) joined with Ḥawwâ', she became pregnant. Then Iblees[113] came to her and said: I am your companion, who caused you to be expelled from paradise. Obey me, or I will cause your child to grow two horns like a deer by which he will puncture your belly when he comes out! So do it! Do it! Thus he tried to frighten them into naming their child 'Abdul Ḥârith, but they did not obey him and a dead child was born to them. When Ḥawwâ' became pregnant a second time, Iblees again approached them and repeated the same demand but again they refused and the child was born dead. She became pregnant a third time and Iblees came to them and made the same demand, reminding them of what had happened before. At this point, they were overcome by love for their (unborn) child and named him 'Abdul Ḥârith. This is why Allah, the All-Mighty, the All-Powerful said: ❨They ascribed to others a share in that which He had given them.❩ *(Qur'an 7: 190)»* (recorded by Ibn Abi Ḥâtim)

Ibn 'Abbâs (may Allah be pleased with them both) informs us in this narration that when Ḥawwâ' became pregnant by Âdam (ﷺ), Allah wished to test them, and so He allowed Satan to come to them and demand from them that they obey him by naming their child 'Abdul-Ḥârith. Satan kept on repeating this demand with threats to the unborn foetus' life, until eventually they gave in out of fear for their child and acceded to his ultimatum. Then Allah saved the child from death as a trial to them, in order to see whether they attributed its safety to Allah or another.[114]

---

[113] Iblees: the name of Satan, the head of the jinn, the primary devil

[114] Not because Allah did not know what they would do, for He knows all things, but in order that their action should be proof either for or against=

Benefits derived from this narration

1. This narration confirms Satan's enmity towards Âdam (ﷺ) and all humankind.
2. It is an obligation to avoid Satan and his evil whispering.
3. Satan is persistent in seducing humankind.
4. Allah may test righteous people by afflicting them with calamities.
5. Human resolve is weak.
6. Love of one's children is a natural instinct with which Allah has endowed us.
7. It is prohibited to name anyone as slave of other than Allah.

Relevance to tawheed and the subject of the chapter

This narration proves that naming one's child as the slave of other than Allah is an act of shirk.

50.3

Qatâdah (ﷺ) said, "They attributed partners to Allah by obeying other than Him, not by worshiping Iblees." (recorded by Ibn Abi Hâtim)[115]

It is also authentically narrated that Mujâhid said, concerning Allah's words ❨If You give us a righteous child, good in every respect❩: "They were afraid that the child would not be human." (narrated by Ibn Abi Hâtim) The same thing was said by al-Hasan, Sa'eed, and others.

=them on the Day of Judgment.

[115] Ibn Abi Hâtim stated this narration has an authentic chain of narrators, but Ibn Katheer and others stated that this narration was weak.

Mujâhid informs us, concerning the above mentioned Qur'anic verse, that the reason Âdam and his wife called their son 'Abdul Ḥârith was fear that he would be born in a non-human form after Satan had deceived them into believing that he had the power to do as he had threatened — may Allah's curse be upon him.

Chapter 51

Allah's divine names and attributes

51.1

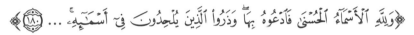Allah (﷿) says:

﴿وَلِلَّهِ ٱلۡأَسۡمَآءُ ٱلۡحُسۡنَىٰ فَٱدۡعُوهُ بِهَا ۖ وَذَرُواْ ٱلَّذِينَ يُلۡحِدُونَ فِيٓ أَسۡمَـٰٓئِهِۦ ... ﴾ (١٨٠)

(سورة الأعرَاف : ١٨٠)

❨The most beautiful names are for Allah, so call on Him by them, and shun those who deny His names...❩ *(Qur'an 7: 180)*

Allah, Most Glorified, informs us in this verse that His names are of the utmost beauty and that He is Most Perfect and Complete in all of His divine attributes. Then He tells us that we should supplicate to Him using these names, in order that our prayers may be answered and that they may be answered quickly. Then He, the Exalted, commands us to avoid those who reject His names or knowingly alter their meanings in order to suit their deviated understanding of tawḥeed. Then He, All-Mighty, All-Powerful, warns us of the justified punishment which awaits those who deny His names and attributes on the Day of Resurrection.

Relevance to tawḥeed and the subject of the chapter

This Qur'anic verse proves that it is forbidden to deny any of Allah's divine names and attributes. Such denial includes bestowing

His names upon His created beings or bestowing the names of His created beings upon Him, for this is shirk in the matter of His names and attributes.

Important notes

1. Mentioning the divine names by which the believer may enter Paradise may be described as being on three levels:

(i) pronouncing the words;

(ii) understanding their meanings; and

(iii) calling upon Allah by them.

2. Some of Allah's names may be pronounced alone, such as *Al-Hakeem* (the Judge). Others may be pronounced together, such as *As-Samee'* (the All-Hearing) and *Al-Baseer* (the All-Seeing), and some only ever be pronounced together, such as *An-Nâfi'* (the Benevolent) and *Ad-Darr* (the Harmer) because Allah's Completeness is not made clear except by this combination. Were one to pronounce Allah's name Ad-Dârr alone, it would not be a word of praise unless Allah's name An-Nâfi' was mentioned along with it.

3. The rule regarding Allah's names and attributes is that we do not ascribe to Him any name or attribute which is not found in the Qur'an or the authentic Hadith of the Prophet (ﷺ). We reject all names and attributes which He and His Messenger (ﷺ) have rejected, and we remain silent concerning matters connected with His names and attributes about which we have no knowledge.

4. It is not permissible to derive names for Allah from the verbs used in the Qur'an to describe Allah's actions. Thus, we may not refer to Him as *Al-Mun'im* (the Provider of Blessings), even though the Qur'an speaks of His *Ni'am* (Blessings), nor is it allowed for us to call Him *As-Sattâr* (the Veiler) even though He has been described as

As-Satteer (derived from the same verb) in an authentic hadith; and whoever does so is in error.

5. Denial of Allah's divine names and attributes is of five types:

(i) Bestowing Allah's names or names derived from them upon idols, as the pagan Quraysh did when they named one of their gods Al-Lât, which is derived from the same root as Allah;

(ii) Ascribing to Allah names which do not befit His Majesty, as the Christians do when they refer to Him as the Father, or as the philosophers do when they refer to Him as the Active Cause, or the Power, and so on;

(iii) Ascribing to Allah attributes which He is far above in His Majesty, such as the Jews' obnoxious claim that He rested on the seventh day (Saturday);

(iv) Changing the meaning of Allah's divine names and attributes and rejecting the true meanings, as did the Jahmites[116] who claimed that Allah is the All-Hearing, but He does not hear and that He is the Living, but He does not live;[117]

(v) Comparing the attributes of Allah with those of His creation, when in truth, we should affirm only that which does not suggest any comparison between Allah and His creation.

51.2

It is reported that Ibn 'Abbâs (may Allah be pleased with them both) said, "Those who belie or deny His names are guilty of shirk." (recorded by Ibn Abi Ḥâtim)

---

[116] the Jahmites: a deviant sect which perverted Islamic beliefs. Although, as a group, they no longer exist, many of their distorted beliefs have been adopted by others.

[117] that Allah's names are just names, without meaning

Relevance to tawḥeed and the subject of the chapter

This narration proves that Ibn 'Abbâs (may Allah be pleased with them both) held that ascribing Allah's names to idols is an act of denial of those names, and it is confirmed that those who do so are guilty of shirk.

51.3

It is reported that Al-A'mash said that they used to ascribe names to Allah which were not His.

Relevance to tawḥeed and the subject of the chapter

This narration is evidence that Al-A'mash was of the view that calling Allah by names which are not His is a denial of the true names of Allah, and it has been confirmed that denial of Allah's names is shirk.

Chapter 52

Saying: 'Peace be upon Allah'

52.1

$\mathcal{I}$t is authentically reported that Ibn Mas'ood (رضي الله عنه) said: «Whenever we prayed behind the Prophet (ﷺ), we used to recite, '*As-Salâm* (Peace) be upon Allah from His slaves and As-Salâm be upon so-and-so and so-and-so', until the Prophet (ﷺ) told us: Do not say, 'As-Salâm be upon Allah,' for verily, He is As-Salâm.» (recorded by Bukhari and Muslim)

Ibn Mas'ood (رضي الله عنه) informs us that when he and the other Companions (may Allah be pleased with them) prayed with the Messenger of Allah (ﷺ), they used to invoke Allah's Peace and Blessings upon Allah and then upon a number of people during the final sitting in the prescribed prayers. The Messenger (ﷺ) forbade them from continuing to do so. He (ﷺ) informed them that As-Salâm is one of Allah's names. Therefore, it is not appropriate that they should invoke Allah's peace and blessings upon Himself, for He is not in need of peace or blessings, rather He is the Owner and Source of all peace and blessings.

Benefits derived from this hadith

1. It is forbidden to invoke peace upon Allah.
2. When Islam forbids a thing, it guides us to that which is better.

3. As-Salâm is one of the names of Allah.

4. It is permissible to supplicate to Allah on behalf of His slaves in prayer.

Relevance to tawheed and the subject of the chapter

This hadith proves that it is forbidden to invoke peace and blessings upon Allah. That is contrary to tawheed, because As-Salâm is a form of supplication on behalf of the weak and those in need, and Allah is neither of these things.

Chapter 53

Saying: 'O Allah, forgive me if You will'

53.1

$\mathscr{I}$t is authentically reported by Abu Hurayrah (رضي الله عنه) that the Messenger of Allah (ﷺ) said: «None of you should say, 'O Allah! Forgive me if You will,' or 'O Allah! Have mercy upon me if You will.' Rather you should always appeal to Allah firmly, for nobody can force Allah to do something against His will.» (recorded by Bukhari) The Messenger of Allah (ﷺ) also said: «One should appeal to Allah with firm determination, for nothing is too much or too great for Allah to give it.» (recorded by Muslim)

Because all of us are wretched and humble before Allah, Most High, and He is Self-Sufficient and Most Praiseworthy, Allah's Messenger (ﷺ) forbade those who supplicate to Allah from adding to their requests the phrase 'if You will'. Saying such suggests a lack of interest on Allah's part in the needs of His slaves. It is not befitting of the true spirit of humility in which the Muslims are supposed to approach their Lord, nor is it fitting to suggest that Allah treats His slaves in such a fickle manner, acceding to some requests, while rejecting others on a whim. Allah, the Exalted, is far above that. In fact, He has informed us that he answers the supplication of everyone who asks Him:

﴿وَإِذَا سَأَلَكَ عِبَادِى عَنِّى فَإِنِّى قَرِيبٌ أُجِيبُ دَعْوَةَ ٱلدَّاعِ إِذَا دَعَانِ ...

(سورة البَقَرَة: ١٨٦) ﴿١٨٦﴾

﴿When My slaves ask you about Me, I am indeed near. I answer the supplication of the suppliant when he asks Me...﴾ *(Qur'an 2: 186)*

Then Allah, Most Glorified, commands us that when we ask Him, we should do so imploringly and beseechingly, whether the request is big or small, since no request is difficult for Him to grant, for He is the Owner of all things in the heavens and the earth, the absolute Disposer of all affairs, and He is Able to do all things.

Benefits derived from this hadith

1. It is prohibited to say, 'If You will,' when supplicating to Allah.
2. Supplication is a part of Islam, and this hadith confirms its effectiveness.
3. The hadith also confirms Allah's completeness and perfection.
4. Imploring Allah firmly, rather than timidly and apologetically, is to think well of Him, Most Glorified, Most High.
5. Allah is free from all imperfection.

Relevance to tawheed and the subject of the chapter

This hadith proves that it is prohibited to use the saying 'if You will' when making supplication to Allah as this suggests some lack or imperfection in Allah, as if He might answer us or not, according to His whim, and such an idea is incompatible with correct tawheed.

Chapter 54

Saying: 'My slave' or 'My lord'

54.1

$\mathcal{I}$t is authentically reported by Abu Hurayrah (ﷺ) that the Messenger of Allah (ﷺ) said: «None of you should say, 'Feed your lord,' or 'Help your lord in performing ablution.' Instead you should say, 'my master' or 'my guardian'. Likewise, none should say, 'my slave' or 'my slave-girl'. Instead you should say, 'my lad' or 'my lass' or 'my boy'.» (recorded by Muslim)

Because Lordship and worship necessitate glorification — and none should be glorified but Allah, All-Mighty All-Powerful — the Messenger of Allah (ﷺ) forbade referring to a slave-owner as 'lord' or to a bonded slave as *'abd* (slave),[118] since this suggests some kind of partnership with Allah, when in fact, we are all Allah's slaves and He is the only Lord. Then, the Prophet (ﷺ) guided us to that which is better and does not connote lordship of the slave-owner or worship on behalf of the slave, and that is to say, 'my lad' or 'my lass' or 'my boy'. This is better and safer for those whom Allah has tested with the responsibility of slave-ownership or the burden of being a slave.

---

[118] While it is true that the word 'abd means slave, it also connotes worship and submission. Thus, it is not permissible to say, for example, "Abdu Aḥmad," meaning the bonded slave of Aḥmad. The word 'abd is only for the slave relationship between human beings and Allah, as Allah refers to His slaves in the Qur'an as *'Ibâdullâh* (the slaves of Allah).

Benefits derived from this hadith

1. It is an obligation to block all roads to shirk.

2. *Ar-Rabb* (the Lord) is one of Allah's names which it is forbidden to ascribe to any other, unless it is linked to something inanimate or inhuman, such as the expressions *rabb al-bayt* (owner of the house) or *rabb ad-dâbbah* (owner of the beast).

3. It is forbidden to call a slave 'abd' or call a slave-girl *'amah'* (a female slave).

4. It is permissible to refer to a slave-owner as the 'master' or 'protector'.

Relevance to tawheed and the subject of the chapter

This hadith prohibits calling the slave 'abd' and the slave-girl 'amah' because this is a form of shirk in matters of worship.

Important notes

1. There are those who have claimed that it is permissible to call the slave-owner *rabb* (lord) and that there is no restriction on this. As proof, they have cited the words of Allah, Most High:

(٤٢ : سورة يُوسُف)   ﴾... ﴿ ... أَذْكُرْنِي عِندَ رَبِّكَ ...﴾

﴾...Mention me to your lord...﴿   *(Qur'an 12: 42)*

They also cite the words of the Messenger of Allah: «...and the amah will give birth to her *rabbah*.» The answer to these claims is that in the Qur'anic verse, the reference is to a time before the mission of Prophet Muhammad (ﷺ), when such terminology had not been forbidden. As for the above-mentioned hadith, what is mentioned here is *rabbah*, which is the feminine form of the word *rabb*, and as such, does not connote lordship. Rather, the word would mean mistress or lady.

2. In this hadith, the Prophet (ﷺ) has permitted reference to a slave-owner as *mawlâ* (protector or guardian), while in another hadith, he (ﷺ) has forbidden it. It may be that the way to understand both of these hadith without inferring any contradiction, is to say that, while it is permissible to do so, it is preferable not to. This would be particularly so in the case of those people who refer to their scholars or sheikhs as *Mawlânâ* (our Protector), for Allah has so described Himself in Qur'an where He tells us to address Him this way:

﴿... أَنتَ مَوْلَىٰنَا فَٱنصُرْنَا عَلَى ٱلْقَوْمِ ٱلْكَٰفِرِينَ ٢٨٦ ﴾   (سورة البَقَرَة: ٢٨٦)

﴿...You are *Mawlânâ* [our Protector] so give us victory over the disbelievers.﴾   *(Qur'an 2: 286)*

Chapter 55

Refusing a person who asks in the name of Allah

55.1

*I*t is reported on the authority of Ibn 'Umar (may Allah be pleased with them both) that Allah's Messenger (ﷺ) said: «If someone asks for something in Allah's name, give it to him; if anyone seeks refuge in Allah's name, give him refuge; if anyone gives you an invitation, accept it; and if anyone does you a kindness, recompense him; but if you have not the wherewithal to do so, pray for him until you feel that you have recompensed him.» (recorded by Abu Dâwood and an-Nasâ'i, both of whom said it was sound)

The Prophet (ﷺ) commands us in this hadith to help whoever asks for assistance in Allah's name in all that does not entail disobedience to Allah and His Messenger (ﷺ) and to protect from evil whoever seeks protection in Allah's name. In addition, Muslims should accept invitations, so long as they do not entail anything forbidden,[119] and respond in kind to those who do favours for us.

---

[119] For example, were one to be invited to a gathering where drinking of alcoholic beverages, playing of music, smoking, or playing of games of chance were taking place, it would not be obligatory to attend; rather, it would be obligatory to decline the invitation.

Then he (ﷺ) said that if we are unable to respond in kind, we should supplicate to Allah on their behalf until we feel that we have repaid them in full. If we do all of these things, the result will be to foster brotherly love, compassion, generosity, and unity within the Muslim community and to put an end to enmity, division, strife, miserliness, and disunity.

Benefits derived from this hadith

1. It is an obligation to give to the one who asks in Allah's name.
2. It is an obligation to defend from evil the one who seeks shelter in Allah's name.
3. It is an obligation to accept a Muslim's invitation to a meal, or a wedding celebration, or a birth celebration, and so on, as long as doing so does not involve anything forbidden.
4. It is an obligation to recompense those who do good to us.

Relevance to tawheed and the subject of the chapter

This hadith proves the obligation to give to whoever asks for something in Allah's name. This proves that it is forbidden to refuse people in need, when they ask in Allah's name, because to do so is to fail to glorify Allah, as is His right upon us, and this conflicts with correct tawheed.

Chapter 56

Saying about what has happened in the past: 'If only...'

56.1

*A*llah (ﷻ) says:

﴿ثُمَّ أَنزَلَ عَلَيْكُم مِّنۢ بَعْدِ ٱلْغَمِّ أَمَنَةً نُّعَاسًا يَغْشَىٰ طَآئِفَةً مِّنكُمْ وَطَآئِفَةٌ قَدْ أَهَمَّتْهُمْ أَنفُسُهُمْ يَظُنُّونَ بِٱللَّهِ غَيْرَ ٱلْحَقِّ ظَنَّ ٱلْجَٰهِلِيَّةِ يَقُولُونَ هَل لَّنَا مِنَ ٱلْأَمْرِ مِن شَىْءٍ قُلْ إِنَّ ٱلْأَمْرَ كُلَّهُۥ لِلَّهِ يُخْفُونَ فِىٓ أَنفُسِهِم مَّا لَا يُبْدُونَ لَكَ يَقُولُونَ لَوْ كَانَ لَنَا مِنَ ٱلْأَمْرِ شَىْءٌ مَّا قُتِلْنَا هَٰهُنَا قُل لَّوْ كُنتُمْ فِى بُيُوتِكُمْ لَبَرَزَ ٱلَّذِينَ كُتِبَ عَلَيْهِمُ ٱلْقَتْلُ إِلَىٰ مَضَاجِعِهِمْ وَلِيَبْتَلِىَ ٱللَّهُ مَا فِى صُدُورِكُمْ وَلِيُمَحِّصَ مَا فِى قُلُوبِكُمْ وَٱللَّهُ عَلِيمٌۢ بِذَاتِ ٱلصُّدُورِ ﴿١٥٤﴾﴾

(سورة آل عِمرَان: ١٥٤)

﴿After distress, He sent down calm on a group of you overcome with slumber, while another group was stirred to anxiety by their own feelings, moved by wrong thoughts about Allah — thoughts which belonged to the Days of Ignorance. They said: Is this matter anything to do with us? Say to them: Verily, the matter is for Allah. — They hide within themselves what they would never reveal to you. They say: If the matter had been left to us, none of us would have been killed here. Say: Even if you had remained in your homes, those for whom death was written would have gone forth to their deaths. —But [all this was] that Allah might test what is in your hearts and purge what is in your hearts, for Allah knows well the secrets of your hearts.》 *(Qur'an 3: 154)*

Allah, Most Glorified, informs us in this verse about the believers upon whom He sent the blessing of slumber after they had been distressed and worried, in order that they might be invigorated and refreshed. Then He tells us that among them were a number of hypocrites, who did not share the believers' faith and whose sole concern was for their own safety. In tones of criticism and rebuke, the hypocrites asked the Prophet (ﷺ) why they should risk their lives in that battle. Allah commanded the Prophet (ﷺ) to inform them that the matter was for Allah to decide, not for him, but that Allah aids whom He wills.

Finally, Allah reveals their hypocrisy. He, the Exalted, says that their faith in His promise and that of His Messenger (ﷺ) was not genuine, for had it been so, they would not have feared to go out and fight. They would have realized that if death is written for someone, the person cannot avoid it, no matter whether in battle or at home. Allah says that all of this was no more than a test of their faith and sincerity and a test to reveal their true natures.

Benefits derived from this verse

1. Good and evil are ordained by Allah, All-Mighty, All-Powerful.
2. Adversity often reveals a person's true nature.
3. Rejection of Allah's divine preordination is a sign of hypocrisy in belief.
4. Taking precautions against any eventuality will not prevent what Allah has decreed from taking place.
5. The verse confirms Allah's divine attribute of possessing a Face.

Relevance to tawḥeed and the subject of the chapter

This Qur'anic verse proves that it is forbidden to reject Allah's decree. One must submit to Allah's divine preordination because that is true tawḥeed.

56.2

Allah, the Exalted, says:

﴿ٱلَّذِينَ قَالُواْ لِإِخْوَٰنِهِمْ وَقَعَدُواْ لَوْ أَطَاعُونَا مَا قُتِلُواْ قُلْ فَٱدْرَءُواْ عَنْ أَنفُسِكُمُ ٱلْمَوْتَ إِن كُنتُمْ صَٰدِقِينَ ۝﴾

(سورة آل عِمرَان: ١٦٨)

❪Those who said about their brethren, while they themselves sat at home: If only they had obeyed us, they would not have been killed. Say: Avert death from your own selves, if you speak the truth!❫

(Qur'an 3: 168)

Allah, Most Glorified, informs us in this verse about what took place in a heated debate between the believers, who had fought valiantly in Allah's cause, and the hypocrites, who had stayed away from the battle and sat at home. The hypocrites belittled the sacrifice made by the believers who had died at the battle of Uḥud due to ignoring the express command of the Prophet (ﷺ) about the positions they were to take on the battlefield. The hypocrites falsely said that if only the believers had followed their example and stayed at home, they would now be alive. Allah, Most High, in response, challenged them: if they spoke the truth, then let them save themselves from death. Certainly, no warning can avert what Allah has ordained.

Benefits derived from this verse

1. Jihad, or struggle in Allah's cause, is a part of Islam.
2. The hypocrites are a danger to the Muslim community.
3. Warnings cannot avert what Allah has preordained.

Relevance to tawḥeed and the subject of the chapter

This Qur'anic proves that it is prohibited to reject Allah's decree. Accepting Allah's divine preordination is an essential part of tawḥeed.

56.3

It is authentically reported by Abu Hurayrah (﷽) that the Messenger of Allah (ﷺ) said: «Seek what benefits you, and seek help only from Allah and do not lose heart. If any adversity comes to you, do not say: 'If I had only acted in such-and-such a way, it would have been such-and-such.' Instead, say: 'Allah has decreed (it) and what He willed, He has done,' for verily, (the word) 'if' opens the way for the work of Satan.» (recorded by Muslim)

Because Islam calls humankind to that which leads to success, prosperity, and the betterment of society, Allah's Messenger (ﷺ) commanded the Muslims to take part in jihad in Allah's cause. Then, in order that they might attain the aforementioned blessings in this life and the hereafter, he ordered them to accept calamities — which are all from Allah's divine preordination — with equanimity, and not to become depressed or open the door to regret or blame by saying things like 'If only I had done such-and-such a thing, I might have avoided this outcome.' Such thoughts and words will only lead to anger and despair, and these are the works of the devil. Instead the Messenger (ﷺ) guided them to that which is better and more worthy, which is to say: 'Allah has decreed (it) and what He willed, He has done.'

Benefits derived from this hadith

1. Undertaking the necessary precautions in order to achieve one's objectives does not conflict with tawḥeed.
2. Human beings have a measure of free will and are not driven helplessly by events.
3. Despair conflicts with seeking help from Allah.
4. It is forbidden to seek help from other than Allah in those matters over which those who are asked have no control.
5. Islam encourages the Muslim to work and be productive.
6. It is prohibited to reject Allah's divine preordination.
7. Good and evil are ordained by Allah.
8. The hadith confirms Allah's divine attribute of will, in a manner befitting His Majesty.
9. It also confirms Allah's divine attribute of action.
10. Belief in Allah's divine preordination is a cure for what ails the heart and leads to mental peace and stability.

Relevance to tawḥeed and the subject of the chapter

This hadith proves the obligation to accept and submit to Allah's divine preordination because this is an essential part of tawḥeed.

Chapter 57

Maligning the wind

57.1

$\mathcal{U}$bayy ibn Ka'b (رضي الله عنه) reported that Allah's Messenger (صلى الله عليه وسلم) said: «Do not malign the wind. If you see that which displeases you, say: O Allah! We ask of You the good of this wind and the good that it is commanded to bring with it; and we seek refuge with You from the evil of this wind and the evil that it is commanded to bring with it.» (recorded by at-Tirmidhi, who said it was sound)

Because Islam has ordered us to be of good character and good manners, the Messenger of Allah (صلى الله عليه وسلم) forbade Muslims from maligning or cursing the wind. This is because the wind is one of Allah's creations. It does not blow or remain still or harm or benefit except by Allah's Command; therefore, vilifying it amounts to vilifying Him Who sent it. Then Allah's Messenger (صلى الله عليه وسلم) informs us that the wind may bear good or ill and it is incumbent upon the believers to ask Allah, the Exalted, for the good and to seek protection with Him from the evil.

Benefits derived from this hadith

1. It is prohibited to malign the wind.
2. It is virtuous to use the above-mentioned supplication when one

sees anything disliked brought by the wind.

3. Supplication is part of Islam and benefits the believers.

Relevance to tawḥeed and the subject of the chapter

This hadith proves that it is forbidden to curse or vilify the wind because doing so amounts to maligning Him Who sent it, and this conflicts with correct tawḥeed.

Chapter 58

Having wrong thoughts about Allah

58.1

$\mathcal{A}$llah (ﷻ) says:

﴿ ... يَظُنُّونَ بِٱللَّهِ غَيْرَ ٱلْحَقِّ ظَنَّ ٱلْجَٰهِلِيَّةِ يَقُولُونَ هَل لَّنَا مِنَ ٱلْأَمْرِ مِن شَىْءٍ قُلْ إِنَّ ٱلْأَمْرَ كُلَّهُ لِلَّهِ يُخْفُونَ فِىٓ أَنفُسِهِم مَّا لَا يُبْدُونَ لَكَ يَقُولُونَ لَوْ كَانَ لَنَا مِنَ ٱلْأَمْرِ شَىْءٌ مَّا قُتِلْنَا هَٰهُنَا قُل لَّوْ كُنتُمْ فِى بُيُوتِكُمْ لَبَرَزَ ٱلَّذِينَ كُتِبَ عَلَيْهِمُ ٱلْقَتْلُ إِلَىٰ مَضَاجِعِهِمْ وَلِيَبْتَلِىَ ٱللَّهُ مَا فِى صُدُورِكُمْ وَلِيُمَحِّصَ مَا فِى قُلُوبِكُمْ وَٱللَّهُ عَلِيمٌۢ بِذَاتِ ٱلصُّدُورِ ﴿١٥٤﴾ ﴾ (سورة آل عِمرَان: ١٥٤)

﴿...[They were] moved by wrong thoughts about Allah — thoughts which belonged to the Days of Ignorance. They said: Is the matter anything to do with us? Say to them: Verily, the matter is for Allah. —They hide within themselves what they would never reveal to you. They say: If the matter had been left with us, none of us would have been killed here. Say: Even if you had remained in your homes, those for whom death was written would have gone forth to their deaths. —But [all this was] that Allah might test what is in your hearts and purge what is in your hearts, for Allah knows well the secrets of your hearts.﴾ *(Qur'an 3: 154)*[120]

---

[120] See 56.1 for the explanation of this verse.

Relevance to tawḥeed and the subject of the chapter

This Qur'anic verse proves that it is forbidden to think ill of Allah. Rather, it is an obligation to think well of Allah, for this is an essential aspect of tawḥeed.

58.2

Allah (ﷻ) says:

﴿وَيُعَذِّبَ ٱلْمُنَٰفِقِينَ وَٱلْمُنَٰفِقَٰتِ وَٱلْمُشْرِكِينَ وَٱلْمُشْرِكَٰتِ ٱلظَّآنِّينَ بِٱللَّهِ ظَنَّ ٱلسَّوْءِ عَلَيْهِمْ دَآئِرَةُ ٱلسَّوْءِ وَغَضِبَ ٱللَّهُ عَلَيْهِمْ وَلَعَنَهُمْ وَأَعَدَّ لَهُمْ جَهَنَّمَ وَسَآءَتْ مَصِيرًا ۝﴾ (سورة الفَتْح: ٦)

﴿And that He may punish the hypocrites, men and women, and the polytheists, men and women, who think evil of Allah. On them is a round of evil. The wrath of Allah is on them. He has cursed them and prepared for them hellfire, and an evil destination it is.﴾ *(Qur'an 48: 6)*

In this verse, Allah, Most Glorified, informs us that the disbelievers from among the hypocrites and the polytheists hold false beliefs concerning Allah. They also wish for the believers defeat and destruction, but Allah will defeat their nefarious plotting. Allah promises them two punishments: one in this world, when their hearts will be crushed at the ultimate success of the Muslims over the disbelievers, and another in the hereafter, when Allah's mighty wrath will overtake them. They will receive no mercy from Him and they will be plunged into hellfire to dwell therein for eternity.

Benefits derived from this verse

1. The hypocrites are the greatest danger to the Muslim Ummah.

2. It is forbidden to think ill of Allah.

3. The Qur'an customarily mentions males before females.

4. Thinking ill of Allah is a sign of hypocrisy.

5. The verse confirms Allah's divine attribute of anger, in a manner befitting His Majesty.

6. In general, it is permissible to curse the disbelievers.

7. The verse confirms the existence of hellfire.

Relevance to tawḥeed and the subject of the chapter

This Qur'anic verse proves that it is forbidden to think ill of Allah. Instead, it is an obligation to think well of Allah because this is an essential aspect of tawḥeed.

Important note

Ibn al-Qayyim said, concerning the first verse:

> The explanation of this thought (of the unbelievers) is that they believed that Allah would not help His Messenger (ﷺ) and that his affair (the religion of Islam) would be forgotten. It is also explained as meaning that the afflictions which befell him (ﷺ) were not from Allah's divine preordination and His wisdom. It is therefore explained as a denial of Allah's divine preordination and wisdom and denial that the matter (or Message) of His Messenger (ﷺ) would be completed and that it would prevail over all religions. These were the evil thoughts of the hypocrites and the polytheists as mentioned in the Qur'an, and they are only that: evil thoughts.
>
> Any person who believes that falsehood will continuously prevail over truth (which is Islamic Monotheism) and will cause truth to disappear, or who denies that things occur in accordance with Allah's decree and His decision, or denies the overriding wisdom

behind His divine preordination, which is deserving of all praise, and thinks that things are due to an aimless, purposeless will — these are the thoughts of those who disbelieve — then, woe to those who disbelieve in hellfire. Most of them think ill of Allah when it concerns that which affects them in particular and what He does to others. No one is saved from such evil thoughts except those who truly know Allah and His divine names and attributes and understand the necessity of His wisdom and the necessity of praising Him.

Let the wise recipients of good counsel look at themselves closely in this matter and repent to Allah and ask His forgiveness for having thought ill of their Lord. If you were to examine such individuals, you would see each of them in distress and anger with what Allah has decreed. They blame and find fault in it and think that it should have been otherwise. In this, some are guiltier than others. Examine yourself. Are you free from such thoughts? If you are saved from it, you have been saved from a great calamity, but if you are not, I cannot regard you as saved.

Chapter 59

Denying Allah's divine preordination

59.1

$\mathcal{I}$bn 'Umar (may Allah be pleased with them both) said, "By Him in Whose Hand is the soul of Ibn 'Umar, if anyone possessed gold as much as the mountain of Uḥud and spent it in Allah's cause, Allah would not accept it from him unless he believed in Allah's divine preordination." Then he (ﷺ) cited as evidence the words of the Prophet (ﷺ): «Faith is to believe in Allah, His angels, His revealed Books, IIis Messengers, the Day of Resurrection, and divine preordination, both the good and bad of it.» (recorded by Bukhari and Muslim)

In this narration, 'Abdullâh ibn 'Umar (may Allah be pleased with them both) swears by Allah, that no matter how much wealth people may spend in Allah's cause, no matter how many righteous deeds they may perform, it will benefit them nothing, and Allah will not accept it from them, if they do not believe in Allah's divine preordination. This is because belief in it is one of the six pillars of faith, as expounded by the Messenger of Allah in a well known authentic hadith, known as the hadith of Jibreel (ﷺ), in which the angel Jibreel visited the Prophet (ﷺ) in human form, in front of a number of the Companions and questioned him about Islam, in order to teach the Muslims their faith. Ibn 'Umar (may Allah be pleased with them both) cited this hadith as proof for what he had said concerning the obligation of belief in Allah's divine preordination.

Benefits derived from this narration

1. Faith consists of six pillars, without all of which faith is invalid.
2. Good and evil are by Allah's decree (*qadr*) and His decision (*qadhâ'*).
3. It is permissible to swearing to something which is beneficial to the community.
4. It is a virtue to confirm the truth of important juristic rulings by swearing to them.

Relevance to tawheed and the subject of the chapter

That narration proves that those who reject Allah's decree are disbelievers because denial of divine preordination is a form of shirk in Allah's Oneness of Lordship.

Important notes

1. Divine preordination consists of four levels:

   (i) Allah's knowledge of events before they take place;

   (ii) His having written them before the creation of all things;

   (iii) His will, which none in creation can evade or resist, nor can they evade His deeds;

   (iv) His creation of all things, by Himself with no partners — and everything that exists besides Him is created.

2. The Prophet (ﷺ) said, in the above-mentioned hadith, that faith is to believe in His divine preordination, both the good and the bad of it, while in another hadith, he (ﷺ) said: «...and evil is not from You.» There is no contradiction here, for what is meant by the latter hadith

is that, while Allah created evil and ordained it, He does not do evil. It may be said that when Allah ordains evil for a person, it is only evil from the point of view of that person, for it is an affliction sent to the person because of some sins the person has committed. However, in Allah's sight, it is not an evil, for it represents Allah's wisdom, justice, and knowledge.

59.2

It is reported on the authority of 'Ubâdah ibn aṣ-Ṣâmit (رضي الله عنه) that he said to his son:

> Son, you will never taste true faith until you know that whatever afflicts you would not have missed you, and whatever has missed you would never have come to you. I heard the Messenger of Allah say: «The first thing Allah created was the pen. He commanded it to write. It said: My Lord, what shall I write? He said: Write down what has been ordained for all things until the establishment of the Hour.» Oh, my son! I heard Allah's Messenger (ﷺ) say: «Whoever dies believing something other than this does not belong to me.» (recorded by Abu Dâwood with a sound chain)

In another narration by Imam Aḥmad, it was reported: «Verily, the first thing which Allah created was the pen, and He said to it: Write. In that very hour all what was to occur (was written) up to the Day of Resurrection.» In another version from Ibn Wahb, Allah's Messenger (ﷺ) said: «Whoever disbelieves in divine preordination, the good and the bad of it, will be burnt in hellfire.» (recorded also by at-Tirmidhi, who graded it 'authentic, but odd')

In this hadith, 'Ubâdah ibn aṣ-Ṣâmit (رضي الله عنه) advised his son that faith has a taste and that none shall savour it except one who believes in Allah's decision and His decree, the good and the bad of it. As proof, he cited the hadith of the Prophet (ﷺ) in which he informed us that Allah commanded the pen to write the destiny of all things up to the Day of Resurrection. The Prophet (ﷺ) said that whoever dies without believing in Allah's decision and His decree would be outside the fold of Islam and the person's eternal abode would be hellfire, where he or she would burn forever — a wretched end.

Benefits derived from this hadith

1. A father should advise and teach his children.
2. The Companions (may Allah be pleased with them) had a precise understanding of matters pertaining to Allah's divine preordination, and they had faith in it.
3. The first of all created things was the pen.
4. The hadith confirms Allah's divine attribute of speech, in a manner befitting His Majesty.
5. Whoever rejects Allah's divine preordination is a disbeliever.
6. It is the last acts in a person's life which are important.
7. The hadith confirms Allah's promise of punishment for those who deny His decree.

Relevance to tawḥeed and the subject of the chapter

This hadith proves that whoever rejects Allah's divine preordination is a disbeliever because this constitutes shirk in the Oneness of Lordship.

Important note

Which was created first, the Throne or the Pen? Some have said that it was the Throne and others that it was the Pen. Those who said it was the Pen cited as proof the above-quoted hadith, understanding the word 'Pen' to be the object of the verb 'created,' while those who said that the Throne was created first cited as evidence a number of authentic hadiths which support this view. The latter group would therefore understand the first hadith to say: "Verily, directly after creating the pen, Allah commanded it to write..."

59.3

It is reported that Ibn ad-Daylami said: "I went to Ubayy ibn Ka'b and said to him: There is some doubt within me concerning divine preordination. Please tell me of something by which Allah might take the doubt from my heart. He said that Allah's Messenger (ﷺ) said: «Even were you to spend gold equivalent in weight to the mountain of Uḥud, Allah would not accept it from you until you believe in divine preordination. Know that what has afflicted you could not be avoided and what did not come to you could never be attained; and if you die believing other than this, then you are one of the inhabitants of hellfire.» I then went to 'Abdullâh ibn Mas'ood, Ḥudhayfah ibn al-Yamân, Zayd ibn Thâbit (may Allah be pleased with them), and all of them told me something similar from the Prophet (ﷺ)." (recorded by Aḥmad and Abu Dâwood)[121]

Ibn ad-Daylami informs us in this narration that he was afflicted by doubts concerning Allah's divine preordination. So he went to Ubayy ibn Ka'b (ﷺ) to seek counsel and guidance from him, in the hope that he might teach him something which would assuage his doubts. Ubayy (ﷺ) then narrated to him a hadith of the Prophet (ﷺ) which explained in simple terms what belief in Allah's divine preordination entails: whatever was written for us will happen, whatever was not written will never happen, and whoever disbelieves

---

[121] Aḥmad, *Musnad*; Abu Dâwood, *Sunan*; and al-Ḥâkim, who authenticated it.

in divine preordination is a disbeliever in Allah, a disbeliever who will never taste the fruits of success, even if the person were to perform innumerable good deeds. Then, in order to assure himself that he understood, Ibn ad-Daylami went to a number of other Companions and asked them the same question, only to receive a similar answer from all of them.

Benefits derived from this narration

1. It is an obligation to seek guidance from knowledgeable people in matters of which one is ignorant.
2. The Companions had broad knowledge and understanding of Islamic beliefs and Islamic jurisprudence.
3. Those who deny Allah's divine preordination are disbelievers.
4. The most important deeds are those performed before a person dies.

Relevance to tawḥeed and the subject of the chapter

This narration proves that those who deny divine preordination are guilty of disbelief because this denial constitutes shirk in the Oneness of Lordship.

Chapter 60

Making pictures of living things

60.1

*O*n the authority of Abu Hurayrah (رضي الله عنه) it is reported that the Messenger of Allah (ﷺ) said: «Allah, the Exalted, said: And who is more unjust than those who try to create the likeness of My creation? Let them create an atom, or let them create a grain of wheat, or let them create a grain of barley.» (recorded by Bukhari and Muslim)

Allah, Most Glorified, informs us in this hadith qudsi, through the speech of His Prophet, Muhammad (ﷺ), that there is no one more unjust than those people who make images of living things, wishing to resemble Allah in His act of Creation. Then He, All-Mighty, All-Powerful challenges such people to create even the smallest and most insignificant of His visible, living creations, which is an atom, or to create the simplest of plant materials, such as a grain of wheat or a grain of barley. This He, the Exalted, does in order to expose their weakness and inability.

Benefits derived from this hadith

1. It is forbidden to make drawings, paintings, or carvings of any living things.
2. Those who make depictions of living things lack proper regard and respect for Allah.

3. Power is Allah's, and He alone has the ability to create what He wills.

4. All other than Allah are weak and incapable of creating even the simplest of things from nothing.

Relevance to tawḥeed and the subject of the chapter

This hadith qudsi proves that depicting living things is forbidden. Making pictures of living things is an attempt to imitate Allah in His act of Creation, which is shirk in Lordship.

60.2

On the authority of 'Â'ishah (ﷺ) it is reported that the Messenger of Allah (ﷺ) said: «The most severely punished of people on the Day of Resurrection will be those who try to make the like of Allah's creation.» (recorded by Bukhari and Muslim)

The Prophet (ﷺ) informs us in this hadith that those who depict living creatures in their drawings, paintings, and carvings, and attempt to imitate Allah in His act of Creation will face the most severe chastisement on the Day of Judgement. They are the worst of people in respect to Allah and the wickedest in committing evil. This is why they are most deserving of Allah's wrath and His punishment.

Benefits derived from this hadith

1. Making pictures of living creatures is strictly forbidden.

2. The hadith is evidence of the reason for the prohibition of depicting living things.

3. Punishment on the Day of Resurrection is in proportion to one's sins.

Relevance to tawheed and the subject of the chapter

This hadith proves that it is forbidden to make pictures of living things. To depict living creatures is an attempt to imitate Allah in His act of Creation, and this is shirk in His Oneness of Lordship.

Important note

People who make images of living creatures will receive the severest punishment on the Day of Judgment if they did so in order to have that image worshipped, because in so doing, they are guilty of disbelief, while if they only intend by their images to imitate Allah, they are also guilty of disbelief.

60.3

It is reported that Ibn 'Abbâs (may Allah be pleased with them both) heard the Messenger of Allah (ﷺ) say: «Every image maker is in the Fire. A soul will be placed in every image made by him, and it will punish him in hellfire.» (recorded by Bukhari and Muslim)

Because the image makers are the wickedest of people in respect to Allah, and the worst of them in performing deeds which Allah has forbidden, the Prophet (ﷺ) informed us in this hadith that on the Day of Resurrection Allah will breathe life into those images of living creatures and those images will punish the people who made them. This punishment in hellfire is the recompense for their evil deeds. Therefore, it behoves every picture maker to fear Allah, the All-Mighty, the All-Powerful and to abandon this evil employment. If they do that, Allah will reward them, for whoever abandons something for Allah's sake will be rewarded with something better by Him, Most High.

Benefits derived from this hadith

1. It is forbidden to make pictures of living creatures.
2. It is permissible to make pictures of things which do not possess a soul.
3. Reward is in accordance with one's deeds.
4. The remuneration which image makers receive for their work is *harâm* (forbidden) because when an action is prohibited, so too is profiting from it.

Relevance to tawḥeed and the subject of the chapter

This hadith proves that it is forbidden to make images of living creatures because doing so constitutes an attempt to imitate Allah in His action of Creation, and this is shirk in Lordship.

60.4

It is reported on the authority of Ibn 'Abbâs (may Allah be pleased with them both) that Allah's Messenger (ﷺ) taught: «Whoever makes images in this life will be charged with breathing life into them, and they will not be able to do so.» (recorded by Bukhari and Muslim)

The Prophet (ﷺ) informs us in this hadith that those who make images of creatures possessing a soul in this life will be ordered on the Day of Judgement to breathe life into them. Allah knows that they will not be able to do so, but He will command them to do it, in order to make clear to them their own powerlessness and weakness and to reproach them for their sin.

Benefits derived from this hadith

1. It is forbidden to make depictions of living creatures.
2. It is permissible to make images of things without a soul.
3. Reward is in accordance with one's deeds.

Relevance to tawḥeed and the subject of the chapter

This hadith proves that it is forbidden to make images of living creatures because doing so is an attempt to imitate Allah in His action of Creation, and this is shirk in Allah's Oneness of Lordship.

60.5

On the authority of Abul Hayâj al-Asadi, it is reported that 'Ali (رضي الله عنه) said to him, "Shall I not send you on a mission on which I was sent by Allah's Messenger (ﷺ)? Do not leave any image without erasing it, nor any elevated grave without levelling it to the ground." (recorded by Muslim)

Because Islam is careful to block all roads to shirk, whether apparent or hidden, 'Ali ibn Abi Ṭâlib (رضي الله عنه) informs us that the Messenger of Allah (ﷺ) charged him with the task of effacing the pictures of living things which he might find and with levelling those graves which had edifices or grave stones over them. This he did in order to protect the Muslims' beliefs from the evils of worship of graven images and adoration of graves, because making pictures of living creatures and building over graves leads to their glorification and reverence and to attributing to them that which they do not deserve — that which is for Allah alone. Anyone who has travelled throughout the Muslim world will have found these forbidden things in profusion — things which make one with correct beliefs shudder and sadden the believer's heart: circumambulation of graves in the manner in which the pilgrims go around the Ka'bah in Makkah, animals sacrificed to the graves' inhabitants instead of their being slaughtered in Allah's name, supplication to the inhabitants of the graves, and many other acts of shirk and innovation unknown to the Messenger of Allah (ﷺ), his Companions (may Allah be pleased with them), or the pious generations who came after them.

Benefits derived from this narration

1. It is an obligation to reject that which is detestable.
2. Making images of living creatures is forbidden.
3. Building over graves is forbidden.

Relevance to tawḥeed and the subject of the chapter

This narration proves that making images of living things is prohibited because doing so amounts to attempting to imitate Allah in His action of Creation, and this is shirk in Lordship.

Important note

This forbiddance of making images includes all living creatures which possess a soul. It is pure fancy to imagine that by putting a line across the neck of the image, or obliterating its features, it becomes permissible.graves leads to their glorification and reverence and attributing to them that which they do not deserve — that which is for Allah, Alone; and anyone who has travelled throughout the Muslim world will have found such things in profusion — things which make one with correct beliefs shudder and sadden his heart: Circumambulation of graves in the manner in which the pilgrims circumambulate the Ka'bah, in Makkah, animals sacrificed to the graves' inhabitants instead of their being slaughtered in Allah's Name, supplication of the graves' inhabitants and many other acts of *shirk* and innovation unknown to the Messenger of

Allah (ﷺ), his Companions or the pious generations who came afer them.

Benefits derived from this narration

1. It is an obligation to reject that which is detestable.
2. Making images of living creatures is forbidden.
3. Building over graves is forbidden.

Relevance to tawheed and the subject of the chapter

This narration proves that making images of living things is prohibited because doing so amounts to attempting to imitate Allah in His action of Creation, and this is shirk in Lordship.

Important note

This forbiddance of making images includes all living creatures which possess a soul. It is pure fancy to imagine that by putting a line across the neck of the image, or obliterating its features, it becomes permissible.

Chapter 61

Frequent swearing

61.1

*A*llah (ﷻ) says:

﴿لَا يُؤَاخِذُكُمُ ٱللَّهُ بِٱللَّغْوِ فِىٓ أَيْمَٰنِكُمْ وَلَٰكِن يُؤَاخِذُكُم بِمَا عَقَّدتُّمُ ٱلْأَيْمَٰنَ فَكَفَّٰرَتُهُۥٓ إِطْعَامُ عَشَرَةِ مَسَٰكِينَ مِنْ أَوْسَطِ مَا تُطْعِمُونَ أَهْلِيكُمْ أَوْ كِسْوَتُهُمْ أَوْ تَحْرِيرُ رَقَبَةٍ فَمَن لَّمْ يَجِدْ فَصِيَامُ ثَلَٰثَةِ أَيَّامٍ ذَٰلِكَ كَفَّٰرَةُ أَيْمَٰنِكُمْ إِذَا حَلَفْتُمْ وَٱحْفَظُوٓاْ أَيْمَٰنَكُمْ كَذَٰلِكَ يُبَيِّنُ ٱللَّهُ لَكُمْ ءَايَٰتِهِۦ لَعَلَّكُمْ تَشْكُرُونَ ﴿٨٩﴾﴾

(سورة المائدة ٨٩ : ٥)

﴿Allah will not call you to account for what is futile in your oaths, but He will call you to account for your deliberate oaths. For expiation feed ten indigent persons what would be average food for your families, or clothe them, or give a slave his freedom. And whoever did not find [the means for that, let him] fast for three days. That is the expiation for the oaths you have sworn, but keep to your oaths. Thus does Allah make clear to you His signs, that you may be grateful.﴾ *(Qur'an 5: 89)*

Allah, Most Glorified informs us in this verse that He will not hold accountable those who make careless oaths, only those who swear knowingly and deliberately. He also tells us that the atonement for one who breaks an oath or swears falsely is to feed ten poor people, without extravagance and without niggardliness, or to clothe them, or to free a believing slave. Whoever does not find means to be able to do any of these things, must fast for three consecutive days. Allah has made this expiation as a solution for us, should we fall into error by making a false oath. Then Allah, the Exalted, commands us Muslims to keep to our oaths and not to make oaths excessively, in order that we might not swear falsely and be thus disgraced before our Lord.

Allah informs us that what He has made plain of His judgements is a blessing from Him, All-Mighty, All-Powerful, for which we should be grateful. Thus Islam, by Allah's Grace and Mercy, makes things easy for us and provides a way out for us from the problems which we sometimes make for ourselves. Allah also called us and encouraged us to free slaves more than fourteen centuries ago, long before the West awoke from its ignorance and claimed the initiative for the abolition of slavery for themselves.

Benefits derived from this verse

1. The verse is evidence of the tolerance and forbearance of Islam.
2. There is no sin and no expiation for unmindful oaths.
3. It is forbidden to deliberately make vain, false oaths.
4. It is an obligation to make expiation for swearing a false oath.
5. Islam had taken the initiative in the abolition of slavery before any other nation.
6. It is forbidden to swear excessively.
7. It is an obligation to preserve one's oaths free from lies.

Relevance to tawheed and the subject of the chapter

This Qur'anic verse proves that excessive swearing is prohibited because doing so diminishes the glorification which is Allah's right and is an imperfection in one's practice of tawheed.

61.2

It is reported on the authority of Abu Hurayrah (ﷺ) that he heard Allah's Messenger (ﷺ) say: «Swearing may benefit (the sale of) commodities, but it will erase the reward (in the hereafter).» (recorded by Bukhari and Muslim)

The Prophet (ﷺ) informs us in this hadith that when sellers swear falsely as to the worth of their goods, they may attain some temporary benefit from it, but in the long term, they will not gain by it. They will lose the reward of it in the hereafter, and loss will come to them from other directions. They might lose their capital or their profits might dwindle to nothing, for Allah does not allow people to profit from disobedience to Him, although He may delay their recompense. Finally, in the end, there awaits the disobedient ones loss-and punishment in the hereafter.

Benefits derived from this hadith

1. It is forbidden to swear excessively.
2. It is forbidden to sell goods by means of swearing.
3. Lying in order to achieve a sale will result in loss in the hereafter.

Relevance to tawḥeed and the subject of the chapter

This hadith proves the forbiddance of excessive swearing without adequate reason because doing so diminishes the glorification which is Allah's right and is an imperfection in one's practice of tawḥeed.

61.3

On the authority of Salmân (ﷺ), it is reported that the Messenger of Allah (ﷺ) said: «There are three types of people to whom Allah will not speak, neither will he bless them, and for them is a severe torment. They are the old white-haired adulterer, the arrogant beggar, and the one who makes Allah as his merchandise since he does not purchase except by swearing (by Allah) and he does not sell except by swearing (by Allah).» (recorded by aṭ-Ṭabarâni with a sound chain of narration)

The Prophet (ﷺ) informs us in this hadith that there are three categories of people to whom Allah will not speak on the Day of Resurrection, nor will He cleanse them of their sins or give them forgiveness. This is because they committed sins without any excuse or justification. The first of these three is the fornicator and adulterer who continues to sin in spite of his advanced years, consequent lessening of sexual urge, and his knowledge that the end of his life is near. The second is the person who behaves arrogantly towards people, though he possesses none of the wealth, rank, or privilege which often leads people to behave this way. The third is one who treats Allah's name with impropriety, frequently swearing by Him, without cause or valid excuse.[122]

Benefits derived from this hadith

1. This hadith confirms Allah's divine attribute of speech, in a manner befitting His Majesty.
2. The hadith is evidence that Allah will not speak to the disobedient ones.
3. Adultery, pride, and the excessive swearing of oaths are all prohibited.

Relevance to tawḥeed and the subject of the chapter

This hadith proves the forbiddance of excessive swearing without reason because doing so is demeaning to Allah, the

---

[122] This is the case with many Arabic-speaking Muslims today. The expression '*Wallâhi* (By Allah)' is used in almost every sentence by some.

Most Glorious, the All-Powerful, and this conflicts with correct tawheed.

61.4

It is authentically reported that 'Imrân ibn Ḥusayn (رضي الله عنه) said: «Allah's Messenger (ﷺ) said: The best of my Ummah is my generation, then those who follow them, then those who follow them.» 'Imrân (رضي الله عنه) added: "I do not know if he mentioned two generations after his, or three." «Then after you, continued the Prophet (ﷺ), there will come a generation who will testify without being called upon to do so, and they will be treacherous and untrustworthy. They will swear oaths, but they will not fulfil them, and obesity will be seen among them.» (recorded by Muslim)

The Messenger of Allah (ﷺ) informs us in this hadith that the best of this community of Muslims are his Companions (may Allah be pleased with them) and the two or three generations who succeeded them, due to their adherence to Islam and their correct beliefs and practices and their freedom from hypocrisy, deviation, and innovation. After them, the good will decrease in this Ummah and evil will increase with each succeeding generation until there will be seen people who will belittle the importance of giving testimony so that they will offer it even before it is requested from them. They will also betray those who place trust in them. When they swear oaths, they will not keep them. They will become so immersed in the life of this world that obesity will become common among them, due to their excessive eating of rich foods and avoidance of physical work or exercise.

Benefits derived from this hadith

1. The hadith establishes the virtue of the first three or four generations of Muslims over their descendants.

2. Treachery is forbidden.

3. It is an obligation to keep one's oaths.

4. It is prohibited to become obsessed with the life of this world and its pleasures at the expense of the hereafter.

Relevance to tawḥeed and the subject of the chapter

This hadith proves that it is forbidden to break or not honour one's oaths because to do so is to demean Allah, in Whose name the oath was taken, and this is in conflict with correct tawḥeed.

Important note

There is no contradiction between this hadith and the words of the Prophet (ﷺ): «The best of witnesses is the one who comes forward with his testimony before he is asked about it.» This latter hadith means that it is preferable for people to present their testimony without being asked in cases where there is a danger that a person may lose rights due to any delay on the witnesses' part. However, in cases where the evidence is known to the person concerned, a witness should not present testimony before being asked.

61.5

On the authority of Ibn Mas'ood (ﷺ) it is reported that Allah's Messenger (ﷺ) said: «The best of people are those of my generation, then those who follow them, then those who follow them, after which, there will come a people whose testimonies will precede their oaths and whose oaths will precede their testimonies.» (recorded by Bukhari and Muslim)

In this hadith, the Prophet (ﷺ) informs us that the best and most virtuous people of this Ummah are the Companions (may Allah be pleased with them), then the first two generations after them, and after them the doors of evil will be opened. Much of what he (ﷺ) told us has already come to pass: apostasy, atheism, materialism, and the following of baseless philosophies have become common, and religious matters and giving testimony are taken lightly by many. People rush hastily into swearing oaths and bearing witness before they are requested to do so, as if these matters are of little importance.

Benefits derived from this hadith

1. The hadith is evidence of the superiority of the first generations of Muslims after the Prophet (ﷺ) over the generations which came later.
2. It is one of the miracles of the Prophet that he predicted events which have since transpired.
3. It is forbidden to hasten to give testimony before one is asked to do so.
4. It is prohibited to swear without cause or necessity.

Relevance to tawḥeed and the subject of the chapter

This hadith proves the forbiddance of hastily swearing oaths because this demeans Allah and belittles His Majesty, and this is in conflict with correct tawḥeed.

61.6

Ibrâheem an-Nakhâ'i said, "When we were children, they used to beat us concerning oaths and testimonies."

Relevance to tawḥeed and the subject of the chapter

This narration shows that some of the salaf used to forbid their children from hastily making oaths and giving testimony, so as to protect them from falling into sin.

Chapter 62

Allah's covenant and the covenant of His Prophet (ﷺ)

62.1

$\mathcal{A}$llah (ﷻ) says:

﴿وَأَوْفُوا بِعَهْدِ اللَّهِ إِذَا عَاهَدتُّمْ وَلَا تَنقُضُوا الْأَيْمَانَ بَعْدَ تَوْكِيدِهَا وَقَدْ جَعَلْتُمُ اللَّهَ عَلَيْكُمْ كَفِيلًا إِنَّ اللَّهَ يَعْلَمُ مَا تَفْعَلُونَ ۩ ﴾(سورة النحل: ٩١)

‹Fulfil the covenant of Allah when you have entered into it, and do not break your oaths after you have confirmed them. Indeed you have made Allah your surety, for Allah knows all that you do.›

(Qur'an 16: 91)

In this verse, Allah, the Exalted, the Almighty commands Muslims to keep their promises because breaking promises is despicable and contrary to the spirit of Islam. Then Allah reinforces this by especially forbidding us from breaking those promises which we have already confirmed. He informs us that those who make promises have made Him their guarantor. He is well acquainted with all that they do, and He will reward good with its like and evil with its like.

Benefits derived from this verse

1. It is an obligation to keep one's promises.
2. It is forbidden to break promises without reason or excuse.
3. Allah's knowledge is all-encompassing.

Relevance to tawḥeed and the subject of the chapter

This Qur'anic verse proves the obligation to keep one's promises. It is forbidden to break one's promises because breaking promises indicates a lack of respect for Allah, and this invalidates correct tawḥeed.

Important note

There is no contradiction between this verse and the words of the Prophet (ﷺ): «Whoever swore an oath, then saw something better than it, he should do that which is better and make expiation for not fulfilling his oath.» (recorded by Muslim) The above verse is a general commandment, while the hadith provides an exception to it when there is the possibility of doing something better than it. However, it is incumbent upon the believer in this case to perform an act of atonement for breaking his or her promise.

62.2

It is reported that Buraydah (ﷺ) said: «Whenever Allah's Messenger charged someone with leadership in the army or sent someone on an expedition, he would admonish him to fear Allah and be good to the Muslims who were with him. He (ﷺ) would say: Fight in the name of Allah and in Allah's cause and fight those who disbelieve in Allah. Do not take excessive booty, do not break treaties, do not mutilate (the enemies' dead), and do not kill children.

When you meet your enemies from among the polytheists, call them to three virtues. If they respond (in a positive manner), respond to them in like fashion and accept it from them and cease making war upon them. Invite them to Islam. If they respond positively, accept it from them and ask them to leave their land and emigrate to the land of the *Muhâjiroon*.[123] Inform them that after migrating, they will be entitled to everything to which the Muhâjiroon are entitled, and they will be under the same obligations as the Muhâjiroon. If they refuse to emigrate, then tell them that they will have the same status as the Bedouin Muslims, subject to the commands of Allah, like other Muslims, but they will not receive any share of the booty or returns of war unless they fight jihad with the Muslims. If they refuse to embrace Islam, then impose the jizyah upon them. If they agree to this, then accept it from them and cease fighting them, but if they refuse, then seek Allah's help and fight them. When you besiege a people in their fort, and they beseech you for protection in the name of Allah and His Prophet, do not grant them the covenant of Allah and His Prophet, but grant them your covenant and that of your companions, for it is a lesser sin if the covenant of you and your companions is broken than if the covenant of Allah and His Prophet is broken. When you besiege a fort and they request you to let them out in accordance with Allah's command, do not let them out in accordance with His command, but do so at your own command, for you know not whether you will be able to carry out Allah's command with regard to them.» (recorded by Muslim)

Buraydah (رضي الله عنه) informs us in this hadith that whenever the Prophet (ﷺ) entrusted anyone with the command of an army or sent anyone in charge of a punitive expedition against the disbelievers, he would order him to adhere to a number of guidelines:

---

[123] *The Muhâjiroon*: The Emigrants; Muslims who fled with the Prophet (ﷺ) from the persecution of Makkah to the sanctuary of Madinah.

1. The leader should be pious and God-fearing in the treatment of his troops and treat them well

2. The army must refrain from excesses, such as taking too much war booty, breaking treaties, mutilating the enemies' dead, and killing non-combatants.

3. The leader must call the enemy to Islam before making war on them. If they accept Islam, he must make peace with them and request them to migrate from the land of disbelief to the city of Madinah, where they will enjoy all the rights and obligations of the other immigrants there. They are under no obligation to migrate, but should they not do so, they will be treated like the nomadic desert Arabs who have embraced Islam. They will receive no share of the spoils of war, unless they join the Muslims in battle.

4. In the event of their refusing to accept Islam, the leader must have them pay the jizyah.

5. Should they refuse to pay the jizyah, the leader must seek Allah's Help and declare war on them.

6. Should the troops besiege the enemy in their fort, they should not grant them the pledge of Allah and that of His Prophet (ﷺ). Instead, they should grant them their own pledge because if their pledge is broken, it will be a lesser sin than if Allah and His Prophet's pledge were broken. Likewise, the leader should not allow them safe passage from the fort by Allah's command, but by his own command and that of his troops.

Benefits derived from this hadith

1. It is part of Islam to choose a good commander and to guide the commander towards correct behaviour.

2. It is forbidden to seize excessive war booty, break treaties, mutilate the war dead, and kill non-combatants, especially children.

3. It is an obligation to call the enemy to Islam before declaring war on them, if the call to Islam has not previously reached them; and it is preferable to do so, if they have been called to Islam previously, but refused the call.

4. If the disbelievers refuse the Muslim commander's call to Islam, he must order them to pay the jizyah or else fight them.[124]

5. It is preferable to emigrate from the land of disbelief to the land of Islam and to call other Muslims to do the same.

6. The spoils of war are only for the Muslims who are fighting jihad and not for the nomadic Arabs, unless they participate in jihad.

7. It is not permissible to grant a covenant in Allah's name or that of His Prophet (ﷺ).

8. It is forbidden to break treaties.

9. Not everyone who resorts to *ijtihâd*[125] reaches the correct conclusion; the one who does so is the person who has sufficient knowledge of Islamic jurisprudence, understanding of the meanings of the Qur'an and Hadith and related Islamic subjects, and uses that knowledge in accordance with the commands of Allah and His Prophet (ﷺ) and with the rules of the science of jurisprudence.[126]

Relevance to tawheed and the subject of the chapter

This hadith proves that it is an obligation to take care of covenants and pledges made in the name of Allah or the name of His Prophet (ﷺ) and protect them from being broken because to betray

---

[124] see section 5.3

[125] *ijtihâd*: Islamic juristic reasoning — resorted to by qualified Muslim scholars in matters where there is no clear ruling from the Qur'an and Sunnah.

[126] It is said that Imam Shâfi'ee was the first Muslim scholar to write down these fundamental rules of Islamic jurisprudence.

Allah's covenant is to demean Him, the Exalted, and this conflicts with pure Islamic tawheed.

Important note

It is obligatory for those who embrace Islam in a land of disbelievers and are unable to declare their faith, due to fear of the consequences, to emigrate to a Muslim land if they are able to do so. It is also preferred for those who are not in fear to do so.

Chapter 63

Swearing by Allah

63.1

*J*t is reported on the authority of Jundub (ﷺ) that Allah's Messenger (ﷺ) said: «A man said: By Allah! Allah will not forgive such-and-such a person. At this statement, Allah, All-Mighty, All-Powerful said: Who is he who swears about Me that I would not forgive so-and-so? I have pardoned him and wiped out your (the swearer's) deeds.» (recorded by Muslim)

According to another narration on the authority of Abu Hurayrah (ﷺ), it is reported that the man who said this was a believing slave. Abu Hurayrah said, "He spoke one word which destroyed his life in this world and in the hereafter."

The Prophet (ﷺ) informs us in this hadith that there were two people, a righteous person and a sinful person. The former condemned the latter and swore that Allah would never forgive that person's sins. Allah became angry at this statement which suggests that anyone may be barred from Allah's mercy and forgiveness and declared that, on the contrary, He had already forgiven the sinner. Allah, the Exalted, further added that He had invalidated the deeds of the righteous man. Thus, due to an injudicious word, the righteous man's deeds were made to count for nothing, while the sinner was forgiven.

Benefits derived from this hadith

1. It is forbidden to swear on Allah's behalf.
2. It is prohibited to make assumptions about Allah.
3. The hadith confirms Allah's divine attribute of speech, in a manner befitting His Majesty.
4. It is an obligation to be cautious when speaking of Allah.
5. Allah's bounty and mercy are vast.
6. The most important deeds are the last ones in a person's life.
7. A person might be forgiven for his or her sins because of the words or actions of another.
8. A person's deeds might be invalidated because of an injudicious word.
9. It is forbidden to bar anyone from Allah's bounty and mercy.

Relevance to tawheed and the subject of the chapter

This hadith proves that it is forbidden to swear on Allah's behalf because to do so is to claim for oneself rights in Lordship which belong solely to Allah.

Important note

There is no contradiction between this hadith and the words of the Prophet (ﷺ): «Verily, among Allah's slaves are those who, when they swear upon Allah, He fulfils it.» (recorded by Bukhari) The first hadith tells us that swearing on Allah's behalf in what entails thinking ill of Him is forbidden and invalidates one's good deeds, while the latter hadith tells us that swearing to something good and beneficial which entails thinking well of Allah is permissible.

Chapter 64

Asking Allah to be an intercessor for His creation

64.1

*I*t is reported that Jubayr ibn Muṭʻim (ﷺ) said: «A Bedouin Arab came to the Prophet (ﷺ) and said: Oh, Messenger of Allah! The people are enfeebled, families are starving, and wealth has perished; so ask your Lord to send us some rain and we will seek Allah's intercession upon you and yours upon Allah. The Prophet (ﷺ) said: Glory be to Allah! Glory be to Allah![127] He continued to do so until the effect of it was apparent in the faces of his Companions (may Allah be pleased with them). Then he (ﷺ) said: Woe to you! Do you not know Who Allah is? Allah's transcendence is far above than that! There is no intercession of Allah upon anyone.» (recorded by Abu Dâwood)[128]

Jubayr ibn Muṭʻim (ﷺ) informs us in this hadith that a Bedouin man came to the Prophet (ﷺ) and complained to him of the deprivation, hunger, and financial loss which they were suffering due to a prolonged drought. He requested from the Prophet (ﷺ) that he

---

[127] Glory be to Allah!: an expression which also means that Allah is Exalted far above any of His creation, free of any imperfection, and without any need.
[128] adh-Dhahabi commented that this hadith was 'very odd indeed'

pray to Allah to lift this affliction from them and send rain, but the method used by this Bedouin man constituted a great wrong upon Allah and His Messenger (ﷺ) — may Allah forgive him — for he sought Allah's intercession upon the Prophet (ﷺ) and that of the Prophet (ﷺ) upon Allah! When the Messenger of Allah (ﷺ) heard this, he became extremely angry and rejected the Bedouin's words. He (ﷺ) began to praise Allah repeatedly, proclaiming His Exaltedness and rebuking the Bedouin. The Prophet (ﷺ) informed him that Allah is Greater than to be called as an intercessor for any of His creation because He possesses all of them and they are under His complete authority. Allah is not asked about what He does, but they will be asked about what they do.

Benefits derived from this hadith

1. It is permissible to seek supplication from the living.
2. It is forbidden to pray for rain from other than Allah.
3. Supplicating to Allah is part of Islam, and the hadith confirms its effectiveness.
4. The hadith is proof of the harmfulness of ignorance.
5. It is an obligation to reject that which is detestable.
6. It is an obligation to proclaim Allah's Exaltedness above all that is not befitting to His Majesty.
7. It is forbidden to seek intercession from Allah with any of His creation.

Relevance to tawḥeed and the subject of the chapter

This hadith proves that it is forbidden to seek Allah's intercession with any of His creation because to do so is to belittle His Majesty and His Greatness, and this is in conflict with correct tawḥeed.

Chapter 65

Safeguarding tawḥeed and blocking all paths to shirk

65.1

$\mathscr{I}$t is reported that 'Abdullâh ibn ash-Shikh-kheer (رضي الله عنه) said: «I went with a delegation of Banu 'Âmir to the Messenger of Allah (ﷺ) and we said (to him): You are our *Sayyid*.[129] He (ﷺ) replied: The Sayyid is Allah, Most Glorified, Most High. We said: And you are the most excellent and superior of us. He (ﷺ) answered: Say what you have to say, or part of what you have to say, and do not let Satan make you get carried away.» (recorded by Abu Dâwood)[130]

The narrator (رضي الله عنه) informs us in this hadith that some of the Companions (may Allah be pleased with them) wished to show their love and respect for the Messenger of Allah (ﷺ) by praising him while in his presence. Though they spoke the truth about him, the Prophet (ﷺ) wished to cleanse their hearts and souls and protect their beliefs from shirk. So, he forbade them from praising him excessively, especially in his presence, in order to protect them from all paths by which the devil might lead them back to the darkness of shirk after they had escaped from it by embracing Islam. Then he (ﷺ)

---

[129] *Sayyid*: Master

[130] with a good chain of narrators

permitted them to praise him in a manner allowed by their religion, befitting his position as Allah's Slave and Messenger.

Benefits derived from this hadith

1. The Prophet had great influence over the hearts and minds of the Companions (may Allah be pleased with them).
2. It is permissible to refer to Allah as *As-Sayyid* (the Master).
3. Excess is an invitation to Satan.

Relevance to tawḥeed and the subject of the chapter

This hadith forbids excessive praise of the Prophet (ﷺ) or anyone else because this is a path that leads to shirk.

Important note

There is no contradiction between this hadith and the hadith which says: «I am the Sayyid of the sons of Âdam.» The latter hadith indicates the permissibility of referring to other than Allah as 'Master', while the former hadith tells us that it is preferred not to do so.

65.2

On the authority of Anas (ﷺ) it is reported: «Some people said: O Messenger of Allah! O the best of us and the son of the best of us! Our Master and the son of our Master! He (ﷺ) replied: You people! Say what you have to say and do not allow yourselves to be seduced by Satan. I am Muhammad, the slave of Allah and His Messenger. I do not like you to raise me above the status assigned to me by Allah, All-Mighty, All-Powerful.» (recorded by an-Nasâ'i with a reliable chain of narrators)

'Anas (ﷺ) informs us in this hadith that a number of people addressed the Prophet (ﷺ) in terms of excessive praise and eulogy and that the Prophet (ﷺ) rejected this, informing them that such was a temptation of the devil, that he might lead them by this means into shirk. Then he informed them of the correct manner of addressing him, which is to say 'Muhammad, the slave and Messenger of Allah', and he told them that he disliked being elevated above the position which Allah had designated for him.

Benefits derived from this hadith

1. The Companions (may Allah be pleased with them) held the Prophet (ﷺ) in high esteem.
2. It is forbidden to excessively praise someone, and the hadith is evidence that excessive praise is one of the works of Satan.
3. The status of the Prophet (ﷺ) is that he is a slave of Allah and His Messenger.
4. It is prohibited to raise the Prophet (ﷺ) above his designated status.

Relevance to tawḥeed and the subject of the chapter

This hadith proves that it is forbidden to elevate the Prophet above his assigned status because this constitutes excess and it leads to shirk.

Chapter 66

Making an unjust estimate of Allah

66.1

*A*llah (ﷻ) says:

﴿وَمَا قَدَرُوا۟ ٱللَّهَ حَقَّ قَدْرِهِۦ وَٱلْأَرْضُ جَمِيعًا قَبْضَتُهُۥ يَوْمَ ٱلْقِيَـٰمَةِ وَٱلسَّمَـٰوَٰتُ مَطْوِيَّـٰتُۢ بِيَمِينِهِۦ سُبْحَـٰنَهُۥ وَتَعَـٰلَىٰ عَمَّا يُشْرِكُونَ ٦٧﴾

(سورة الزُّمَر: ٦٧)

﴿No just estimate have they made of Allah, such as is due to Him. On the Day of Resurrection, the whole earth will be in His grasp and the heavens will be rolled up in His right Hand. Glory to Him! High is He above the partners they attribute to Him.﴾ *(Qur'an 39: 67)*

Allah, Most Glorified, informs us in this verse that the polytheists do not glorify Allah as is His right because they worship others beside Him, when He is the Owner of everything and Able to do all things. He will hold the whole world and the heavens and the earth in His right Hand on the Day of Resurrection, and He is Exalted far above that which they attribute to Him.

Benefits derived from this verse

1. Those who worship others beside Allah do not glorify Him as is His right upon them.

2. It is an obligation to glorify Allah and to abstain from attributing to Him that which does not befit His Majesty.

3. The verse confirms that Allah possesses Hands, in a manner befitting His Majesty.

Relevance to tawheed and the subject of the chapter

This Qur'anic verse proves the obligation to glorify Allah as is His due right, which means affirming His Oneness and abstaining from shirk.

66.2

It is reported that Ibn Mas'ood (رضي الله عنه) said: «A rabbi came to Allah's Messenger (ﷺ) and he said: O Muhammad! We are told that Allah will put all the heavens on one Finger, and the earths on one Finger, and the trees on one Finger, and the water and the dust on one Finger, and all the other created beings on one Finger. Then He will say: I am the King. Thereupon, the Prophet (ﷺ) laughed until his molar teeth were visible, and this was a confirmation of the rabbi's words. Then the Prophet (ﷺ) recited: ﴿No just estimate have they made of Allah such as is due to Him. On the Day of Resurrection, the whole of the earth will be in His grasp.﴾» (recorded by Bukhari) In another narration by Muslim, it is stated: «...and the mountains and the trees on one Finger, then He will shake them saying: I am the King, I am Allah.» In a narration of Bukhari, it states: «Allah will put the heavens on one Finger and the rest of creation on one Finger.»

Ibn Mas'ood (رضي الله عنه) informs us in this hadith that a Jewish rabbi came to the Prophet (ﷺ) and told him that the Jews find in their scriptures that on the Day of Judgement, Allah will place the heavens on one Finger, the earths on one Finger, the trees on one Finger, the water on one Finger, and the dust on one Finger. In another narration, it says that He will place the water on one Finger and all of the rest of creation on another Finger. Thus, Allah reveals something of His might and power and His complete control over all affairs and His sole right to be worshipped.

Benefits derived from this hadith

1. There is some agreement between the Scripture of the Jews and Islam in that they both confirm that Allah has Fingers, though they are unlike our fingers and exactly how they are is unknown to us.
2. The hadith is evidence of Allah's might and His ability to do all things.
3. Laughter for a specific reason is not bad manners.
4. It is an obligation to accept the truth, whatever its source.
5. The hadith confirms two of Allah's divine names:

   (i) Allah, which constitutes proof of Allah's sole right to be worshipped and

   (ii) *Al-Malik* (the King), which proves His divine attribute of ownership.

6. The hadith confirms Allah's divine attribute of speech, in a manner befitting His Majesty.

Relevance to tawḥeed and the subject of the chapter

This hadith proves the obligation to glorify Allah through tawḥeed, and this is not done except by abstaining from every kind of shirk.

66.3

It is narrated on the authority of Ibn 'Umar (may Allah be pleased with them both) that Allah's Messenger taught: «Allah will fold up the heavens on the Day of Resurrection and then He will take them in His right Hand and say: I am the King, where are the tyrants? Where are the arrogant ones? Then He will fold up the seven earths and take them in His left Hand and say: I am the King, where are the tyrants? Where are the arrogant ones?» (recorded by Muslim in marfoo' form)

Ibn 'Umar (may Allah be pleased with them both) informs us that he heard from the Prophet (ﷺ) that on the Day of judgement, Allah, Most Glorified, will fold up the seven heavens and take them in His right Hand and He will fold up the seven earths and take them in His left Hand. As He folds each of them, He will call out to the tyrants and the arrogant people, making them realise their insignificance by His Words: 'I am the King.' He makes it clear to them that He is the true Owner of all things. He is perfect in every respect and there is no weakness or defect in Him. All those who claim kingship or sovereignty are in fact weak and feeble, powerless in His grasp. He will not be asked about what He does, but they will be asked.

Benefits derived from this hadith

1. The hadith confirms that Allah possesses two Hands, both right and left.
2. The hadith confirms Allah's divine attribute of speech, in a manner befitting His Majesty.
3. The hadith confirms Allah's name: *Al-Malik* (the King), from which is inferred His ownership of all things.
4. There are seven earths.
5. Tyranny and arrogance are forbidden.
6. Allah is perfect and infallible.

Relevance to tawḥeed and the subject of the chapter

This hadith proves the obligation to glorify Allah, All-Mighty, All-Powerful, by declaring tawḥeed and practising it in all one's affairs and abstaining from all manner of shirk.

66.4

It is reported that Ibn 'Abbâs (may Allah be pleased with them both) said: "The seven heavens and the seven earths are no more in Allah's Hand than a mustard seed in the hand of one of you." (Ibn Taymiyah authenticated it)

Ibn 'Abbâs (may Allah be pleased with them both) informs us in this narration that the seven heavens and the seven earths — in spite of their enormity — are in comparison to Allah's Hand as insignificant as a mustard seed in a human hand. This is a comparison between the heavens and the earths and a mustard seed, not a comparison between Allah's Hand and the hand of humans because nothing resembles Allah, either in His attributes or in His Self.

Benefits derived from this narration

1. The heavens are seven.
2. The earths are seven.
3. Ibn 'Abbâs confirms that Allah possesses a Hand.

Relevance to tawḥeed and the subject of the chapter

This narration proves the overwhelming Might and Power of Allah and the insignificance of His creation. Thus, it is an obligation to glorify Allah alone, without any partners, by professing His Oneness in word and deed.

66.5

Ibn Jareer said: «Yoonus told me that Ibn Wahb informed him that Ibn Zayd said that his father told him that Allah's Messenger said (ﷺ): The seven heavens are no more in comparison to the Kursi than seven dirhams set in a shield.» Abu Dharr (ﷺ) said: «I heard Allah's Messenger (ﷺ) say: The Kursi is no more in comparison to the 'Arsh than an iron ring thrown in a vast desert.» (recorded by Ibn Jareer in his *Tafseer*)[131]

The Prophet (ﷺ) informs us in both of the above narrations that Allah possesses a Kursi (Footstool) and an 'Arsh (Throne) and that they are both immense, though the 'Arsh is greater than the Kursi. The comparison of the seven heavens to the Kursi is that of seven dirham coins set in a shield, while the comparison of the Kursi to the 'Arsh is as that of a ring thrown in a vast desert. It has been reported in another hadith on the authority of Ibn 'Abbâs (may Allah be pleased with them both) that the Kursi is the resting place of the Feet of the Most Beneficent and that none can estimate its vastness but He, Most Glorified, Most High.

Benefits derived from these two hadiths

1. The hadiths confirm the existence of Allah's 'Arsh and His Kursi and that they are both His creations.
2. Making comparisons is a valid way of teaching in Islam.
3. The hadiths are evidence of Allah's greatness and glory.

Relevance to tawheed and the subject of the chapter

These hadiths both prove the obligation of glorifying Allah by professing His Oneness and abstaining from all manner of shirk.

---

[131] authenticated by Ibn Ḥibbân, al-Ḥâkim and Ibn Ḥajar

66.6

It is reported that Ibn Mas'ood (ﷺ) said, "Between the lowest heaven and the next is the distance of five hundred years, and between each of the seven heavens is the distance of five hundred years. The distance between the seventh heaven and the Kursi is also five hundred years and between the Kursi and the water is also five hundred years. The 'Arsh is above the water, and Allah is above the 'Arsh, and nothing is hidden from Allah of your deeds." (a sound narration recorded by Ibn Khuzaymah)

Benefits derived from this narration

1. There is a distance between each of the heavens, between the seventh heaven and the Kursi, between the Kursi and the water, and between the water and the 'Arsh, each equivalent to five hundred years' travel.
2. The narration confirms the existence of the Kursi, the water, and the 'Arsh, which is above them.
3. The narration confirms Allah's divine attribute of being above His creation.
4. Allah's knowledge encompasses all things.
5. The narration is evidence of Allah's might and majesty.

66.7

It is reported on the authority of Al-'Abbâs ibn 'Abdil Muttalib (ﷺ): «Allah's Messenger (ﷺ) said: Do you know what is the distance between the heaven and the earth? We said: Allah and His Messenger know best. He (ﷺ) said: The distance between them is five hundred years, and the distance between one heaven and the next is five hundred years, and the dimension of each heaven would take five hundred years to travel. There is a sea between the seventh heaven and the 'Arsh which has between its lowest and highest ends the distance equivalent to that between the heavens and the earth. Allah, the Exalted, is above that and nothing is withheld from Him of the deeds of the sons of Âdam.» (a weak hadith recorded by Abu Dâwood and others)

Allah's Messenger (ﷺ) informs us in this hadith that the distance between each of the seven heavens, and between the earth and the lowest heaven, and between the seventh heaven and the 'Arsh is equivalent to five hundred years' travel. The breadth of each heaven is likewise five hundred years. Finally, Allah is above His 'Arsh, and nothing of His creation is hidden from Him.

Benefits derived from this hadith

1. The hadith is proof of the distances between the heavens and the earth, between each heaven, and between the seventh heaven and the 'Arsh.
2. The seven heavens are separate from each other.
3. The heavens are masses with a defined breadth.
4. The hadith is evidence of the position of the water.
5. The hadith is evidence of the existence of the 'Arsh.
6. The hadith confirms Allah's divine attribute of being above His creation.
7. Allah's knowledge is all-encompassing.

Relevance to tawḥeed and the subject of the chapter

This hadith proves the obligation to glorify Allah by professing and practising tawḥeed and abstaining from all manner of shirk.

Conclusion

﴿قُلْ إِنَّ صَلَاتِي وَنُسُكِي وَمَحْيَايَ وَمَمَاتِي لِلَّهِ رَبِّ الْعَالَمِينَ ۝ لَا شَرِيكَ لَهُ ۚ
وَبِذَلِكَ أُمِرْتُ وَأَنَا أَوَّلُ الْمُسْلِمِينَ ۝﴾ (سورة الأنعام: ١٦٢–١٦٣)

❨Say: Verily, my prayer, my sacrifice, my living, and my dying are
for Allah, the Lord of the worlds. He has no partner. And of this I
have been commanded, and I am the first of those who submit [to
Him].❩ *(Qur'an 6: 162-163)*

O Allah! We seek Your refuge from knowingly associating
others with You, and we seek Your forgiveness from associating
others with You unknowingly.

Glossary of Islamic terms*

abu (or abi)	أبو، أبي	father (of)
aḥâd	آحاد	a category of hadith describing narrations that are related by one or two narrators who in turn related it from one or two narrators until the chain ends at the Prophet (ﷺ), or a narration that is related by a group of narrators who constitute a number that is still fewer than the minimum requirement for the mutawâtir narration
ahl as-Sunnah wal-jamâ'ah	أهل السنّة والجماعة	'people of the Sunnah and the community'
'ajwah	عجوة	a specific variety of dates that come from Madinah
alḥamdulillâh	الحمد لله	all praise is for Allah
Allâhu akbar	الله أكبر	Allah is the Greatest
âmeen	آمين	O Allah, accept our invocation; amen
Anṣâr	أنصار	'helpers': the Muslim citizens of

---

* The Arabic words are transliterated according to the conventions of the Transliteration Chart found in this book. If a word has become part of the English language (i.e., is found in a dictionary of Standard English), that spelling is used in this book and appears first in this Glossary, with the transliterated form in brackets after it.

		Madinah who gave refuge to the Prophet (ﷺ) and the other Muslim emigrants from Makkah
'aqeedah (pl. 'aqâ'id)	عقيدة	belief system that is based upon a firm conviction in all the fundamentals of faith and of the oneness of Allah; firm creed that one's heart is fixed upon without any wavering or doubt, and that excludes any supposition, doubt or suspicion
'aṣr	عصر	mid-afternoon; the obligatory prayer at that time
as-salâmu 'alaykum	السلام	a greeting, which means 'peace'
astaghfir Allâh	أستغفر الله	I seek Allah's forgiveness
bid'ah	بدعة	innovation, *esp.* undesired innovation in matters of religion
bismillâh	بسم الله	in the name of Allah
ḍa'eef	ضعيف	a grade of hadith: weak
Dajjâl	الدّجّال	Antichrist (anti-Christ)
da'wah	دعوة	disseminating the teachings of Islam and calling people to accept and embrace Islam
dhikr Allâh	ذكر الله	remembrance of Allah; specifically, remembering Allah through praising and supplicating to Him
dhimmi	ذمّي	protected or covenanted people; non-Muslims who must pay the jizyah in lieu of zakât

dinar (deenâr)	دينار	originally, a gold coin; a unit of currency
dirham	درهم	a silver coin; a unit of currency
du'â'	دعاء	supplication; invocation
eemân	إيمان	faith; belief in all the six pillars of the creed of Islam
Eid ('eed)	عيد	*lit.* festival; the two celebrations: one at the end of Ramadan and the other at the culmination of the Hajj
fajr	الفجر	dawn; the obligatory prayer at that time
fiqh	فقه	Islamic jurisprudence; understanding or interpreting Islamic law
fitnah	فتنة	*lit.* trial, temptation; (attempting to sow) discord between Muslims
fiṭrah	فطرة	the natural inclination (of humans) instilled by Allah
ghareeb	غريب	*lit.* 'strange' or 'unusual': a category of hadith in which at some points in its chain there is only one narrator
ghayb	الغيب	*lit.* 'unseen'; a term used to denote phenomena or aspects that cannot be known using ordinary human faculties
ghusl	غسل	ritual shower necessary after a major impurity, e.g., after sexual intercourse or at the end of the menstrual period

Hadith (ḥadeeth)	حديث	the collected statements and actions of Prophet Muhammad (ﷺ) that with the Qur'an form the basis of Islamic law
hadith (ḥadeeth)	حديث	a statement or action of Prophet Muhammad (ﷺ) that was remembered and recorded by his Companions and followers
hadith qudsi	حديث قدسي	'sacred hadith': a hadith communicated to Prophet Muhammad (ﷺ) by Allah, but that is not part of the Qur'an
Hajj (ḥajj)	حج	the major pilgrimage to the Sacred Mosque, site of the Ka'bah at Makkah, to be undertaken by every able Muslim once in his/her lifetime
halal (ḥalâl)	حلال	permitted according to Islamic law
ḥaneef	حنيف	one who believes as Prophet Ibrâheem believed, i.e., a monotheist, although s/he may not yet have heard of or accepted Islam
ḥarâm	حرام	forbidden according to Islamic law
ḥasan	حسن	a grade of hadith: acceptable or reliable
ḥasan ghareeb	حسن غريب	a category of hadith that is sound, although at some points in its chain there is only one narrator
Hijrah	هجرة	migration: *esp.* the migration from Makkah to Madinah by Prophet Muhammad (ﷺ) and his

Companions that marks the start of the Islamic calendar

Ḥikmah	حكمة	*lit.* wisdom; it also refers to the Sunnah of Prophet Muhammad
'ibâdât (sg. *'ibâdah)*	عبادات	acts of worship
Iblees	إبليس	another name for Satan in Arabic
iḥrâm	إحرام	the state of consecration for Hajj or 'umrah; the special clothing worn by the pilgrim in such a state
iḥsân	إحسان	goodness, perfection, excellence; to worship Allah as if you see Him, but even if you do not see Him you know that He sees you
ijmâ'	إجماع	consensus: a method of deriving rulings in jurisprudence
ijtihâd	إجتهاد	to use one's knowledge of the Qur'an and the Sunnah to derive rulings on matters not specifically mentioned in either source of Islamic law
inshâ' Allah	إنشاء الله	God willing
isnâd	إسناد	the chain of narration through which a hadith can be traced back to the Prophet
isrâ' and *mi'râj*	الإسراء والمعراج	the night journey of the Prophet (ﷺ) from Makkah to Jerusalem and then up to visit heaven
istighfâr	إستغفار	seeking forgiveness from Allah
istiḥsân	إستحسان	a form of analogy in jurisprudence

istishâb	إستسحاب	in jurisprudence, a proof which involves a presumption of continuity
jâhiliyah	جاهلية	*lit.* 'ignorance'; the age of spiritual darkness before Islam
jayyid	جيد	a grade of hadith: good
Jibreel	جبريل	the Arabic name for Gabriel (ﷺ), the archangel who transmitted the verses of the Qur'an and other communication from Allah to Prophet Muhammad (ﷺ)
jihad (jihâd)	جهاد	struggle or striving (in Allah's cause)
jinn *(plural of jinni)*	جن	non-human, rational beings created by Allah from fire, often referred to as 'demons' or 'devils'; They have free will like humans: some are Muslims, others disbelievers; some are obedient to Allah, others disobedient. Satan is a jinni. Some people try to 'foretell' the future by contacting a jinni. Some disobedient jinn mislead people into thinking that they can tell them what will happen in the future, near or far, or that the jinn can provide people with riches or some sort of power.
jizyah	جزية	a tax levied on the people of the Scriptures when they are under the protection of a Muslim government; it is in lieu of the alms tax paid by Muslims

jumuʿah	جمعة	Friday; *also*, the midday congregational prayer of that day
juzʾ (pl. ajzâ')	جزء	a section of the Qurʾan equal to one thirtieth of the text
Kaaba (Kaʿbah)	الكعبة	the House of Allah in Makkah, originally built by Prophets Ibrâheem and Ismâʿeel, and which Muslims face wherever they pray
khabâ'ith	خبائث	evil deeds
khabr	خبر	*lit.* news, report: a narration of any kind
khaleefah (pl. khulafâ')	خليفة	caliph; head of the Islamic state
khaleel	خليل	a very close friend
Al-Khulafâ' ar-Râshidoon	الخلفاء الراشدون	the four 'Rightly-guided Caliphs' who governed after the death of the Prophet (ﷺ)
khuṭbah		sermon or speech; specifically, the sermon given during the Friday congregational prayer
kufr	الكفر	disbelief in Allah and/or what He has revealed
lâ ilâha illâ Allâh	لا إله إلى الله	there is none worthy of worship other than Allah
al-Lawḥ al-Maḥfoodh	اللَّوح المحفوظ	the Preserved Tablet in Heaven on which Allah's words and decrees are written
Laylat al-Qadr	ليلة القدر	the 'Night of Destiny' or 'Night of Power' in which the Qurʾan was first revealed, and in commemoration of

which Muslims are supposed to spend some nights of the month of Ramadan in prayer and supplication, seeking Allah's forgiveness

madh-hab	مذهب	school of juristic thought
maḥram	محرم	a degree of consanguinity precluding marriage; a man whom a woman may never marry due to the close blood or marriage relationship. e.g., father, brother, son, uncle, and father-in-law
marfoo'	مرفوع	*lit.* 'elevated': a category of hadith that is traceable up to the Prophet (ﷺ) where the Companion narrates, 'The Messenger of Allah (ﷺ) said...'
ma'roof	المعروف	lit. act(s) of kindness; in Islamic discourse it refers to all that Islam ordains
Marwah	المروة	one of the two hills between which pilgrims must hurry back and forth during the rites of the Hajj and the 'umrah
al-Masjid al-Aqṣâ	المسجد الأقصى	the 'Farthest Mosque', mentioned in the Qur'an (17: 1)
al-Masjid al-Ḥarâm	المسجد الحرام	the Sacred Mosque in Makkah where the Kaaba is situated
matrook	متروك	*lit.* 'abandoned': a term used by Hadith scholars to describe someone considered to be an unreliable narrator

mawqoof	موقوف	*lit.* 'restricted': a category of hadith that is actually not concerning a saying or action of the Prophet (ﷺ), but rather concerns sayings or actions of the Companions
mu'aḍḍal	معضّل	a category of hadith: a narration whose chain is missing two narrators or more
mu'allal	معلّل	a category of hadith: a narration that is apparently sound, but contains a hidden defect/weakness
mu'allaq	معلّق	a category of hadith: a narration whose chain is not connected to the Prophet
muḍṭarib	مضطرب	a category of hadith in which the different narrations of the same hadith differ, either in the text or the chain, without the possibility of preferring one narration to the others, simply because they are all equal in their authenticity and in the fact that they are related by trustworthy narrators
Muhâjiroon (or Muhâjireen)	مهاجرون	*lit.* emigrants (of any kind); in Islamic discourse this term is used to refer to people who emigrate to safeguard their religion, and specifically, the Muslims who migrated with Prophet Muhammad (ﷺ) from Makkah to Madinah

mujâhid　مجاهد　one who strives in the way of Allah;
(pl. *mujâhideen*)　a fighter in jihad

mujtahid　مجتهد　a person qualified to exercise ijtihâd
(pl. *mujtahideen*)

mujtahidoon　مجتهدين　Scholars who use their knowledge of
the Qur'an and the Sunnah to derive
rulings on matters not specifically
mentioned in either source of Islamic
law; i.e., they practice ijtihâd

munâfiqoon　المنافقون　hypocrites; those people of Madinah
who outwardly professed Islam, but
secretly opposed the Prophet (ﷺ)

munkar (1)　المنكر　lit. something disavowed;
abominable act(s); in Islamic
discourse it refers to all that Islam
has forbidden

munkar (2)　منكر　a category of hadith which is related
by only one narrator, who is neither
upright nor precise; technically, it is
a weak hadith that contradicts an
authentic hadith

munqaṭi'　منقطع　a category of hadith: a narration in
which one narrator — who is not a
Companion — is missing, or if an
obscure narrator is mentioned

mursal　مرسل　a category of hadith: a narration that
a tâbi'ee ascribes to the Prophet (ﷺ)
without mentioning the Companion
that he took it from

musnad　مسند　a compilation (made by his student)
of the hadiths related by an Imam

musṭalaḥul-ḥadeeth	مصطلح الحديث	Hadith criticism
mutawâtir	متواتر	a category of hadith describing narrations that are related by a group of upright and trustworthy narrators who also related from a group of upright and trustworthy narrators, and so on, until the narration ends at the Prophet (ﷺ)
muttaṣil	متصل	lit. 'connected': a category of hadith: a narration whose chain is connected all the way to the Prophet (ﷺ)
muṭlaq	مطلق	a category of hadith: unrestricted
nubuwwah	النبوّة	The term 'prophethood' is not in the English dictionary, but is an invented term, formed along the pattern of 'childhood' and 'motherhood', as a noun reflecting a particular state of being. It is meant to translate the meaning of the Arabic word nubuwwah, which has no one-word equivalent in English, but which could be translated as meaning 'the state of being a prophet', and is also used to refer to 'all things that have to do with being a prophet'. The term 'prophethood' has since become common in English-language Islamic discourse.
qadr	القدر	divine predestination; destiny; power; exact measure

qibla (qiblah)	القبلة	the bearing from the Kaaba to any point on Earth; the direction that all Muslims must face in prayer
qiyâm al-layl	قيام الليل	lit. 'standing the night'; getting up to pray supererogatory prayers during the late night and early morning before fajr; see *tahajjud*
qiyâs	قياس	analogy: a method of deriving rulings in jurisprudence
Ramadan (Ramaḍân)	رمضان	the ninth month in the Islamic calendar; the month of obligatory fasting; the month in which the first verses of the Qur'an were revealed
ribâ	الربا	usury; charging interest on debt
riyâ'	الرياء	showing off; esp. when it is an act of worship, but done with the intention of letting people see one doing it
ruqyah	الرقية	to recite a part of the Qur'an (such as *Soorat al-Fâtiḥah*) or to supplicate to Allah using words prescribed by the Messenger of Allah (ﷺ) in authentic hadiths in order to obtain relief from illness
ṣadaqah	صدقة	voluntary charity; in the Qur'an and Hadith it is often used to refer to *zakât*
Ṣafâ	المروة	one of the two hills between which pilgrims must hurry back and forth during the rites of the Hajj and the 'umrah

ṣaḥeeḥ	صحيح	a grade of hadith: sound or authentic
salaf	السلف	the pious predecessors: the earliest generations of the righteous followers of Islam
salâm	السلام	peace; the greeting of peace
ṣalât or ṣalâh	صلاة	formal prayer: a combination of physical postures, recitation and supplication
seerah	سيرة	biography
shâdh	شاذ	a category of hadith in which a trustworthy narrator contradicts the narration of one who is more trustworthy
shahâdah	الشهادة	testimony, *usu.* the statement *lâ ilâha illâ Allâh, Muḥammadun rasool Ullâh*
sharia (shari'ah)	شرعة	Islamic law derived from the Qur'an and the Sunnah
shaykh	شيخ	teacher, mentor; scholar
shirk	الشرك	associating partners with Allah
soorah or soorat	سورة	chapter of the Qur'an
subḥân Allâh	سبحان الله	glory be to Allah
Sunnah	سنَة	the practice and collected sayings of Prophet Muhammad (ﷺ) that together with the Qur'an forms the basis of Islamic law
tâbi'oon (sg. tâbi'ee)	التابعون	those who knew or met any of the Companions and transmitted hadiths from them

tadlees	تدليس	any form of deception, whether innocent or otherwise, when relating a narration
tafseer	تفسير	exegesis: commentary, or explanation of the meanings (*usu.* of Qur'anic verses)
ṭâghoot	طاغوت	idols; everything evil that is worshipped
tahajjud	تهجُّد	voluntary night prayer offered between 'ishâ' and fajr
tahârah	الطهارة	state of ritual purification
tahiyyât	التهيات	*lit.* greeting: a formula recited in the sitting position of the prayer that contains words that indicate the glorification of Allah, His eternal existence, His perfection, and His sovereignty
taqwâ	التقوى	fearful awareness of Allah; being mindful of Allah; pious dedication; being careful not to transgress the bounds set by Allah
tasbeeḥ	تسبيح	the recitation of phrases glorifying Allah; saying *subḥân Allah*
tashahhud	التشهد	the testimony that states that there is none worthy of worship other than Allah, He has no partners, and that Muhammad (ﷺ) is His Slave and His Messenger
ṭawâf	طواف	circumambulation of the Ka'bah

tawḥeed	التوحيد	the Oneness of Allah: that He alone deserves to be worshipped and that He has no partners
'uboodiyyah	عبودية	servitude, slavery
Ummah	أَمَة	community or nation: *usu.* used to refer to the entire global community of Muslims
'umrah	عمرة	a minor, non-obligatory pilgrimage to Makkah
unseen		a term used to denote phenomena or aspects that cannot be known using ordinary human faculties
uṣool al-fiqh	أصول الفقه	principles of Islamic jurisprudence
witr	وتر	*lit.* an odd number: a single unit of supererogatory prayer, to be prayed any time after the evening (*'ishâ'*) prayer and before the call for the dawn prayer
wuḍoo'	وضوء	ablution required before prayer or touching the Qur'an
zakât (zakâh or zakât)	زكاة	obligatory charity: an 'alms tax' on wealth payable by Muslims and to be distributed to other Muslims who qualify as recipients
zakât al-fiṭr	زكاة الفطر	obligatory charity at the end of the fast of Ramadan, payable in kind
Zamzam	زمزم	the blessed spring of water that Allah caused to gush out at baby Ismâ'eel's feet; located near the Ka'bah

Names mentioned in this book

Arabic names and their English equivalents

Âdam	Adam
'Eesâ	Jesus
Fir'awn	Pharaoh
Ḥawwâ'	Eve
Ibrâheem	Abraham
Isrâ'eel	Israel or Jacob
Jibreel	Gabriel
Maryam	Mary
Moosâ	Moses
Nooḥ	Noah
Sulaymân	Solomon